乾象

THE QIANLONG EMPEROR
TREASURES FROM THE FORBIDDEN CITY

Zhang Hongxing

With preface by Craig Clunas
And special contributions
by Zhu Chengru, Liu Lu,
Nie Chongzheng, Yu Hui
and Yang Danxia

National Museums of Scotland Publishing Limited

Front cover: Detail of *The Qianlong emperor in formal court robe* (no. 5) with design modification in placement of two seals.

Published by
NMS Publishing Limited
National Museums of Scotland
Chambers Street
Edinburgh EH1 1JF

British Library Cataloguing in Publication Data
A catalogue record for this book is available from the British Library

ISBN 1 901663 77 9

Project management and design by Elizabeth Robertson of NMS Publsihing Limited

Printed and bound by Keyline of Newcastle Limited, United Kingdom

CONTENTS

FOREWORDS

At the invitation of the National Museums of Scotland, I was given the great honour of representing the Palace Museum in Beijing at the formal opening of the 'Forbidden City, Treasures of an Emperor' at the Royal Museum in Edinburgh. I was also delighted to be asked to contribute a foreword to this book which accompanies the exhibition.

The Palace Museum is a museum of international standing established on the foundation of the imperial palaces of the Ming (1368–1644) and Qing (1644–1911) dynasties, China's final two imperial dynasties which together lasted for more than five hundred years. The reigns of the Kangxi and Qianlong emperors saw the sun at its zenith over imperial China, a sun that was slowly to set during the final decades of the Qianlong period. The Qianlong emperor was the supreme sovereign of the Qing dynasty, and one of imperial China's most outstanding rulers, excelling in both military skills and cultural achievements. He held the reins of power in China for 60 years, and lived for 89, both records for China's imperial rulers. The living legacy of the Qianlong emperor's golden age is the vast collection of works of art and craft that the emperor amassed in his lifetime. These form the core of the Palace Museum collections.

This exhibition is made up of paintings, works of calligraphy and precious objects from the reign of the Qianlong emperor. Some of the exhibits are well known and well loved, while others are being seen in public for the first time. The paintings include not only the startling works produced collaboratively by court artists from China and Europe, but also works by the Qianlong emperor himself. I am sure these treasures from the east will meet with the approval of the Scottish public.

The opening up of Sino-Western communications has advanced the exchange of Chinese and British culture. Although the British public is by no means ignorant of Chinese works of art, this is the first time that art from the imperial court will have been on view in Scotland. In the past these works were stored deep within the imperial palaces and the forbidden gardens, where only the emperor himself could appreciate them. Today, following all kinds of changes in the world and the speeding up of globalisation, people from all over the world are able to view them. Art knows no boundaries. Let us hope that these precious treasures of traditional Chinese culture receive a warm welcome from the Scottish people.

I would like to take this opportunity to express my heartfelt thanks to all those colleagues who have put in so much hard work and I wish the exhibition every success.

Professor Zhu Chengru
Deputy Director of the Palace Museum, Beijing

Opposite:
Detail of *The elderly Qianlong emperor in formal court robe* (no. 76). The sense of fatigue on the face of the emperor contrasts with the freshness of his appearance in 1735 when he had just succeeded the throne (front cover).

The title of this book contains three elements which are certain to create a sense of anticipation. 'Forbidden City' can only mean the vast imperial palace at the heart of Beijing, no less mysterious and intriguing since becoming accessible to tourists. 'Treasures' is no exaggeration as the following pages about the art and patronage of a great emperor clearly demonstrate. 'Emperor' refers to the Qianlong emperor who was one of the great figures in the long history of a great civilisation, revered as much for his success as a leader as for his art and patronage.

The National Museums of Scotland have a fine tradition of collecting, researching and exhibiting Chinese culture and art. The Ivy Wu Gallery of Chinese, Japanese and Korean Art was opened in 1996 for the display of our own collections. Since 1998 we have had a curatorial post dedicated to Chinese art which is shared with the Department of Fine Art in Edinburgh University where the postholder, the author of this book, teaches courses on the subject.

In the summer of 1997 we mounted an exhibition on the historical trade links between China and Scotland, entitled 'Precious Cargo'. This aroused great interest in China and its culture, and led us to arrange our first major loan exhibition from China, 'Chinese Paintings from the Shanghai Museum', in 2000. The exhibition which this book accompanies, 'Forbidden City, Treasures of an Emperor', is our next step in developing closer and more meaningful ties with sister institutions in China. It has only been possible through the generosity, co-operation and hard work of colleagues in the Palace Museum, Beijing. We are grateful for their efforts on our behalf to bring some of their outstanding national treasures to the United Kingdom for the first time.

In his foreword Professor Zhu describes the importance and significance of this exhibition. I fully concur with his remarks. It is our duty as a national museum not just to concentrate on our own Scottish heritage, but to show the best of other cultures to our visitors, many of whom come from other countries. I believe that we in the West have not always been good at appreciating the great achievements of other civilisations. This is a wonderful opportunity to broaden our understanding.

I have already mentioned our indebtedness to our Chinese colleagues for this book and the exhibition. I would also like to thank our sponsors, Dawson International PLC, who have developed the 'Forbidden Cashmere' collection in their Ballantyne cashmere range as part of their innovative support of the exhibition. We are also very grateful to the Dunard Fund and Napier University for their generosity.

Dr Gordon Rintoul
Director of the National Museums of Scotland

Opposite:
Gentleman, accompanied by a boy servant carrying a lute, walking across an idealistic landscape. Detail from *Copy of 'Brewing tea' by Tang Yin* (no. 47). To give texture to the rock in the foreground the emperor has used a dry brush.

BALLANTYNE
CASHMERE

Intrigue... fascination... inspiration – these are the feelings evoked by the Forbidden City. That was our reaction when the opportunity arose to become involved with the exhibition 'Forbidden City, Treasures of an Emperor' at the National Museums of Scotland in 2002.

This priceless art collection from the Palace Museum in Beijing made instant connections with us as the world's leading cashmere business, Dawson International PLC. Cashmere is the world's most luxurious and expensive natural fibre and the highest quality raw cashmere fibre comes from China, where we have connections stretching back over 100 years.

We then began to see parallels between the heritage, quality and beauty of the Forbidden City collections and our own premium brand, Ballantyne Cashmere. But more than this we saw the opportunity to do what we do best as a business: to push the boundaries of cashmere and challenge ourselves to do something different – something that would inspire our own creative thinkers and excite and involve our customers.

The result is the 'Forbidden Cashmere' collection, a limited range of one-off cashmere garments inspired by the exhibition, created by some of the world's most talented contemporary designers, with whom we have worked closely over many years.

United Kingdom designers include Clements Ribeiro, Scott Henshall, Shelley Fox, Ann Louise Roswald, Brett Munro and Queene & Bell; from France Lucien Pellat-Finet; and from the United States, Lutz & Patmos.

We are also delighted that Ballantyne Cashmere's guest designer, Matthew Williamson, has given his support for this initiative by designing two exclusive Forbidden Cashmere designs. Matthew Williamson is a great admirer of Chinese art and his creations will feature as the centrepiece of the Forbidden Cashmere collection.

It has been a pleasure for us to work with such a professional and committed team within the National Museums of Scotland – our thanks to everyone involved. Sincere thanks are also due to all of the designers and production team who have turned inspiration into reality.

Paul Munn
Chief Executive
Dawson International PLC

The exhibition was also supported by:

DUNARD FUND

ACKNOWLEDGEMENTS

This book is the result of a larger project that includes the first ever exhibition devoted to the Qianlong emperor and images related to him. As the project is based exclusively on the collections of the Palace Museum in Beijing, it has taken the vision and commitment of the National Museums of Scotland to bring it to Edinburgh. There my greatest debt is to Mark Jones, former Director, for his inspirational initiative, as well as to Lord Wilson of Tillyorn, Chairman of the Board of Trustees, and to Dr Gordon Rintoul, present Director, for their unfailing support. To all the rest of my colleagues in the museum who have helped enormously with the project in various ways, I would like to extend my personal thanks. All my colleagues in the University of Edinburgh, and in particular Robert Hillenbrand, have also been great sources of encouragement.

Essential to the early conception of the project were the Ninth International Symposium on the History of the Qing Dynasty and the 75th Anniversary of the Palace Museum in Beijing in the summer of 2000, and the Universities' China Committee in London. Thanks to Zhu Chengru, Deputy Director of the Palace Museum and organiser of the symposium, it was possible for me in a very short time to appreciate the rich collections of Qing court art and to encounter the leading Chinese scholars in the field. I was particularly fortunate to have discussions on the Qianlong emperor with Zhou Yuanlian and Gao Xiang from the Chinese Academy of Social Sciences, and I am greatly indebted to the curators of the Palace Museum, five of whom have become my principal collaborators on the book.

In Britain, Craig Clunas from the University of Sussex has provided a preface to the book as well as his overwhelming support, for which I am particularly grateful. In the preparation of the book, I have benefited greatly from the constant encouragement of Roderick Whitfield, Ann Paludan and Anita Chung and from the writings of many historians and art historians who have been acknowledged wherever possible. I am equally indebted to the 18 members of the University of Edinburgh's honours course in Chinese art (Spring 2002) who studied the topic with me. Their enthusiastic participation in the course not only helped to clarify the problems of the topic, but also made the writing a much more enjoyable experience.

The editorial work has been carried out by Susan Leiper, whose professionalism and expertise have pulled the text together. The essays by five experts from the Palace Museum were translated by Julian Ward and Frances Weightman, and the Chinese characters in the book were written by my wife Ruihua. I would like to thank this team who, along with Liz Robertson, designer, Cara Shanley and Lesley Taylor of National Museums of Scotland Publishing, have responded to a demanding schedule and exacting requests with extreme patience and care.

PICTURING COSMIC GRANDEUR

乾象

The reign of the Qianlong emperor (1736–95), who held sway as ruler of the Great Qing dynasty (1644–1911) over an enormous area of East and Central Asia, spanned most of the first century of Scotland's history after the Act of Union of 1707. Born at a time when many in the Qing empire and in Scotland remembered the vicious civil wars of the 1680s, the emperor lived on to be a contemporary of Walter Scott, into an era widely understood (at least by the élites of both countries) as one of relative peace and internal stability. Over the course of that near-century, European engagement with China and its civilisation intensified in both an intellectual and a commercial sense, to a point where it stood on the brink of violent threat to that stability. Thus the thinkers of the Scottish Enlightenment, in their creation of theories of trade, of political economy, and of civil society, would have been aware of the example of the Qing empire, and educated people in eighteenth-century Edinburgh would have been able in their reading to encounter the title of its ruler. In the two principal languages of the empire, the title of the ruler, Qianlong in Chinese and Abkai Weheyihe in Manchu, means something like 'Pillar of Heaven' or 'Cosmic Grandeur' and embodies the claim of this extraordinary man to reign by virtue of a mandate bestowed by the cosmic forces of heaven itself.

Besides the mandate of heaven, the imperial clan to which the Qianlong emperor belonged, the Aisin Gioro, was extremely fortunate in its genes. These provided it with a steady supply of long-living males – only four emperors were needed to take the dynasty from 1644 to the eve of the nineteenth century. These four men, each one a son of his predecessor, shared more than simple longevity in that all were distinguished for the seriousness with which they took the task of ruling their vast domain. They (and the tutors who instructed them) had constantly before their eyes the negative example of their imperial predecessors, the Zhu family who had supplied the rulers of the Ming dynasty (1368–1644). Then, as Qing historians understood it, a succession of idle, pleasure-addicted and at best semi-competent rulers had frittered away a great legacy of imperial foundation in a downward spiral of lassitude and futility. The mistake would not be repeated. The first four Qing emperors were men of extraordinary stamina and energy who drove themselves hard and expected others to follow. Long hours at the desk dealing with mountains of paperwork were interspersed with lengthy audiences, court conferences and gruelling tours of inspection. This was emperorship as hard work.

The practices of culture meant hard work also. The Qianlong emperor's production of vast numbers of poems, his amassing of an unparalleled collection of antiquities from China's past, his patronage of ateliers of painters, enamellers, weavers, carvers, lacquerworkers, clockmakers and artisans in a hundred different crafts – all this formed part of *wen*. *Wen* means 'culture', sometimes in the narrow sense of 'literature', but more often in the wider sense of 'pattern',

Opposite:
Detail of *The Qianlong emperor in ceremonial armour on horseback* (no. 16). Although the artist had access to the emperor's armour to copy, he has made various modifications (compare the armour in no. 32) to achieve the effect of greatness.

the cosmic 'pattern' which holds human activity and the powers of the universe in equilibrium. It is the sustenance of this pattern that is an emperor's greatest duty; ignore it, and the mandate of heaven may be withdrawn. Thus when the Qianlong emperor devoted time to what we now categorise as 'artistic' activities, he was in no sense being frivolous or neglecting his duties as a ruler. In one striking example, he devoted vast amounts of attention to a colossal boulder of jade, discovered in the late 1770s near the town of Khotan, in the far west of the empire. He selected from the enormous imperial art collection an early painting showing the legendary emperor Yu the Great taming the primeval flood at the dawn of human history, and hence making civilised life possible. He approved a full-sized wax model of this scene in three-dimensional form. He then ordered a wooden version of this made, to be transported with the 5330 kg jade boulder to the southern city of Yangzhou, where he felt the craftsmen in jade were more skilled than those available to him in Beijing. He had the wooden model returned to Beijing so he could try it out in various locations; meanwhile 150,000 working days were being spent in the laborious carving of the piece, over a period of nearly eight years. He then composed the lengthy text which palace craftsmen engraved on the boulder over the course of a year after its return in 1787. This object, the largest jade carving in the world, remains in the Palace Museum in Beijing, in the spot chosen for it. The labour of anonymous craftsmen and the care of the emperor come together here in a massive physical testimony to the beneficence of heaven, which had favoured the dynasty's recent extension of its sway into the 'New Dominion' of Central Asia by revealing this miraculously large gem. The jade carving was the emperor's response to this favour (see photo, p. 161). It was an acknowledgement of his responsibility to make the world of civilisation, of *wen*, possible, just as his ancient predecessor had done millennia before.

Such an example of imperial grandeur is too large ever to leave Beijing, but many of the pieces in the present extraordinary selection of work from the Qianlong court bear witness to the same impulses which produced it, and to the almost unprecedented seriousness with which the Qianlong emperor addressed the visual imagery of rulership. There must be more images of the Qianlong emperor than of any other Chinese ruler; indeed there may be more of him than of all the others in history put together. These paintings express a wide variety of contexts of viewing and display: some ritual, some more informal and personal. They show the emperor as the embodiment of *wen*, of culture, as well as the personification of its complementary partner *wu*, the 'martial' virtues of warrior leadership and the vigorous manly activities of hunting and wilderness travel. They display a variety of identities, from the emperor as adept of the mysteries of Daoism, or as earthly manifestation of a fearsome Buddhist deity, to the emperor as revered father of a respectful and loving family unit, the basic building block of human society. They show him able to command the allegiance of visitors from the remotest corners of the inhabited world, like the Italian missionary artist Giuseppe Castiglione, equally with that of the scholar officials of the Han Chinese élite.

In addition to pictures of the emperor, there are works in this book which display the imperial person in other significant ways. Perhaps most important for contemporary Qing viewers would have been the samples of the emperor's own calligraphy, the traces of his brush which were at the same time understood as images of his own bodily presence. The rituals performed at the reception, viewing and installation of the emperor's works of calligraphy (another form of *wen*) consisted of the same bodily gestures and prostrations as would have been shown to the emperor himself. The same was true of the pictures he produced, as he inserted himself as a practitioner into the history of both calligraphy and painting, the two most highly valued of élite visual arts. And by inscribing the masterpieces in the imperial collections with additional critical comments on the occasion of viewing his treasures, he ensured that the culture of the past as well as of the present fell under his imperial gaze.

The great scope of the imperial collections formed in the Qianlong reign has deeply coloured our understanding of the art of China's past, by acting like a vast filter. Surviving into museum collections to this day, the enormous store of cultural riches amassed by the Qianlong emperor has sometimes come to seem as if it *is* Chinese culture, and the material excluded by him has been correspondingly marginalised, or has not been preserved. Until quite recently, the glories of China's pre-Qing cultural history contained in the palace collection have perhaps blinded scholarship to what is extraordinary or distinctive about that court culture in itself. Only in the past two decades have many of the pictures and artefacts displayed here been exhibited, published, discussed and allowed to travel. In travelling, they carry into the four corners of the globe the ideology of cosmic grandeur and benign universal rulership which brought them into being, and 'all under heaven', *tianxia*, are made aware of the Qianlong emperor's just and all-encompassing sway. He would surely have thought it no more than his due.

Professor Craig Clunas
University of Sussex
February 2002

INTRODUCTION

Zhang Hongxing

The Qianlong emperor was the most powerful and most complex of China's rulers to occupy the Forbidden City. During his 60-year reign China's dynastic power increased dramatically and the nation became one of the wealthiest in the world. As well as being a pre-eminent monarch, the emperor is universally regarded as the greatest patron of the arts in China since late medieval times. The objects and works of art that he commissioned and collected make up the core of the former palace collections, now divided between the Palace Museum in Beijing and its counterpart in Taipei. Within the Forbidden City itself the majority of the architectural work undertaken after the completion of the first phase of building in the early fifteenth century dates from his reign. It may not be an over-exaggeration then to claim that the Qianlong emperor single-handedly represents the splendour of the Forbidden City.

However, this book is not a survey of the life of the Qianlong emperor or of court art during his reign, although both are deserving of study.[1] By presenting a selection of more than 80 works of art and objects from the Qianlong court, the book attempts to address the question: how did the Qianlong emperor see himself? The book is primarily concerned with pictorial representations of the emperor, in various genres from portraits to documentary paintings and religious hangings. It also deals with his image as projected through writings, pictures and objects: verses he composed, pictures he painted and objects that he collected, commissioned or used such as jades, seals, furniture, clothing, weapons, treasure boxes and ritual objects, some bearing his personal symbols and inscriptions. By looking at this extraordinary array of exhibits, we can gain something of an insight into the kind of self-image this opulent eighteenth-century Chinese monarch sought to project.

Over the last two decades the self-image of the Qianlong emperor, as projected by visual images of him, has attracted the attention of a number of specialists. There are studies of the scrolls depicting the emperor's tours of inspection to the south and his hunting expeditions.[2] The portraits of the emperor in various guises such as bodhisattva, Daoist priest, warrior and scholar have been examined, some in great depth.[3] A full picture of the emperor based on some of the most familiar pictures of him has been attempted.[4] There is also a general study of the emperor's self-image, but it is based on an analysis of textual evidence – official and private histories, works of fiction and drama, and miscellaneous notes. Considering the importance the emperor attached to the visual aspects of his image, and given the fact that he chose to inscribe verses and inscriptions on so many objects, there is an overwhelming need for a portrait of the man based on the visual material related to him, incorporating recent scholarship.

In terms of the study of self-image, the Qianlong emperor is an ideal subject as it is something that concerned him deeply. To begin

Opposite:
Detail of *Hongli, the future Qianlong emperor, gathering fungus* (no. 3). This delicate monochrome image evokes the spirituality of the future emperor.

The Qianlong emperor receiving the British embassy in the Garden of Ten Thousand Trees, Rehe, by William Alexander (1767–1816), 1796, watercolour on paper, H 40 cm, W 60.6 cm, British Museum. This picture makes an interesting comparison with *Imperial banquet in the Garden of Ten Thousand Trees, Rehe* (no. 21), as both depict the same kind of event.

with he was fortunate to be blessed with physical fitness and the stamina required of a conscientious ruler. He was a man of slender build and upright bearing and remained so until old age, partly due to his love of outdoor activities. When not engaged in hunting or travelling he kept to a simple daily routine: he got up around six o'clock in the morning, went to bed at midnight, and ate only two meals a day, each lasting no more than 15 minutes.[5] He enjoyed drinking tea, did not partake of wine, and would seldom stay at evening functions beyond nine o'clock.

Yet the simplicity of his private life did not seem to prevent him from being glamorous and gracious in public. Lord Macartney, the British envoy of George III who was sent to China to meet the emperor in 1793, recorded his impression of him on the day of his reception, Saturday 14 September, eleven days before the emperor's eighty-second birthday: 'Among other things, he [the Qianlong emperor] asked me the age of my King, and being informed of it, said he hoped he might live as many years as himself, which are eighty-three. His manner is dignified, but affable, and condescending, and his reception of us has been very gracious and satisfactory.'[6]

As a man constantly under public scrutiny, the Qianlong emperor was meticulous about his dress and appearance. Before having a robe made he would take pains to check the drawing prepared by the imperial dressmaker and comment on it before it was sent to be made up at one of the imperial textile factories in the south.[7]

He approached his portraits equally seriously, attaching great importance to likeness. According to one of the Jesuits at court, Father Benoist (1715–74), acting as interpreter for the portraitist Brother Joseph Panzi (*c.* 1733– before 1812) who painted the Qianlong emperor in 1773, the emperor spent hours sitting for the artist. Benoist recalled in a letter: 'Both Brother Panzi and I noticed with surprise that never, during all the sittings, some of which were extremely long, did the Emperor lean against the cushions at the back ... he made various movements in talking, moving the hands, head and chest, but never moved his legs, or changed his position.[8] On one occasion the emperor invited Panzi to examine his features at close quarters, drawing his attention to a small imperfection, a tuft of hairs above one eye, and requesting him not to exclude it from the painting.

Physical attributes aside, what aspect of his self-image did the emperor most want to project? First and foremost was his desire to represent Chinese emperorship. A Chinese emperor was a universal ruler, the embodiment of every major function of society. First of all he was the religious head of state, the son of heaven and mediator between heaven and earth. Next, the emperor had to be an exemplary family man, filial son to his parents, loyal husband to his wife, and loving father to his children. The monarchical system also required him to be a guardian of the law and an efficient administrator, and to work hard for his subjects' well-being. Yet the emperor should not allow himself to be buried by mountains of official documents; he must find opportunities to patronise and, even better, to engage in the practice of literature and art. An emperor who failed to leave behind a major cultural project would not be remembered as an enlightened ruler. To complement his cultural pursuits the emperor was expected to excel in martial skills, to be a mighty commander capable of quelling rebellions and guarding frontiers.[9] Thus, when we look at all the different images of the Qianlong emperor in this book (nos 2, 3, 5, 16, 17, 21, 26, 30, 31, 35, 36, 53, 54, 56–59, 76), it is important not just to see them as different moments in the emperor's life, but to understand them as displaying the many different roles required of him. As a whole the self-image of the Qianlong emperor conforms to the notion of Chinese emperorship – he portrays himself as an omnipotent monarch, a universal ruler.

Although omnipotence was central to the notion of Chinese rulership, in reality few Chinese emperors aspired to be this universal man, and still fewer had the talent or luck to become one even if they were willing. The reason for this lies partly in the notion itself: it comprises too many conflicting values. Only a handful of rulers were sufficiently resourceful to handle the contradictions successfully. The Qianlong emperor was one of them. His success derives mainly from his ability to 'localise' his various roles and perform each in its appropriate place. This localisation is graphically illustrated by the way in which the many images of him were displayed. For instance, his hunting images (nos 16, 30, 31 and 36) were not displayed in the Forbidden City, the seat of the son of heaven, but in the Summer Palace in Rehe (Chengde) on the edge of the steppes where the emperor conducted his annual autumn hunting expeditions. These pictures were hung in the reception hall of the palace where their primary audience was Manchu warriors and their Mongol allies, the very people in whom the dynasty's military foundation lay. In stark contrast are the *thangkas* showing the emperor as a bodhisattva (no. 17) which were hung in the lamaist temples and monasteries in Beijing, Rehe and Lhasa. Since the very idea of a Chinese emperor as a Tibetan bodhisattva would have been considered hugely arrogant to any Han Chinese Buddhist, these *thangkas* were made only for display within their specific religious context. In the same way, the portraits of the emperor dressed as a Han Chinese scholar (nos 53, 54 and 59) and the emperor's own paintings and works of calligraphy were kept in his own private rooms in the Forbidden City and his various imperial villas, and in the private gardens that he frequented in southern China. Their targeted audience was not the Manchus, Mongols or Tibetan lamas, but the emperor himself. The way in which he separated his roles according to the different cultures of his empire is crucial to understanding the Qianlong emperor's view of monarchy. He created a new version of Chinese emperorship in which the universal ruler was able to adapt to the diversity of the people, thereby emphasising that diversity. The Qianlong emperor meant all things to all men.

In a wider sense the Qianlong emperor's reconstruction of the notion of the royal self was part of his aim to create a multicultural China. This enterprise in turn was deeply rooted in the cultural identity of the Qing ruling house itself and influenced by the emperor's acute awareness of it. The Qianlong emperor was a member of the Manchu, a group of people descended from the Tungus. The Tungus had lived in northeastern China since prehistoric times and spoke a language related to Turkic and Mongolian, all three belonging to the Altaic family. They were hunters, fishers and food gatherers. In the first century CE various tribes moved to the north and west and eventually occupied most of Siberia. Those who were left behind formed the direct ancestors of the Manchu. The Manchu were distinct from other Altaic people for their unique position as the nexus of the major cultures of East Asia. Under the influence of the Han Chinese they developed a form of agriculture and animal domestication to complement their own hunting and gathering, and in the early seventeenth century they devised their own written language, adapted from Mongolian script.

The Manchu moved into China proper and established their ruling seat in Beijing in 1644. They adopted the dynastic name Qing, meaning pure. The first century of Qing rule witnessed a huge wave of

Detail of *The Qianlong emperor seeking pleasure* by Jin Tingbiao, undated, handscroll, ink and colour on silk, L 320 cm, H 167.4 cm, Palace Museum, Beijing

欽定四庫全書　御製詩三集 卷二十七　十一

題宮中行樂圖一韻四首

喬樹重巒石逕紆前行廻顧後行呼松年粉本東山趣石渠寶笈藏劉松年此幅喜其結構古雅因令金廷標摹為宮中行樂圖摹作宮中行樂圖

小坐溪亭清且紆侍臣莫謾襍傳呼閼氏來備九嬪列較勝明妃出塞圖

幾間壺裏小遊紆憑檻何須清蹕呼詎是衣冠希漢代丹青寓意寫為圖圖中衫履即依松年式此不過丹青遊戲非慕漢人衣冠向為禮器圖序已明示此意

瀑水當軒落澗紆巖邊馴鹿可招呼林泉寄傲非吾事

Printed version of the poem inscribed on the painting *The Qianlong emperor seeking pleasure* by Jin Tingbiao. From the third collection of the emperor's poems, *Four Treasuries* edition. The small characters in the second and third columns from the left address the issue of dress.

sinicisation whereby the early emperors – the Qianlong emperor's father and grandfather in particular – tried to adapt to the sophisticated culture of the Chinese in order to maintain their rule. What was unique in the case of the Qianlong emperor was that while he immersed himself deeply in Chinese culture, he was to develop in adulthood a strong sense of his Manchu identity. His revival of the imperial hunt, his consolidation of the banner system, his construction of Tibetan monasteries and temples in Rehe, and his military expeditions to eastern Turkestan all show a different approach to Manchu rulership to that of his father and grandfather. His multiculturalism was influenced by his ethnic uniqueness.

Perhaps because of his awareness of his Manchu identity, the Qianlong emperor used his images with extraordinary discretion. Most interesting in this respect are those portraits in which he wears Han Chinese robes (nos 2, 3, 35, 53, 54, 56, 57, 59 and 76). The emperor was well aware that by dressing in this way he was in danger of violating the dress code, established by his Manchu forebears, which banned the wearing of Han costume, even if these were just pictures

Detail of treasure box (no. 9). The *qian* trigram is carved in the centre of the sandalwood tray.

and not reality. As a result, all these portraits were kept in his private living quarters and studies in his various palaces, and only a very few privileged people were permitted to see them. To prevent these portraits from being misinterpreted at court, the emperor went as far as to note in an inscription on the painting *The Qianlong emperor seeking pleasure* by Jin Tingbiao that he was dressed as a Han Chinese in the picture purely for entertainment and not because he was an admirer of Han dress.[10] In contrast to some of the other types of picture of him, the image of the emperor as scholar or scholar artist was his 'private' image. It was in his private space that he was able to be frank about the different roles he played in public, and on one painting he wrote that he was not at all concerned about the inconsistency between these roles (no. 59). These 'private' portraits therefore not only add a critical dimension to his self-image, but they also open a door to the innermost world of the Qianlong emperor.

For any ruler who remained on the throne for such a surprisingly long time there was a danger that he might retreat into his own realm and neglect the outside world. The Qianlong emperor was to become just such a victim of his long reign. Before he had ascended the throne at the age of 24 the young prince had been known by his personal name Hongli. Over the following six decades the young man called Hongli was gradually to fade from his consciousness and he came to identify himself more and more with his reign title 'Qianlong'. This title contains two words: *long*, meaning greatness or grandeur (which sounds the same as another character *long* meaning dragon); and *qian*, the name of the first of the eight trigrams, the basic set of three-line figures used in ancient divination. As described in the classic book on divination, the *Book of changes (Yijing)*, originated during the early Western Zhou dynasty (eleventh century–771 BCE), the trigram *qian* consists of three unbroken lines and represents the qualities of creativeness, activeness and strength. Applied to the natural and human world it stands for heaven, male and father. The Qianlong emperor had the trigram carved on his treasure box (no. 9), on his personal seals (back cover), and depicted on his portraits (no. 57). Furthermore, he acted in accordance with the instructions for the trigram given in the sacred book. The text on the movement of the trigram reads: 'The movement of heaven is full of power. Thus the superior man makes himself strong and untiring.'[11] The emperor had worked tirelessly throughout his life. In his declining years he had the words 'strong and untiring' from the text carved into his seal in an attempt to prevent himself from feeling tired.

Eventually, having ruled for 60 years – a complete cycle according to the *ganzhi* year-count – he retired from the throne, the final act of a sagacious ruler. This last attempt to mould his self-image, to leave his subjects with the impression that he had been a true emperor sage, was probably made only after consulting the meaning of the trigram *qian* in the *Book of changes*. On the subject of the last phase of the tireless active movement, represented by the top line of the hexagram *qian*, the text reads:

> The dragon exceeds its proper bounds,
> There will be occasions for repentance.

An explanation is then given in the commentary:

> The phrase 'exceeds its proper bounds' means that the dragon knows how to advance but not how to retire, how to survive but not how to be dissolved, how to obtain but not how to let go. He alone is the sage who, knowing progression and retrogression, coming into being and passing away, never loses his true nature. Truly he alone is the sage.[12]

Notes

1 The art of the Qianlong reign has been the subject of an exhibition (see Chou and Brown 1985). In late 2002 there will be a major exhibition in Taipei of the cultural activities of the emperor entitled 'Opulent Bounties of Heaven: Emperor Ch'ien-lung's Grand Cultural Enterprise'.

2 Hearn 1988; Yang Boda 1993

3 Farquhar 1978; Crossley 1999

4 Kahn 1985; Wu Hung 1995; Zito 1997

5 Hummel 1949, vol. 1: 372; Dai Yi 1992: 4–5

6 Cranmer-Byng 1962: 123

7 Chen Juanjuan 1994.2: 84–5

8 Danby 1959: 134; Beurdeley 1972: 102

9 Ellen Uitzinger in *De Verboden Stad* 1990: 71–91

10 *YZSSJ* 1771: *juan* 27

11 Wang Bi: *juan* 1. Translation from Wilheim 1965: 8

12 Wang Bi: *juan* 1. Translation from Needham 1956: 283

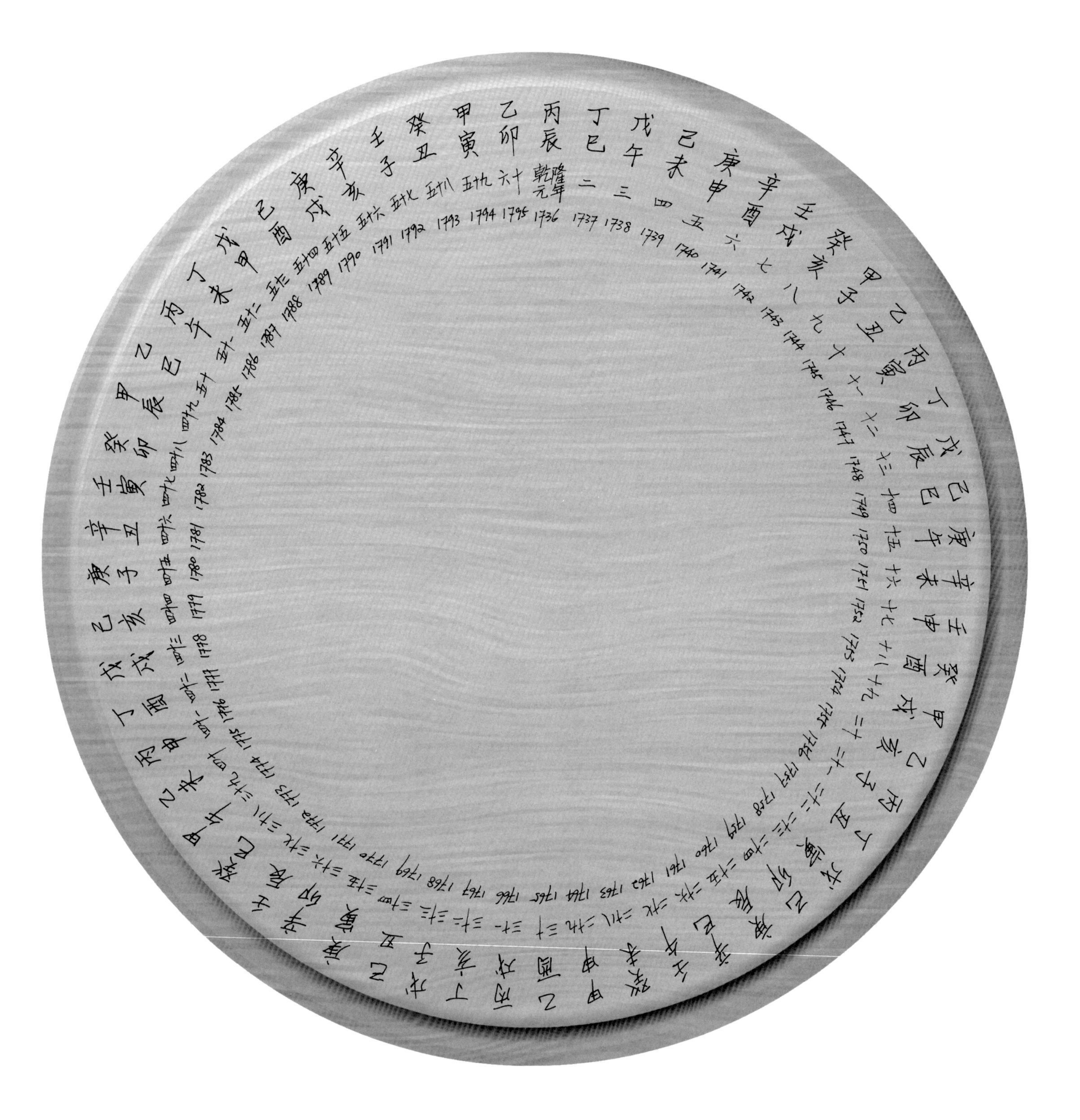

This diagram records the 60-year reign of the Qianlong emperor in three different year-counting systems. The innermost ring shows the Gregorian system, which was not adopted in China until 1912. Before that date the Chinese used both the regnal and the *ganzhi* systems to record years. The middle ring represents the regnal system which dates from the Shang dynasty: the year of the ruler's accession is counted as year one, the following year as year two, and so on. The outer ring shows the *ganzhi* dating system, which officially began in the first century CE. It is based on two sets of counters – the so-called ten heavenly stems and the twelve earthly branches – and is called the Cycle of Cathay in treaty port English. The cycle is formed by taking one counter from each set and putting them together to make 60 unique combinations. As the Qianlong emperor ascended the throne officially in 1736 and abdicated in 1796, his reign therefore completed the cycle.

IMAGES OF THE QIANLONG EMPEROR

SPRING'S PEACEFUL MESSAGE

The Qianlong emperor was born as Hongli to the Aisin Gioro family in Beijing on the thirteenth day of the eighth month of the fiftieth year of the reign of his grandfather the Kangxi emperor (25 September 1711). He was the fifth son of Yinzhen, and the only son of his mother, then his father's young concubine. At that time even royal nurseries were not exempt from infant mortality: of Hongli's nine half-brothers and four half-sisters, nine died before reaching maturity. That Hongli survived must have seemed to his parents a sign of some miraculous immunity.

Hongli had a happy childhood. Not only did his parents lavish affection upon him, but at the age of eleven he won the heart of the elderly Kangxi emperor who brought him to live in the Forbidden City. Contemporary anecdotes record their close relationship. In the palace the young Hongli was not lacking in companions closer to him in age, with his best friends including his brother Hongzhou (1712–70), his father's very young brother Yinxi (1711–58) and the Third Cangca Khutuktu of Inner Mongolia, Rolpa'i Dorje (1717–1805?).

The situation changed dramatically when Hongli's grandfather died. The struggle for succession had been horrendously bloody, and when Hongli's extremely able father won the battle and became the Yongzheng emperor, all his opponents were either imprisoned or executed. To ensure that such a succession crisis should not be repeated after his own death, the Yongzheng emperor implemented the secret selection of heir apparent. Thus, in 1723, the young Hongli was secretly singled out. Thereafter his life was carefully planned around a strict educational curriculum comprising Chinese classics, history, poetry, the Manchu language, horse-riding and shooting. He had twelve hours of schooling a day.

Although Hongli was not told outright what the future held in store for him, he was sensitive to his father's display of favouritism towards him and was quick to grasp opportunities to prove that he deserved special treatment. He also recognised early the potential benefits of art on a possible path to the throne. At the age of 20 he presented to the court a selection of the fruits of his studies (no.4). At the age of 24 he made the acquaintance of Giuseppe Castiglione, the talented Italian missionary painter who had served under both his father and grandfather, and this prompted a portrait of Hongli by the artist (no. 3). Both the anthology of his studies and the portrait were indications by the young prince to the court that he was in possession of the qualities required of an heir apparent.

The date of Hongli's inauguration ceremony was chosen to coincide with the Spring Festival of 1736, to reinforce the idea that his succession was a cosmic new beginning. From that day on his name became taboo. Even using the characters that made up his name was forbidden unless some of the strokes were modified. Various terms were adopted to refer to the emperor, the most common being his reign title Qianlong, which means cosmic grandeur.

Opposite:
Detail of *Spring's peaceful message* (no. 2). The young Hongli accepts a sprig of plum blossom from his father, an allusion to his father's trust in him and to his right to rule.

1

The Kangxi emperor in military attire

Second half of 17th century
Hanging scroll, ink and colour on silk
L 112.2 cm, W 71.5 cm

The Kangxi emperor was the grandfather of the Qianlong emperor and the third son of the Shunzhi emperor, the first Qing emperor after the conquest of China. He came to the throne in 1661 at the age of seven and ruled the empire for 61 years, a reign matched in length only by that of his grandson. The Kangxi emperor was an extremely able ruler who had demonstrated unusual determination and sagacity at an early age. From the age of eight he was assisted by a regent, but he succeeded in removing him and assumed full power at the age of 14.

Throughout his life the Kangxi emperor was an avid traveller. He took pride in having been to every corner of his empire: 'Rivers, lakes, mountains, deserts – I've been through them all.' One of the emperor's reasons for travelling was to win the support of the large Chinese population. He also went on hunting expeditions and he loved ranging in the forests in the south of the Manchu heartland. Hunting was more than just a form of entertainment: on hunts the emperor would train thousands of warriors to shoot, to set up camp and to ride in formation, thereby strengthening Manchu martial virtues. This emphasis on robust military virtue led to territorial expansion and the securing of frontiers during his reign. In the war against the Dzungars in the far west of the empire in the 1690s, the Kangxi emperor led the expedition personally, defeating the brilliant Dzungar warrior-leader Galdan and forcing him to commit suicide.

For the most part of his long reign the Kangxi emperor was renowned for being an open-minded, conscientious ruler. He was a great admirer of the Jesuit missionaries for their knowledge of and skills in mathematics, mechanics, medicine, astronomy and art, and he employed them at court as painters, astronomers, cartographers and advisers on foreign affairs. He also granted them the right to preach freely in China. The Kangxi emperor showed genuine concern for his subjects, with the result that his reign saw a period of great prosperity and peace.

This is one of the two portraits known to us of the emperor in his youth. The other, which also belongs in the Palace Museum in Beijing, shows him practising calligraphy. The similarity in the details of the face in each portrait would suggest that both convey a strong likeness of the young emperor.

EXH: Museu de Arte de Macau 2000: no. 1
LIT: Hummel 1949, vol. 1: 327–31; Spence 1974: xi–xxvi

2

Spring's peaceful message

Attributed to Giuseppe Castiglione
Qianlong period (1736–95)
Hanging scroll, ink and colour on silk
L 68.8 cm, W 40.6 cm
Inscription: one by Hongli, dated 1782
Seals: five of Hongli

The subject of this painting has for long been an art historical riddle. There has been much speculation about the identification of these two men who stand by a clump of bamboo against a dazzling azure background. Some scholars have identified the young man on the right as the Qianlong emperor in his princedom, and the older man as a palace attendant. Others believe that the painting is a metaphoric portrait of the different stages of life and that both figures represent the Qianlong emperor. It is now generally agreed that the painting depicts the Qianlong emperor as a young prince receiving a sprig of plum blossom from his father the Yongzheng emperor. Plum blossom is often included in Chinese New Year paintings, being appreciated by mythical figures. As harbinger of spring, it symbolises the coming of the new year and the cyclic nature of life. In the present picture, the plum blossom may allude to Yongzheng's trust in his son as the crown prince to whom he will pass on the mandate of heaven and the guarantee of another peaceful reign.

Towards the upper right corner of the painting is a poem written by the Qianlong emperor, not at the time the painting was executed, but when he was 71 years old, in 1782. The poem adds a very personal touch to an intimate family painting, revealing the elderly emperor's awareness of time and of his own mortality: 'In portraiture [Lang] Shining is masterful; he painted me in the days of my youth. The white-headed one who enters the room today cannot recognise who this is' (trans Wu Hung).

The inscription also reveals the identity of the painter: Lang Shining is the Chinese name given to Giuseppe Castiglione (1688–1766), the brilliant Italian Jesuit missionary painter at court. Castiglione was born in Milan in 1688, and may have received some artistic training before entering the Society of Jesus in 1707. He went to China as a Jesuit brother in 1715 and entered the late Kangxi emperor's court as a painter. It was not easy for a painter from Europe to work for a Chinese patron, but Castiglione soon gained the respect of each of the emperors he served. He was admired in particular by the elderly Yongzheng emperor and by the Qianlong emperor for his skill in European painting techniques and for his willingness to accommodate these to a completely different cultural environment. In this painting Castiglione shows a grasp of Chinese symbolism and an ability to compromise his skills: in keeping with Chinese preferences, he does not use the technique of *chiaroscuro,* the depiction of light and shade, in the painting of the two figures.

The precise dating of the painting is problematic. It has been argued by Wu Hung that it must have been commissioned by the Qianlong emperor only after his accession to the throne in 1736, for had it been painted before his accession it would have revealed the identity of Hongli as the future emperor, which was a closely guarded secret.

EXH: Museu de Arte de Macau 2000: no. 20
LIT: Beurdeley 1971: 11–60, 97–106; Kahn 1971: 77; Yu Zhuoyun 1982: 90, 95; Wu Hung 1995

寫真世寧擅繢我少
年時入室皤然者不
知此是誰
壬寅暮春御題

何來瀟灑清都客逍遙為愛雲
烟碧筠籃滿貯仙巖芝芒鞵不
踏塵寰迹人世蓬萊鏡裏天霞
巾彷彿南華仙誰識當年真面
貌圖入生綃屬偶然
長春居士自題

3

Hongli, the future Qianlong emperor, gathering fungus

Attributed to Giuseppe Castiglione
Datable to 1734
Hanging scroll, ink on paper
L 204 cm, W 133 cm
Inscriptions: one by Hongli, undated; one by Liang Shizheng, dated 1734
Seals: three of Hongli; two of Liang Shizheng

There is no record of any portrait of Hongli, the future Qianlong emperor, as a young child, and this painting is the only known portrait of him before he became emperor. The inscription to the left, by Liang Shizheng (1697–1763), one of his tutors, is dated 1734, which would suggest that the painting was probably made in that year, the year prior to Hongli's accession to the throne, and when he was 23 years old. The painting may well have been commissioned by the prince himself rather than by his emperor father, as indicated by his own inscription in the upper right corner in which he uses one of his own chosen literary names: 'Inscribed by Changchun jushi, the Eternal Spring Scholar, himself.' The fact that such a portrait was made in 1734 is testimony to Hongli's elevated position by this time.

What is of particular interest is that Hongli is shown not in the normal attire of a prince, but dressed as a Daoist priest with a *lingzhi* fungus in one hand and caressing a deer with the other. The entire picture is executed in ink, with no costly use of pigments. The picture conforms to the conventional treatment of a Daoist subject, the search for the fungus of immortality in a land abounding in plants and flowers, with woods full of deer, also symbolic of longevity.

Such treatment of an imperial figure is not unprecedented: the emperor's father, the Yongzheng emperor, who was known to be a secret student of Daoism, had more than once had himself depicted as a Daoist figure wandering in a wild landscape. The portrait may well be a tribute by Hongli to his father, as well as showing his own aspirations for a spiritual life. This concern with the cultivation of the mind is spelt out clearly in the inscription, which may be rendered as follows:

> Who is this unrestrained palatial sojourner,
> Wandering freely amidst clouds and mist of jade green?
> His bamboo basket overflowing with fungus from the cliffs,
> His sandals of straw not stained with the dust of the world,
> He seems to live in a mythical land.
> His robe is similar to that of a Daoist.
> Who knows the true self of this youth?
> Or does the picture capture just the one time
> he happened to don such robes?

The painting does not bear a signature. The discrepancy between the accomplished rendering of the faces and the less sophisticated treatment of the folds of the robes suggests that it may be a collaborative work by a Jesuit artist and his Chinese pupil. The striking similarity between the treatment of Hongli's face in this picture and in the formal portrait (no. 5) suggests that both are by the same artist, probably Castiglione.

EXH: Museu de Arte de Macau 2000: no. 46
LIT: *LSTQJ* 1758: *juan* 20; Wu Hung 1995

4

Prefaces to the anthology of studies from the Hall of Delight in Doing Good

1730

Manuscript: 14 volumes, ink on paper

Case: black lacquer

Case: H 48 cm, L 24 cm, W 17.5 cm

In the autumn of 1730, just after his nineteenth birthday, Hongli, the future Qianlong emperor, presented to the court a selection of the fruits of his formal education of the previous seven years. This comprised his own essays, examination exercises, poems, historical sketches, letters, homilies, prefaces and colophons. This lacquer case contains the prefaces to the anthology, written by 14 people, including his brother, uncles, friends and court officials. Each preface is written in an album and slots neatly into the portable case with 14 shelves and a protective cover.

From this anthology of the prince's studies it is obvious that his education had concentrated on giving him an understanding of imperial leadership and of the role of the emperor in history and politics. The writings present prescribed views of good and bad, and are an orthodox guide rather than a set of personal opinions. He himself made this clear in the preface: '"Knowing is not difficult, but taking action is." I often refer to the words I have written as mirroring my actions. Were I incapable of self-examination to the point where words and action had no relevance to each other, were I capable of knowing but not of acting – would this not be to my shame?' (trans Harold Kahn). To ensure that his actions might be compared with his words, he had the anthology placed on a table where it would be easily accessible.

The title of the work is taken from the name of the prince's study, which was located in a remote and secluded corner in the northwest of the Forbidden City, just in front of his residence (see Liu Lu in this book, p. 158). The name, the Hall of Delight in Doing Good, alludes to the emperor's desire to be a powerful yet humble leader. According to the emperor,

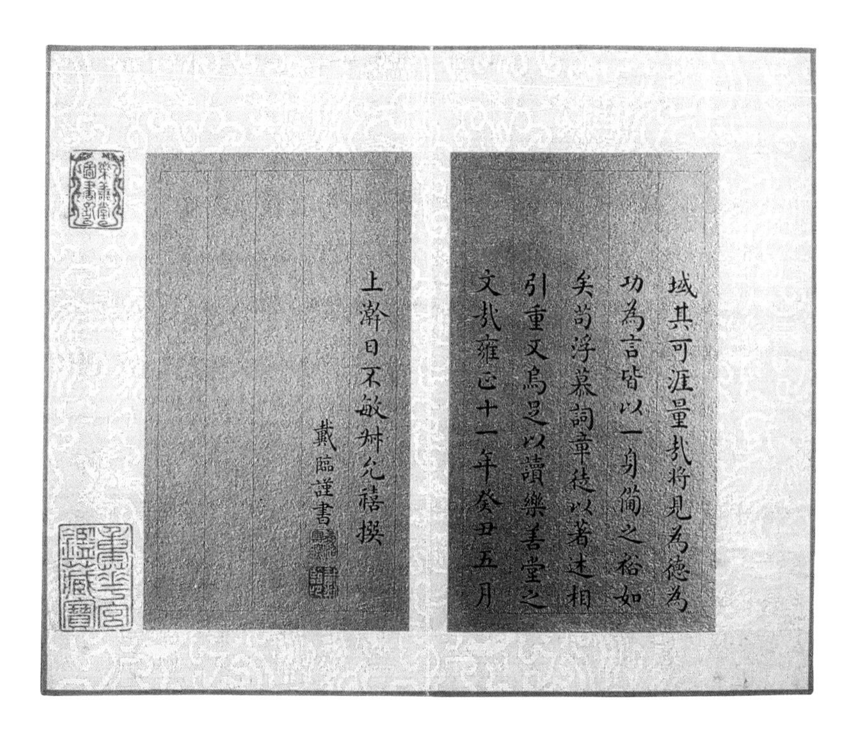
域其可涯量哉將見為德為
功為言皆以一身備之裕如
矣豈浮慕詞章徒以著述相
引重又烏足以讀樂善堂之
文哉雍正十一年癸丑五月
上澣日不敏弟允禧撰
戴臨謹書

the name originated from the words of the great Chinese philosopher Mencius who wrote: 'The great Shun [one of the legendary sage rulers] ... takes delight in learning from others so that he may practise only what is good.' These words point to the ultimate aspiration for a monarch: modesty. Without humility and an open mind, a monarch could be but a despot, never a sage. 'Delight in doing good' thus became the Qianlong emperor's motto for success.

EXH: Palace Museum 2000: no. 40
LIT: Khan 1971: 101, 168–72; Zhu Jiajin 1986: 191; Palace Museum 2000: 123

5

The Qianlong emperor in formal court robe

Anonymous
Datable to 1735
Hanging scroll, ink and colour on silk
L 242 cm, W 179 cm
Seals: three of Hongli

This portrait is unsigned and undated, but may be attributed to Giuseppe Castiglione and dated to 1735. In that year Castiglione painted a handscroll showing the newly inaugurated Qianlong emperor with his wife the Xiaoxian empress (no. 6) and eleven concubines. This scroll is now in the Cleveland Museum of Art. A comparison of the treatment of the emperor's facial features in the two paintings leaves little doubt that both portraits were the work of the same artist in the same year.

What is puzzling is how the present portrait might have been used. It falls within the genre of 'ancestor portrait', with the emperor shown full length but seated, in a rigidly frontal, symmetrical and restrained pose. The emperor's expression is sombre and detached, and his clothing, the throne and the floor are all highly patterned. Within the Qing court such ancestor portraits were used in ritual ceremonies. According to studies by Evelyn Rawski, it is recorded that after the death of the Yongzheng emperor, his portrait was hung in the Palace of Complete Harmony, his former princely palace. There daily rituals were performed in front of the portrait between the time of death and the burial. Apart from their use in funerary rites, imperial portraits were worshipped in places such as the Shouhuangdian, the imperial family ancestral hall, at New Year, when the emperor and his sons would offer sacrifices before the portraits.

It is uncertain however whether the present portrait was ever used for ancestral worship since there are at least three portraits of the elderly Qianlong emperor (see no. 76). As the present portrait depicts the emperor as a young man just after his accession to the throne, it should perhaps be regarded as an inauguration portrait. Should such an interpretation be correct, the omission of a reference to the sitter's name or to a specific event, and the detailed attention to the cosmic motifs on the fabric of the robe take on a new meaning. This is not an effigy of the emperor, but an emblem of his special place in the cosmos, as a semi-sacred being, a mediator between heaven and earth.

EXH: *De Verboden Stad* 1990: no. 1; *A Cidade Proibida* 1992: no. 1; Museu de Arte de Macau 2000: no. 21
LIT: Chou and Brown 1985: 23–4; Rawski 1998: 286–7; Stuart and Rawski 2001: 45, 52–8

6

The Xiaoxian empress in formal court robe

Anonymous
Datable to 1735
Hanging scroll, ink and colour on silk
L 194.8 cm, W 116.2 cm

This portrait of the Xiaoxian empress, the Qianlong emperor's first wife, was probably painted by Castiglione at the same time as the inauguration portrait of the emperor (no. 5). In the similar painting in the Cleveland Museum of Art she is placed next to the emperor.

The Xiaoxian empress was born in 1712 to a Manchu family which had a special relationship with the royal family. The empress's grandfather had served the Qianlong emperor's grandfather, the Kangxi emperor. It was thus not surprising that she was chosen to be the wife of Hongli in 1727 when she was 15 years old. By all accounts they had a loving relationship. To Hongli she was a symbol of the decency of the Manchu way of life.

In 1748 the empress accompanied her husband on a trip to offer sacrifices at the Temple of Confucius in Qufu in Shandong province, the hometown of Confucius. On the return journey, in Jinan, the provincial capital, which was notorious for its cases of malaria, the empress was struck down with the disease and died in Dezhou on the border of Shandong province long before the imperial retinue returned to the palace. In his sorrow, the emperor decided to reintroduce state mourning for the empress, a Chinese tradition that had not been practised since the Manchus came to power. According to the statute, mourning lasted for 100 days, during which time officials throughout the empire had to wear traditional hemp mourning garb and refrain from all manner of pleasure. At some stage during the mourning period it was reported to the emperor that several officials in the provinces had shaved their heads. Interpreting this as a sign of betrayal, the emperor had the men executed. This incident has been singled out by Norman Kutcher as not simply the angry over-reaction of a man in mourning but as a sign of the Qianlong emperor asserting his power to solve a crisis arising from the clash of Manchu and Han Chinese cultures.

EXH: *De Verboden Stad* 1990: no. 2; *A Cidade Proibida* 1992: no. 2; *Die Verbotene Stadt* 1997: no. 25; Museu de Arte de Macau 2000: no. 22
LIT: Chou and Brown 1985: 23–4; Kutcher 1997

7

The Xiaosheng empress dowager in formal court robe

Anonymous

Qianlong period (1736–95)

Hanging scroll, ink and colour on silk

L 229 cm, W 140 cm

The Qianlong emperor's mother came from Niohuru, one of the eight famous Manchu families. Her family was related through her father's side to Eidu (1562–1621), the famous warrior-companion of Nurhachi, founder of the Qing dynasty. She entered Prince Yong's house at the age of eleven in 1704, and her rise was slow initially. In 1723, the Yongzheng emperor's first year on the throne, she was promoted to the third rank, only rising to the second in the late years of the emperor's reign. When her only son Hongli acceded the throne she was immediately proclaimed the empress dowager. She had a long life, dying at the age of 85 in 1777, when her emperor son himself was already 66 years old.

The Xiaosheng empress dowager loved the outdoor life. She accompanied her son on four of his six southern tours of inspection, as well as going to the sacred Buddhist mountain Mount Wutai in Shanxi province, and three times to Mount Tai and the Temple of Confucius in Shandong province. The third time she visited Mount Tai she was 84 years old. She also travelled regularly, until the age of 84, with her son to Rehe (Chengde) in the southern part of the Manchu heartland for the autumn hunt. Although the emperor lived in close contact with his mother, she had little intellectual influence and played a very private role as mother.

According to the Palace Museum, this portrait of Xiaosheng was painted on her eightieth birthday. There is another similar portrait of her, also undated, in the Palace Museum collection.

LIT: Khan 1971: 85–97; Dai Yi 1997: 53–9

8

Imperial seal inscribed 'Treasure of the son of heaven'

After 1748

Gold

L 11.71 cm, W 11.7 cm, H 10 cm

No imperial document was complete or fully sanctioned without the imprint of the state seal, the final and literal stamp of authority. This seal, which was for the use of the Qianlong emperor, is inscribed 'Treasure of the son of heaven' in Manchu seal script, a script invented at the request of the emperor. As this script came into use only in 1748, the present seal cannot have been made before that date. The base of the seal is square, and it has a dragon-shaped grip. It is made of gold, one of the favoured materials for seals, the others being jade, bronze and silver.

The basic form and function of seals were established as early as the Han dynasty (206 BCE – CE 220). The state seal system of the Qing dynasty was set up early in the reign of the Shunzhi emperor. The Board of Rites was given responsibility for seal casting, the Grand Secretariat for the selection of the script, and the Board of Works for the materials with which to make them, with the exception of gold and silver which were under the remit of the Board of Revenue. When a seal was cast there was a ritual to promulgate its existence. These rituals were carried out by each emperor until the Qianlong emperor who placed such importance on the state seal as the symbol of imperial authority that he sought a further elaboration to the system.

According to the new regulations set out in 1746, the number of designated state seals was set at 25, a figure based on the emperor's study of the *Book of changes (Yijing)*. The figure referred to the number of reign periods that the emperor envisaged as ideal for the dynasty. This casts an interesting light on the emperor's views on dynastic history: he thought of a dynasty as something living, that would be born, grow and die. Each seal had a particular function. The present seal was for use on documents related to the sacrifices offered to mountain and river spirits.

Stricter rules regarding the storage of seals were also imposed. All seals were placed in the Hall of Union in the Forbidden City, and were overseen by a keeper. Each time a seal was required, an official was sent from the inner court with the responsibility of collecting it and then returning it immediately after use.

EXH: Ledderose and Butz 1985: no. 11; *De Verboden Stad* 1990: no. 74; *A Cidade Proibida* 1992: no. 74

LIT: Guo Fuxiang 1992: 14–15; Xu Qixian 1995

9

Treasure box

Qianlong period (1736–95)

Lacquer, inlaid, containing jade disc and red sandalwood tray

Box: H 7 cm, D 11.4 cm

This box was made to contain a precious object, in this case a jade *bi* disc, symbol of heaven (see no. 68). As most such boxes have become separated from the treasures they once contained, this one allows a rare insight into the use of a court lacquer box. It was probably a New Year gift to the emperor from a courtier.

The box is of brownish-red lacquer in the shape of a six-petalled lotus flower. The centre of the lid bears an image of the god of longevity superimposed on the Chinese character for spring, *chun*. This decoration is inlaid with various colours of lacquer, a technique known as *tianqi*, literally 'filled in'. The six scenes around the lid depict spring outings.

Fitting snugly inside the case, and resting on a red sandalwood tray, is a jade *bi* disc. The centre of the sandalwood tray is raised to allow the disc to slot neatly over it and the area is carved with the Qianlong emperor's regnal device. This device is made up of the first of the eight trigrams in the Chinese divinatory system (meaning heaven and male), pronounced *qian*, and dragons, pronounced *long*. Together the two sounds are homophonous with the reign title of the emperor, Qianlong. The design ingeniously suggests that the Qianlong emperor had received the mandate of heaven and embarked on a new reign (see Introduction, p. 22).

EXH: Palace Museum 2000: no. 63

10

Pair of elephants carrying vases

Qianlong period (1736–95)
Jade, cloisonné enamel, sandalwood
Each H 36 cm

The elephant is a symbol of strength and wisdom and as such became identified with the Buddha Sakyamuni. The Buddha is said to have been conceived when a small white elephant entered his mother's womb. The elephant is also the mount of the bodhisattva Samantabhadra (see no. 58) and the bearer of the Buddha's alms bowl.

The Qing court received elephants as gifts from lands to the south such as Thailand. They were kept by the imperial procession guard for use in state rituals. In grand ceremonies they would carry vases on their backs and walk ahead of the imperial cortège, as symbols of the strength of the dynasty and of the peaceful reign period. As the favourite imperial symbol, elephants were made in a variety of materials by the imperial workshops and used in various contexts. Elephant-shaped wine vessels of bronze, *xiangzun*, were placed in the Imperial Ancestral Temple and used for imperial ancestor worship.

This pair of carved jade elephants flanked the throne in one of the throne halls in the Forbidden City.

EXH: Ledderose and Butz 1985: no. 15
LIT: *DQHDT* 1899, vol. 2, 1427; Ju Shicheng 1981

11

Pair of incense burners

Qianlong period (1736–95)
Jade, gilded copper
Each H 120 cm

Like the jade elephants above, this pair of incense burners shaped as pavilions was also for use in a throne hall. They were commonly placed at the two front corners of the throne platform to act as air fresheners. These burners, made of jade and gilded copper, decorated with cosmic motifs such as dragons surging amidst clouds, were intended to project an image of the emperor's residence as a representation of heaven on earth.

EXH: Ledderose and Butz 1985: no. 16

12

The Qianlong emperor's semi-formal court robe

Datable to 1759–95
Satin, embroidered with gold and silk
L 144.5 cm

This winter robe was worn by the Qianlong emperor on less formal occasions such as state banquets and annual festivals. A more formal robe was worn at grand sacrifices and at the inauguration ceremony (no. 5). The cut of the robe is typical of Manchu-style dress. The sleeves are tight fitting, tapering to distinctive flared cuffs which would have protected the hands from the cold. The lower half of the robe is split at the front and back for ease of movement, a visible remnant of the Manchus' equestrian roots.

However, the decoration tells us much about the place of the emperor in the Chinese world picture. The robe is of brilliant yellow, the colour reserved solely for the emperor, the empress and the empress dowager. The shimmering golden light that would have emanated from its surface was symbolic of the divine nature of the son of heaven.

The imperial symbolism is further revealed by two sets of decorative motifs. The first is a set of nine dragons, the number representing the nine zones, or the furthest corners of the empire ruled by the emperor. Four frontal dragons radiate from the neck: on the chest, the back and the shoulders, representing the four cardinal points. The four dragons in profile on the skirt, two at the front and two at the back, indicate the directions midway between the cardinal points. The ninth dragon is hidden on the inner flap of the skirt. The second group of symbols consists of the sun, the moon, a constellation, mountains, a dragon, a pheasant, a pair of cups, waterweed, grain, fire, an axe, and the symbol *fu,* meaning good wishes. These are the twelve emblems associated with imperial authority.

This robe can be securely dated to after 1759, for in that year new regulations were issued regarding items for use at state occasions. These regulations stipulated that the twelve emblems could be used on imperial robes.

To make a dragon robe such as this one took at least one year. In Chen Juanjuan's study of surviving court documents regarding clothing, she records that the first stage in the process was a drawing: a painter in the imperial workshop was asked to create a design and his drawings had to be approved by the emperor. The drawings were then sent to one of the imperial textile factories, in either Nanjing or Hangzhou. As the robe was made, the complete process was recorded, including materials, techniques, packing details, and transportation costs.

LIT: Medley 1982: 1–30; Pang 1989: 80–3; Chen Juanjuan 1994.2: 84–5

13

The Qianlong emperor's informal jacket

Qianlong period (1736–95)
Gauze
L 145 cm

When not engaged in public duties the emperor wore a more informal jacket, somewhat similar in cut to his formal and semi-formal robes. However, informal clothing gave the emperor greater freedom to wear materials, colours and designs of his choice. This summer jacket is made of plain pale yellow gauze, woven with concealed medallions.

14

Ceremonial court necklace

Qianlong period (1736–95)
Coral
L 126 cm

Court necklaces were worn by the emperor, empresses, princes, dukes and civil servants above the fifth rank with court robes at ceremonies and festivals. This necklace has 108 beads, divided evenly by four large beads known as Buddha's heads. The short strings of beads, two on the left and one on the right, are called *jinian,* commemoration beads. The gourd-shaped bead at the top end of the central string is known as the Buddha's pagoda. These names point to the Buddhist origins of the court necklace. This red coral necklace was worn by the emperor when he made his annual sacrifice to the sun, as red is the colour specified in the court regulations for the emperor's attire on this occasion. The emperor was required to wear different necklaces for different sacrifices: lapis lazuli when making sacrifices to heaven, amber for earth, and turquoise for the moon.

EXH: Pang 1989: no. 36
LIT: *DQHDT* 1899, vol. 2, 1859; Chen Juanjuan 1994.2: 92; 1994.3: 52–4

15

Equatorial armillary sphere

Qianlong period (1736–95)
Gilded bronze, wood
H 70 cm

This armillary sphere consists of three rings (*armilla* is the Latin for a ring) which make up a skeletal celestial sphere. The outermost upright ring is called the meridian ring (for measuring degrees above the horizon), the horizontal ring perpendicular to it is the immobile equatorial ring, and the innermost ring is the ecliptic (an imaginary band set at an angle to the earth's horizon around which the celestial bodies apparently move). Armillary spheres were used to calculate equatorial degrees of longitude and latitude and to obtain the positions of stars in equatorial coordinates.

Observational armillary spheres were developed by the ancient Greeks and also independently in China where they became an important item of observatory equipment from the first century. Most Chinese observational armillary spheres were, like this one, of the equatorial form and many had an automatic rotation mechanism. Western and eastern traditions converged in the seventeenth century with the arrival of Jesuit missionaries in China.

Many of these Jesuit missionaries brought with them a sound training in the sciences. Their collaboration with Chinese scientists encouraged the development of scientific knowledge, particularly mathematics and astronomy. One of the most famous Jesuit astronomers was Ferdinand Verbiest (1623–88) who had been greatly influenced by the Danish astronomer Tycho Brahe, the last western astronomer to make extensive use of the armillary sphere for the purpose of observation. Verbiest went on to become the director of the Beijing observatory which had been established in the Yuan dynasty (1279–1368). He was responsible for refitting the observatory in the 1670s and for equipping it with instruments, including an equatorial armillary sphere based on Tycho Brahe's designs.

The present instrument was probably made about 1744, possibly by the Jesuit Ignatius Kogler and his Chinese collaborators at the Beijing observatory.

UNIVERSAL RULER

More than his grandfather and father before him, the Qianlong emperor was determined to stem the erosion of Manchu identity among those Manchu who had settled in China proper over the previous hundred years of the dynasty. As early as 1739 he reinstated the grand military review of the capital banner troops (no. 34), and two years later he revived the annual royal hunting expedition on the steppes of the Manchu heartland (no. 30). His early reign also witnessed the vigorous restructuring of the banner system to consolidate Manchu values (no. 33). He repeatedly reminded the Manchu how vital it was for them to have a command of their native language and to develop the skills of horse-riding and shooting (*guoyu qishe*).

The emperor's insistence on the revival of Manchu identity was not an isolated action, but was closely connected with his renewed initiative to consolidate dynastic rule over the Mongols in the north. As the emperor himself clearly stated, one of the main reasons why he went hunting annually in Rehe was to maintain ties with the Mongols (no. 21). The emperor's emphasis on the Mongol connection was both strategic and ideological. He started to learn the Mongol language in 1743, and in 1745 he converted the palace where he was born into the largest lamasery in Beijing to show his endorsement of the religion worshipped by the Mongols since the fourteenth century, lamaism. In the same year he was baptised.

This emphasis on the Mongol connection influenced the emperor's decision to launch the expensive wars of the 1750s against the Western Mongols who had long posed a threat to Qing authority in Mongolia and Tibet. Victory over the Western Mongols gave the Qing control of the entire northwest frontier region which included eastern Turkestan and Tibet. On completion of the campaign at the end of 1759, the Qianlong emperor sought to project himself not just as emperor of China but as ruler of an Asian empire, as *cakravartin* or the universal ruler of the Buddhist world (no. 17).

Cakravartin is an ancient Indian term meaning literally a ruler whose chariot wheels roll everywhere. Likewise, the Qianlong emperor was a man on the move. During his lifetime he made numerous grand tours throughout his empire (no. 26) and when not on tour divided his time between the Forbidden City, his summer palaces and his country mansions.

The Qing empire of the post-conquest period comprised different regions with distinct cultures. In order to integrate these various peoples the Qianlong emperor adopted a multicultural approach to his rule. This can be seen in his construction projects in the Forbidden City and elsewhere, in the compilation of *The Four Treasuries* (no. 22), multilingual dictionaries and Buddhist sutras (no. 20), in the recruitment of court artists from wide-ranging backgrounds, and above all in the eclectic styles of the works produced by these artists to glorify their emperor.

Opposite:
Detail of *The Qianlong emperor as the manifestation of Manjusri and Dharmaraja* (no. 17).

16

The Qianlong emperor in ceremonial armour on horseback

Attributed to Giuseppe Castiglione
1739 or 1758
Hanging scroll, colour on silk
L 322.5 cm, W 232 cm

There are conflicting opinions as to the date of this magnificent equestrian portrait of the Qianlong emperor. One theory dates it to 1739 because the emperor appears quite youthful (he would have been 28 years old in 1739), and because the first grand military review was conducted in that year (see no. 34). However, no documents have been found to support this date for the painting.

Another opinion holds that the portrait was linked to a diplomatic event. In the autumn of 1758 the court heard that the Buruts, a Muslim tribe living in the Tarim Basin, had sent envoys to pay homage to the emperor. This announcement came as the emperor was involved in a military campaign in the Tarim Basin to put down a group of dissident Uyghur Muslims led by two brothers, Khozi Khan and Burhan-al-Din. As the campaign was not proving successful the emperor realised that the allegiance of the Buruts might increase his support against the Uyghur dissidents. In order to impress the Burut envoys and to mark the allegiance, grand receptions were arranged. The first of these was held in Mulan, the imperial hunting ground in Rehe, where the envoys were invited to join the imperial hunt and attend a lavish state banquet. The emperor then invited them to the court in Beijing, an exceptional favour as, according to court regulations, envoys on their first visit were received only in Rehe. On 3 November the emperor held an audience for the envoys in the Hall of Supreme Harmony, and on 5 December there was a grand military review at the South Park, the imperial hunting reserve outside Beijing. According to Liu Lu's reading of the court archives, the emperor asked Castiglione to paint a portrait of him to be hung in the South Park on the day of the review. This may be that very portrait.

According to a description by Lord Macartney, Britain's first ambassador to China in 1793, the emperor was short, about 1.6 metres in height. However, in this portrait he is portrayed as tall, assertive and radiant in his armour. In one sense this equestrian portrait can be seen as a typical example of the importation of a European style of portrait to the Qing court. The so-called Spanish pose of the horse, with one leg raised, can be found in many portraits of mounted European rulers. Yet the painting is not an exotic form of glorification of the emperor within the European pictorial idiom. Rather, it represents a new type of monarch. As Pamela Crossley has argued, this image is a visual amalgamation of the different concepts of monarchy held by the various cultural groups who made up the Qing empire: his pose astride the horse, his left hand holding the rein and his right a riding crop in the Mongolian manner, presents us with the emperor as a northern frontier lord. His ceremonial armour of bright yellow embroidered with golden dragons shows him to be a Chinese son of heaven; and the conical helmet embellished with gold stylised Sanskrit characters makes him a protector of Tibetan Buddhism (see no. 32). This portrait shows, for the first time, that the emperor was not simply ruler of China but of a multicultural Asian empire.

EXH: *Die Verbotene Stadt* 1997: no. 125
LIT: Zhu Jiajin 1988; Crossley 1999: 272–80; Liu Lu 2000.4

17

The Qianlong emperor as the manifestation of Manjusri and Dharmaraja

Datable to 1760
Gouache on cloth
H 108 cm, W 63 cm

This portrait of the Qianlong emperor takes the form of a *thangka,* a wall hanging used for meditation in Tibetan Buddhist worship. The majority of *thangkas* bear images of deities, but some have religious scenes, visions of paradise and portraits of lamas. Usually two artists, normally monks, are involved in the production of a *thangka* – one draws the design and another applies the paint.

This *thangka* portrays the Qianlong emperor as a pre-eminent figure in the sacred Buddhist realm. Dressed in a monk's robe and seated on a cushion, he has his right hand in *vitarka mudra,* the gesture of persuasion. In his left he holds the wheel of law, an emblem commonly associated with early Tibetan rulers and later with the Dalai Lamas as it suggests that the ruler is *cakravartin,* the one who set the world in motion. Various ritual objects are placed on the altar. On the front of the altar is an inscription in Tibetan naming the emperor as manifestation of Manjusri, bodhisattva of wisdom, Lord of the Human World, and of Dharmaraja, king of the Buddhist faith. The identification of the Qianlong emperor with Manjusri is highlighted by the addition near his shoulders of a sword and scriptures, two of the attributes of Manjusri. This painting can be considered as a lineage portrait in the sense that the emperor's spiritual teacher, the Grand Lama of Beijing and the Third Cangca Khutuktu of Inner Mongolia, Rolpa'i Dorje (1717–86), is seated above him in the sky among buddhas, attendant deities and flying monks. Below, monks flank a pool of lotus blossoms. Towards the lower edge of the painting are the three guardian deities of the religion.

Seven similar portraits of the emperor are known to exist: five in Beijing, one in the Potala Palace in Lhasa, and one in the Freer Gallery of Art in Washington DC. This portrait is characterised by its fantastic scenes of gardens and skies. Before entering the collections of the Palace Museum in Beijing it was stored in the Puning Monastery in Rehe, a Sino-Tibetan-style monastery, modelled on the Samye Monastery in Tibet, that was constructed to commemorate the victory over Davatsi, leader of the Western Mongols, in Dzungaria in the northwest in 1755. The painting was commissioned in memory of the same event, to highlight the religious cause of the military campaign.

It has been suggested that the design of the painting was probably supervised by Rolpa'i Dorje. While the iconography is typically Tibetan, the style of the *thangka* shows a blend of European and Sino-Tibetan elements. The subtle modelling of the emperor's face suggests that it could have been the joint work of Giuseppe Castiglione and a Mongol lamaist monk artist at court.

EXH: Ledderose and Butz 1985: no. 39
LIT: Dagyab 1977: 24–8, 40–5; Bartholomew 1997: 117; Bruckner 2000: 8–22; Stuart and Rawski 2001: 118–21

18

Kapala, human skull bowl

Qianlong period (1736–95)
Bone, gilded copper
H 22 cm

The *kapala,* Sanskrit for skull, is used both in Hindu India and in Buddhist Nepal and Tibet. In Tibet a *kapala* is made from the skull of a donor, usually a holy man of great wisdom. Only with the approval of the lama can a skull be made into a ritual utensil. In tantric rituals a *kapala* is placed on the altar as a reminder of the impermanence of all things, and its main function is as a container of offerings for divinities. It is sometimes filled with wine or cakes, symbolising the blood or flesh of the demon, in the hope that deities such as Dharmapala, defender of the faith, will partake of them.

This *kapala* has a gilded rim and a gilded copper cover with a flaming pearl at the top serving as a handle. The cover is decorated with the eight auspicious emblems of Buddhism amidst scrolling flowers, and the gilded base is adorned with flame motifs. Three small human heads project from the corners of the triangular stand on the base.

LIT: Chang and Hsu 1999: nos 64, 72

19

Portable Buddhist shrine and ritual objects

Qianlong period (1736–95)

Nan wood, sandalwood, coral, turquoise, gilded silver

Case: L 33.5 cm, W 14 cm, H 29 cm

This portable case opens to display a miniature Buddhist shrine and eleven utensils for use in worship. The shrine is made of *nan* wood (cedar) and is of Han Chinese style. Inside the shrine is a small coral bodhisattva seated on a lotus-flower base made of turquoise. In Buddhist rituals the three basic types of utensil are incense burner, candleholder and flower vase. In ordinary daily worship people use sets of five utensils, *wujuzu*, which comprise a pair of flower vases, a pair of candleholders and one incense burner. The present elaborate set comprises two candleholders, two incense burners, a flower vase, five lamp holders and a box, all of gilded silver. As the niche for each utensil is specially cut to fit the utensil exactly and prevent it from moving around inside the box, it seems likely that the set was for use by the imperial family when travelling.

20

Bodhisattva Manjusri's Commendation of Sakyamuni

Qianlong period (1736–95)

Sutra folios: ink on gold-flecked paper

Sutra covers: gilded red sandalwood, protected with silk

Base: gilded copper, turquoise, coral

Outer case: glass, gilded copper

Case: L 23.5 cm, W 12 cm, H 19.5 9 cm

This magnificent case is the external protection for a sutra, the *Commendation of Sakyamuni*. The sutra is inscribed on gold-flecked folios in four languages, from top to bottom: Manchu, Mongol, Tibetan and Han Chinese. It is not known when the Han Chinese translation of the sutra first appeared, nor do we know the name of its translator. Each folio is bordered with the curse of Manjusri in stylised Sanskrit characters (*lanca*).

Both the front and back covers of the sutra are made of red sandalwood and gilded. On the outside of the front cover is written the curse of Manjusri in early Tibetan script, and on the inside is the title of the sutra with images of the Buddha Sakyamuni and the bodhisattva Manjusri. The back cover is decorated with the four guardian kings: Dhritarashtra, king of the east, Virupaksha, king of the west, Virudhaka, king of the south, and Vaishravana, king of the north. Three layers of silk, embroidered with designs of the eight treasures, are laid on top of both front and back covers.

Inside the case the sutra is placed on a gilded sumeru base inlaid with turquoise, coral and other precious materials. The book is further protected by another cover made of glass inset into gilded copper frames. The glass panes are also painted with the eight auspicious emblems of Buddhism, *bajixiang,* namely the wheel of the law, the banner of victory, the knot, conch-shell, lotus, jar, a pair of fish, and the canopy, as well as other Sino-Tibetan designs.

Such a sumptuous sutra was obviously not for daily reference, but for display in a lamaist temple in the palace to show the emperor's reverence for it.

EXH: Palace Museum 2000: no. 76

21

Imperial banquet in the Garden of Ten Thousand Trees, Rehe

Attributed to Giuseppe Castiglione and others
Dated 1755
Hanging scroll, ink and colour on silk
L 419.6 cm, H 221.5 cm
Inscription: part of artist's signature, dated 1755

This monumental painting, one of the largest in the Palace Museum collection, is executed on a single piece of silk more that four metres long. The silk was probably made in the imperial textile factory in Hangzhou which would have had the facilities to make such a piece. The painting was not mounted initially in scroll format but was made as a type of wall painting, *tieluo*, meaning literally to paste on and then remove. Yang Boda has argued that the painting was made for a wall in the Hall of Pleasant Breezes, the main reception hall in the Summer Palace in Rehe, and was only mounted in its present format in the 1970s.

The Garden of Ten Thousand Trees was the prairie district in Rehe, and was designed to evoke the landscape of Mongolia. The garden contained not only a huge number of trees but also the re-creation of a Mongolian campsite, in which temporary yurts and low fences could be erected for outdoor imperial banquets. Such banquets were commonly held in the hunting season for the lords of Dzungaria and the religious leaders of Mongolia and Tibet. During his reign the Qianlong emperor held numerous significant receptions, including one for the Western Mongols from Dzungaria and one for the Panchen Lama. It was also here that Lord Macartney, Britain's first envoy to China, was received in 1793.

The painting shows a typical imperial banquet in a recreated camp. Within the yellow fences a large imperial yurt occupies the central area towards the back. To each side of the yurt are musical instruments, and in front of it are two rows of tables set for a meal. There is also a tent for the display of imperial gifts, and there is equipment for acrobatic performances after dinner.

The Qianlong emperor, dressed in blue and seated crosslegged on a sedan chair in the midst of his impressive entourage, approaches from the left. What is special about this painting is that it is the visual record of an actual imperial banquet in held 1754 for the Western Mongols from Dzungaria, who can be seen, in their Dzungar costumes, kneeling in rows to the left of centre. In that year the Qianlong emperor hosted two banquets, one in the spring for the Derbet tribe, and the other in the autumn for the Khoits. Both tribes had migrated to China as a result of recent internal unrest in Dzungaria. Yang Boda argues that the painting depicts the reception of the former tribe. However, both events were equally instrumental in the emperor's grand plan for the conquest of the Dzungars in 1755. It was at such banquets and the associated events in Rehe that the emperor formed a coalition with the Western Mongols for a military campaign.

The remnants of an artist's signature can be made out in the lower left corner, but the name is illegible because of damage to the silk. Nevertheless, according to Yang Boda, the court archives mention the artists who participated in the commission, namely Giuseppe Castiglione, Jean-Denis Attiret, Ignatius Sickelbart and a number of Chinese court painters.

EXH: Ledderose and Butz 1985: no. 27; *De Verboden Stad* 1990: no. 10; *A Cidade Proibida* 1992: no. 10
LIT: Beurdeley 1971: 52; Zhang Zhansheng 1986; Yang Boda 1993: 178–210; Forêt 2000: 43–9

22

Catalogue of The Four Treasuries

1782

Manuscript in four scrolls, ink on paper

Case: sandalwood

Case: L 39 cm, W 32 cm, H 9 cm

In emulation of the major cultural enterprises of previous dynasties, the Qianlong emperor launched an ambitious project to review and transcribe books published from 1773 to 1782. After the review of over 10,000 titles, the entire texts of 3461 works, arranged in four categories – classics, history, philosophy and *belles-lettres* – were copied on to the best paper in four identical sets for the four imperial libraries: in the Forbidden City, the Summer Palace near Beijing (Yuanmingyuan), the Summer Palace in Rehe, and Mukden (Shenyang). Each set comprises a total of 36,000 volumes. They are known as the emperor's *Four Treasuries*. The reviews and comments on individual works were also compiled in the form of a catalogue, which is still considered the most indispensable reference book in the field of bibliography.

The present catalogue is a list of the 3450 works copied for the imperial libraries. Each of the four scrolls represents one of the categories into which the works were arranged. The catalogue was presented to the emperor in 1782.

LIT: Hummel 1949, vol. 1: 120–2

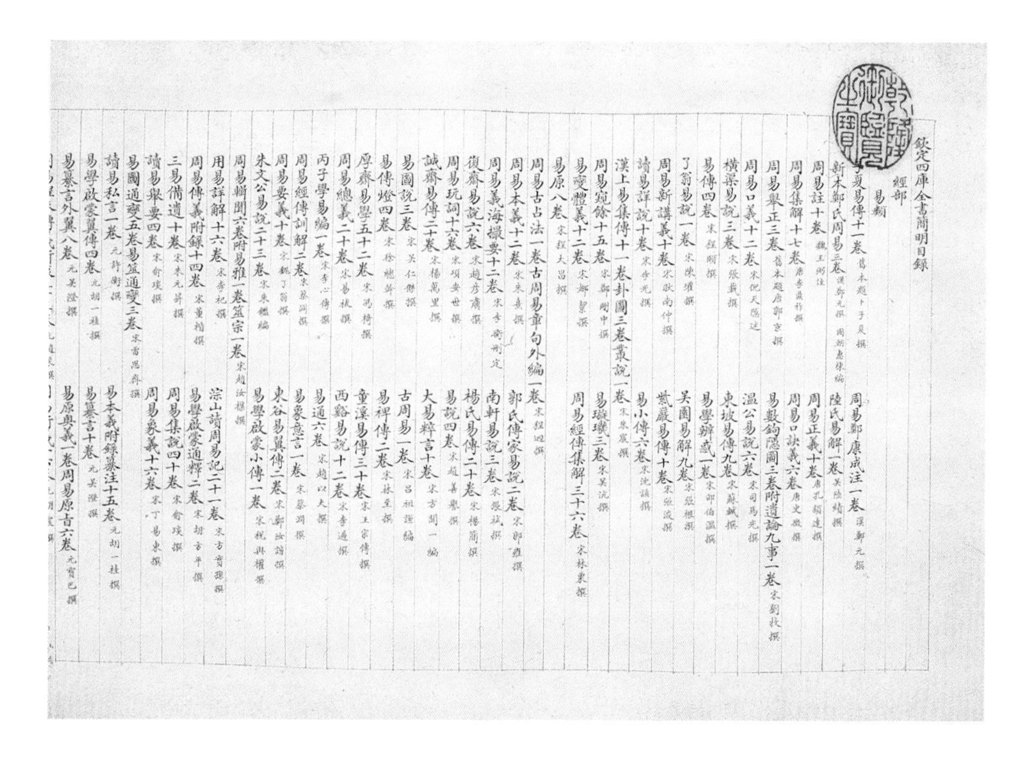
欽定四庫全書簡明目錄
經部
易類
子夏易傳十一卷 舊本題卜子夏撰　周易鄭康成注一卷 漢鄭元撰
新本鄭氏周易三卷 漢鄭元撰 國朝惠棟編　陸氏易解一卷 吳陸績撰
周易註十卷 魏王弼注　周易正義十卷 唐孔穎達撰
周易集解十七卷 唐李鼎祚撰　周易口訣義六卷 唐史徵撰
周易舉正三卷 舊本題唐郭京撰　易數鈎隱圖三卷附遺論九事一卷 宋劉牧撰
周易口義十二卷 宋倪天隱述　溫公易說六卷 宋司馬光撰
橫渠易說三卷 宋張載撰　東坡易傳九卷 宋蘇軾撰
易傳四卷 宋程頤撰　易學辨惑一卷 宋邵伯溫撰
了翁易說一卷 宋陳瓘撰　吳園易解九卷 宋張根撰
周易新講義十卷 宋耿南仲撰　紫巖易傳十卷 宋張浚撰
讀易詳說十卷 宋李光撰　易小傳六卷 宋沈該撰
漢上易集傳十一卷卦圖三卷叢說一卷 宋朱震撰
周易窺餘十五卷 宋鄭剛中撰　易璇璣三卷 宋吳沆撰
易變體義十二卷 宋都絜撰　周易經傳集解三十六卷 宋林栗撰
易原八卷 宋程大昌撰
周易古占法一卷古周易章句外編一卷 宋程迥撰
周易本義十二卷 宋朱熹撰　郭氏傳家易說二卷 宋郭雍撰
周易義海撮要十二卷 宋李衡刪定　南軒易說三卷 宋張栻撰
復齋易說六卷 宋趙彥肅撰　楊氏易傳二十卷 宋楊簡撰
周易玩詞十六卷 宋項安世撰　易說四卷 宋趙善譽撰
誠齋易傳二十卷 宋楊萬里撰　大易粹言十卷 宋方聞一編
易圖說三卷 宋吳仁傑撰　古周易一卷 宋呂祖謙編
易傳燈四卷 宋徐總幹撰　易裨傳二卷 宋林至撰
厚齋易學五十二卷 宋馮椅撰　童溪易傳三十卷 宋王宗傳撰
周易總義二十卷 宋易祓撰　西谿易說十二卷 宋李過撰
丙子學易編一卷 宋李心傳撰　易通六卷 宋趙以夫撰
周易經傳訓解二卷 宋蔡淵撰　易象意言一卷 宋蔡淵撰
周易要義十卷 宋魏了翁撰　東谷易翼傳二卷 宋鄭汝諧撰
朱文公易說二十三卷 宋朱鑑編　易學啟蒙小傳一卷 宋稅與權撰
周易輯聞六卷附易雅一卷筮宗一卷 宋趙汝楳撰
用易詳解十六卷 宋李杞撰　淙山讀周易記二十一卷 宋方實孫撰
周易傳義附錄十四卷 宋董楷撰　易學啟蒙通釋二卷 宋胡方平撰
三易備遺十卷 宋朱元昇撰　周易集說四十卷 宋俞琰撰
讀易舉要四卷 宋俞琰撰　周易象義十六卷 宋丁易東撰
易圖通變五卷易筮通變三卷 宋雷思齊撰
讀易私言一卷 元許衡撰　易本義附錄纂注十五卷 元胡一桂撰
易學啟蒙翼傳四卷 元胡一桂撰　易纂言十卷 元吳澄撰
易纂言外翼八卷 元吳澄撰　易原奧義一卷周易原旨六卷 元保巴撰

If the banquet held in Rehe in 1754 (no. 21) heralds the beginning of the military campaign on the northwest frontier, the one in the Purple Light Pavilion in Beijing in 1761 marks its victorious completion. In the interim the Qing army had conquered the Western Mongols in Dzungaria in two wars in 1755 and 1756. From 1757 to 1759 the army was expedited further to the south of Tianshan to suppress a group of Muslim dissidents. As a result, the whole of the northwest border region, on both sides of the Tianshan, was brought under the control of the Qing empire.

To celebrate his unprecedented territorial expansion, the emperor chose the Purple Light Pavilion in the Sea Palaces for a state banquet. The banquet was held on the second day of the New Year 1761. Among the 107 guests were the army officers who had commanded the campaign, the lords of Dzungaria, and the leaders of the Muslim groups from eastern Turkestan who had just been subjugated. This painting of the banquet is part of a larger programme to commemorate the military victory. Some works were displayed at the banquet: one hundred portraits of Qing army officers hung on the walls of the pavilion, and engravings were made in stone of the emperor's war poems and displayed in the rear courtyard – these are visible at the end of this scroll.

EXH: Ledderose and Butz 1985: no. 30; *De Verboden Stad* 1990: no. 11; *A Cidade Proibida* 1992: no. 11; Museu de Arte de Macau 2000: no. 32
LIT: Wu Kong 1994

23

Imperial banquet in the Purple Light Pavilion, Beijing

Yao Wenhan

Datable to 1761

Handscroll, ink and colour on silk

L 486.5 cm, H 45.8 cm

Inscriptions: artist's signature, undated

Seals: one of the artist; twelve of Hongli; one of the Jiaqing emperor

合羣聯珠

壽宇同遊

慈寧燕喜

香林千衲

萬國來朝

回人獻伎

24

Display of jubilation

Anonymous

Late 18th century

Album of eight leaves, ink and colour on silk

Each leaf H 97.5 cm, W 161.2 cm

Inscriptions: one title inscription by Hongli on each leaf

Seals: one of Hongli on each leaf

The Qianlong reign was not short of magnificent displays. As well as major annual festivals and great sacrifices, the court organised grand tours, hunting expeditions, military reviews, banquets, birthday celebrations for the emperor and his mother, parties for the elderly and receptions for envoys from overseas. Many of these celebrations assumed a national scale and were carried out in full grandeur.

This set of album leaves records eight of those grand occasions, namely, *Tributes from ten thousand countries, Gathering of provincial officials and nobles from colonies, Uyghurs performing, Elderly commoners travelling to the capital, Celebration for imperial officials over the age of seventy, Birthday celebration at the Palace of Compassion and Peace, Extending happiness to Tibetan Buddhist temples,* and *Thousands of incense sticks burning.* The name of the occasion is given in the inscription on each work. While the painting of the emperor's mother's birthday celebration is a visual record of the moment when the emperor and his concubines paid tribute to the Xiaoshen empress in her residential palace, some of the other album leaves rely less on fact than on imagination. The most far-fetched is *Tributes from ten thousand countries* in which envoys from abroad, holding banners and carrying exotic tributes, wait obediently outside the Gate of Supreme Harmony for an audience with the emperor. Here art has clearly assumed the role of cultural propaganda.

The album was probably created to celebrate a particular occasion but it is not known which one.

EXH: Museu de Arte de Macau 2000: no. 38

25

Illustrated tributaries of the Qing empire

Ding Guanpeng and others

Datable to 1751–75

First of a set of four handscrolls, 59 sections, ink and colour on paper

L 1941.3 cm, H 33.6 cm

Inscriptions: 59 in Manchu and Han Chinese on painting proper; one by Hongli on frontispiece, undated; four by Hongli, dated 1761, 1763, 1771 and 1775 respectively; one colophon of Liu Tongxun, undated; one colophon of Liang Shizheng, undated
Seals: five of Hongli; one of Liu Tongxun; two of Liang Shizheng

These ethnographic portraits formed part of the documentation about the peoples of the world which was stored in the map room of the imperial archives. Wei Dong's study shows that the work was commissioned and carried out between 1751 and 1775. Numerous courtiers, governors and governor-generals of the frontier regions, as well as artists, were involved in its production. Four court artists, Ding Guanpeng, Jin Tingbiao, Yao Wenhan and Zheng Lianggong, were chosen for the final execution of the four scrolls, each artist being responsible for one. It has been suggested that the four scrolls in the collection of the Palace Museum, which are unsigned, are copies of the originals, by the same painters, on the grounds that the first sequel to the imperial catalogue records four scrolls of the same titles but with the artists' signatures on the works.

The four scrolls, which fall under the general title *Illustrated tributaries of the Qing empire*, can be understood as illustrating the concept of the Chinese world order, in which the nations of the world were structured in a hierarchical and concentric manner with China at the centre surrounded by vassal states, and uncivilised barbarians on the periphery. This scroll, the first, depicts the peoples with diplomatic relations with the Qing, while the remaining three record the ethnic groups in the frontier provinces whose relationship to the Qing was domestic. A detailed look at the portraits of the men and women and their accompanying texts can tell us much about the relationship of the so-called tributaries to the Qing and about the relationship between the Qing and other countries.

Visual sources for the portraits are diverse. For example, the outfits worn by the British lady and gentleman could have been copied from illustrated books brought to court by European missionaries, or from designs sent by British traders to China for reproduction on export ceramics. The texts above the portraits bear witness to the curiosity of the eighteenth-century Chinese court about different cultures and their customs. The text above the British couple may be rendered as follows:

> British dress is similar to that of The Netherlands. The nation is wealthy. Men are commonly dressed in *duoluorong* (woollen flannel) and like drinking alcohol. Women, before marriage, bind their waists to make them narrow. They wear short tops and long dresses and let their hair flow loosely over their shoulders. When going out they wear an overcoat. Some people carry a snuff bottle in a little bag made of golden thread.

EXH: Museu de Arte de Macau 2000: no. 42
LIT: Wei Dong 1992; *AAS Abstract* 1995

英吉利國夷人
英吉利亦荷蘭屬國夷人頎長相似國頗富男子多著哆囉絨喜飲酒婦女未嫁時束腰欲其纖細披髮垂肩短衣長裙出行則加大衣以金縷合貯鼻煙自隨

小西洋國夷人
小西洋去中土萬里廣於大西洋遣夷目守之衣冠狀貌與大西洋略同常佩鬯刀鼓兵器夷婦青帕蒙首著長衣團領緝幅於前摺袖單顏喜執繡帕以習針黹

蘿圖式廓

26

The Qianlong emperor on his first inspection tour of the south

Xu Yang

Datable to 1764–70

Twelfth of twelve handscrolls, ink and colour on silk

L 1027 cm, H 68.9 cm

Inscriptions: one by the artist, dated 1770; one by Yu Minzhong, undated

Seals: two of the artist; two of Yu Minzhong; seven of Hongli

Beginning in 1751, the Qianlong emperor made altogether six grand tours to the south, to the lower Yangzi River valley, the economic and cultural heartland of China. His grandfather the Kangxi emperor had carried out similar tours of inspection. Departing from the capital, the Qianlong emperor headed south along the Grand Canal (see map, p.142). He examined major river dykes and conservation projects, paid homage to sacred mountains and cultural sites, and visited commercial cities as far south as Hangzhou, before returning to the Forbidden City. Each tour, of approximately three months, was meticulously planned and conducted in the most lavish fashion.

Equally lavish in scale was the pictorial record of these tours commissioned by the emperor. In 1764 he ordered the first tour to be depicted, following a precedent set by his grandfather. The finished paintings, a set of twelve spectacular scrolls, were presented to him in 1770 as part of his sixtieth birthday celebrations (by Chinese reckoning a child is one year old at birth; hence, born in 1711, the emperor was 60 in 1770). As documentary evidence they are invaluable in their wealth of detail: imperial paraphernalia, official ceremonies, views of cities and the countryside, and the daily lives of people at the time. The painter, Xu Yang, was a native of

Suzhou who had presented himself to the emperor when he passed through the city on his first tour (see Nie Chongzheng in this book, p. 164).

According to Nie Chongzheng, the emperor had commissioned two versions of the scrolls, one on silk and the other on paper. While the version on paper is now in the collection of the Chinese History Museum in Beijing, the twelve silk scrolls are scattered around the world: scroll number 2 is at Sotheby's, New York; scroll number 3 is in the Musée des Beaux Arts in Nice; scroll number 4 in the Metropolitan Museum of Art in New York; scroll number 5 in Keitaro Tanaka in Tokyo; and scroll number 9 and this present one are in the Palace Museum in Beijing.

The present painting records the final episode of the tour, the emperor's return to the Forbidden City along the south-north axis. The scroll opens with an impressive view of the Meridian Gate at the southern end of the city, followed by a long and detailed section showing the emperor's entourage and the imperial insignia, which stretches as far as the Gate of Dignity and beyond.

EXH: Museu de Arte de Macau 2000: no. 35
LIT: Chou and Brown 1985: no. 9; Hearn 1988: 185, n 18

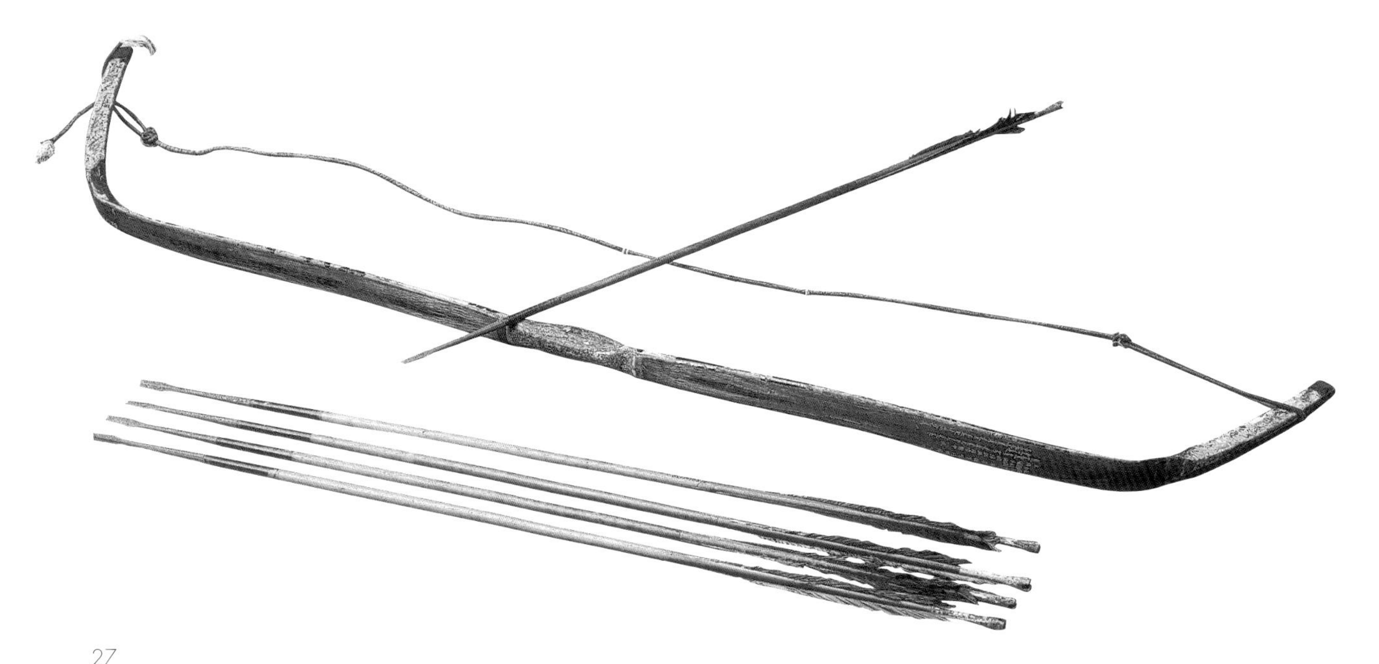

27

The Qianlong emperor's bow, arrows, quiver and bow container

Qianlong period (1736–95)

Bow: mulberry wood, L 145 cm, W 25 cm

Arrows: lacquered birch, L 93.5 cm

Quiver: leather covered with satin woven with gold and silver thread, L 38 cm

Bow container: leather covered with satin woven with gold and silver thread, L 76 cm

The Qianlong emperor wore his bow and arrows on two occasions – the military review and the hunt. We know that he used this bow at the imperial hunting grounds in Rehe from the gilded inscription on the back, in both Chinese and Manchu, which reads: 'In the twenty-second year of the Qianlong reign [1757] the emperor took the surrendering Dzungars on a hunt. He hit a deer with this bow at Yimianhuoluo hunting ground.'

The core of the arrows is made of birch, and the shape of the metal heads categorises them as *meizhen,* plum tree needles, one of the three major types of arrow used by the Manchu army.

The bow and arrows would have been carried by the emperor in their containers, attached to the body by a belt. The bow container is made of leather covered with fine satin woven with gold and silver thread, and the sides are fastened together and reinforced with strips of green leather. The container is embossed with iron plaques covered with silver. The quiver is of leather, covered with the same material as the bow container. The belt for carrying the containers is covered with bright yellow satin, lined with red brocade and inset with gilded iron plaques.

LIT: *DQHDT* 1899: vol. 3, 2175, 2204; Wang Zilin 1994

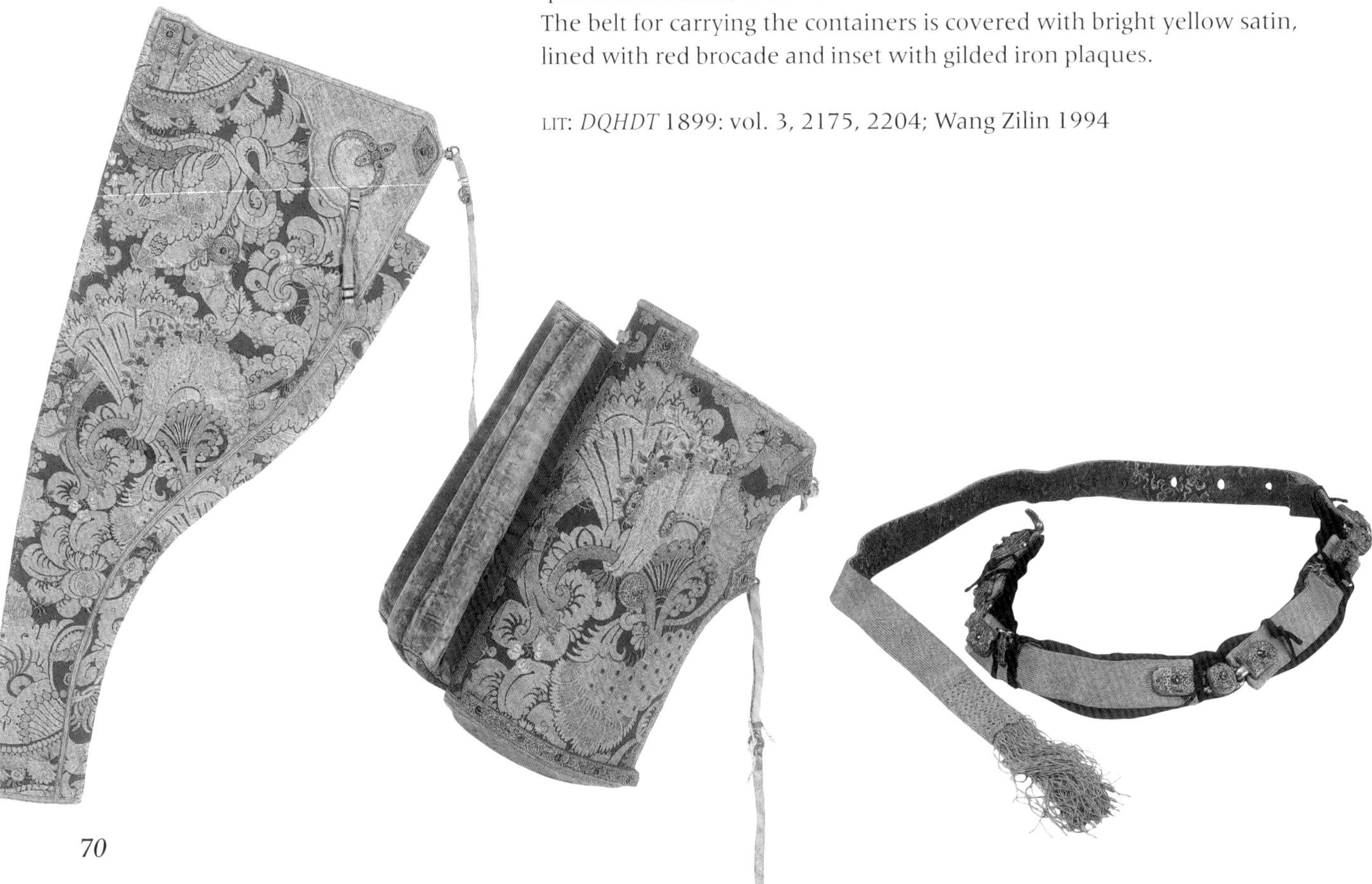

28

Antler chair

Datable to 1763
Deer antler, sandalwood
H 131 cm, W 90 cm, D 72 cm

The early and mid-Qing emperors commissioned numerous antler chairs. The earliest surviving chair was made in the reign of Huangtaiji (1627–43), son of the founder of the Manchu dynasty, Nurhachi, and its second ruler, and is preserved in the Shenyang (Mukden) Palace Museum. However, it is not clear whether such chairs belong to the traditional repertoire of furniture of the Manchu hunters of the northeast, or whether they were an invention of the Huangtaiji emperor as part of his programme to assert the Manchu identity of the dynasty. The Qianlong emperor undoubtedly saw the antler chair as a symbol of traditional Manchu values and was eager to preserve it.

This chair is made of sandalwood adorned with three pairs of antlers: one pair for the seat, one for the armrests and one for the back. The inscription, a stanza of eight lines, on the back of the chair tells us that in 1763 the emperor went on a hunting expedition at the imperial hunting ground in Rehe, and on that occasion the keeper of the hunting ground presented him with the antlers from the hunt. The emperor instructed a craftsman to use them to make this chair. At the end of the inscription the emperor confirms that he was having this chair made not just to preserve Manchu material culture, but also to remind the younger generation of Manchus of their equestrian roots and of the need for military virtue.

LIT: *YZSSJ* 1771: 1305 (644); Hu Desheng 1986: 84–5; Wan Yi 1988: pl. 70; Rawski 1998: 316–17, n 89, fig. 1

29

Ten imperial horses

Jean-Denis Attiret

Datable to 1739–45

Album of ten leaves, ink and colour on paper

Each leaf H 24.4 cm, W 29 cm

Inscriptions: artist's signature on leaf 10, undated; name of each horse written in Manchu on each leaf; poem on page opposite each leaf (not shown): 1–5 composed by Zhang Zhao, 6–10 by Liang Shizheng, transcribed by Ji Huang, undated

Seals: two of the artist; 18 of Hongli: seven on leaf 1, one on each of leaves 2–9, and three on leaf 10

Throughout his life the Qianlong emperor had a strong affection for his horses, many of which he had portrayed by the Jesuit missionary artists. Although horses had been a popular subject in Chinese painting since the Tang dynasty (618–907), the emperor seems to have preferred the European naturalistic treatment of his horses to a more traditional Chinese linear rendering.

This set of ten portraits of horses by Jean-Denis Attiret shows an interesting intermarriage of European and Chinese painting techniques: the naturalistically rendered horses are superimposed on landscapes painted in Chinese style. The name of each horse appears beside it in Manchu. Attiret, born in Dôle near Dijon in eastern France, was a Jesuit missionary who came to China in 1739 and worked for the Qianlong emperor as a court painter.

EXH: Ledderose and Butz 1985: no. 114

30

Calling for deer

Giuseppe Castiglione

Datable to 1741

Hanging scroll, ink and colour on silk

L 319 cm, H 267.5 cm

Inscriptions: three pieces of writing by Hongli, two transcribed by Wang Youdun, dated 1749 and 1753 respectively, one by Yu Minzhong, dated 1774

Seals: four of Wang Youdun; two of Yu Minzhong

The title of this painting in Manchu would be *Mulan*, the traditional name for the deer-calling hunt and also the name given to the imperial hunting ground in Rehe. The Manchu had a distinctive technique for deer hunting whereby the hunters would enter the forest early in the morning, and one would blow upon a horn to mimic the sound of a stag in heat. This would lure the doe to within shooting distance.

The painting depicts the deer-calling hunters just as they are entering the forest. The third rider from the front, astride a white horse and with a red bow case at his side, is the Qianlong emperor. Accompanying him are twelve mounted figures who look after his weapons, his steeds, telescope, hound and eagle. There is also a camel with a freshly killed deer on its back. The whole cavalcade is vividly and realistically painted. The figures of the emperor and others in the foreground are depicted in accordance with the techniques of European portraiture. They are also in proportion to each other and to their surroundings, which creates a sense of depth to the composition. The close attention to detail in the riders and horses would suggest that they were painted from life, by the missionary painter Giuseppe Castiglione, while the Chinese-style landscape backdrop would appear to be by the hand of a Chinese court painter.

This painting is of particular importance because it records the Qianlong emperor's first hunting expedition in Rehe in 1741 after much debate over the value of the hunt. There had been no royal hunt for several decades as it was not favoured by the Yongzheng emperor. So when the Qianlong emperor proposed its reintroduction as a court institution early in 1741 his court officials tried to dissuade him, fearing criticism of a pleasure-seeking culture at court. The emperor however defended his support for the hunt by arguing that it was not pure sport, but a means of preserving the Manchu way of life and of maintaining the dynastic alliance with the Mongols.

The Qianlong emperor's three inscriptions on the painting are also worthy of note. The one on the upper left, transcribed by one of his ministers Wang Youdun (1692–1758), is a rhapsody on the techniques of deer calling, written in 1749. The emperor stresses that the hunter should apply Confucius' five virtues – kindness, righteousness, decorum, wisdom and trust – to the hunt. For instance, the hunter should not pursue a deer that the first shoot has missed. Four years later, in 1753, the Qianlong emperor wrote another rhapsody, transcribed on the upper right. In contrast to the moralistic overtone of the first inscription, here the emperor suggests, in the form of a dialogue with a fictional partner, that the deer-calling hunt is an ideal way for men to commune with nature. He describes the feeling of ecstasy to be had by lingering in the magical world of the forest in the evening and observing every nuance of the deer's sounds and movements. The third inscription, transcribed by another minister Yu Minzhong (1714–80), was written in 1774 when the emperor was an elderly man. Here the emperor reviews the painting, regretting with a hint of sadness the passing of all the principal men in the picture. From this we know that the twelve mounted figures are his ministers and bodyguards, including Fuheng, the younger brother of his wife, the Xiaoxian empress. Although the emperor fails to identify any of them, it is possible, judging from age, that the seventh mounted figure is Fuheng.

EXH: Ledderose and Butz 1985: no. 45
LIT: Wang Baoguang 1983; Yang Boda 1993: 147–8

31

Imperial dinner at the hunting ground

Giuseppe Castiglione
Dated 1749
Hanging scroll, ink and colour on silk
L 313 cm, W 189 cm
Inscriptions: artist's signature, dated 1749
Seals: one of the artist

Among the many images of the Qianlong emperor this painting is particularly difficult to categorise. From its subject matter it could be considered as an informal portrait, *xinletu,* of the emperor since the dinner is not a state banquet. Yet the artist's emphasis on culinary activities makes it almost like a genre picture.

In the foreground men are busy skinning animals, chopping meat, making soup and barbecuing – each activity depicted in great detail. The emperor, in contrast, is relegated to the rear of the scene where he does not command our immediate attention. The painting, like the antler chair (no. 28), may have been intended to show the emperor's endorsement of Manchu values, in this case a simple existence devoid of extravagance.

EXH: Museu de Arte de Macau 2000: no. 28

32

The Qianlong emperor's ceremonial armour

Datable to 1739
Jacket and skirt: satin embroidered with silk
Helmet: black lacquer on ox hide core, inlaid with pearls
Jacket: L 76 cm
Skirt: L 70 cm
Helmet: D 21 cm

The Qianlong emperor wore this ceremonial armour on state military occasions. Each of the padded parts of the armour is covered with bright yellow satin embroidered with cosmic motifs in coloured silk threads, and lined with blue satin. The segments are joined together by loops and toggles. To evoke the effect of real armour, the sleeves are decorated with strips of golden thread. The helmet of black lacquer over an ox hide core is decorated with pearls and inscribed with *dharani*, protective magic formulae in Sanskrit, marking the wearer as a believer in Tibetan Buddhism. The strong similarity between this armour and that in the emperor's equestrian portrait (no. 16) suggests that this was Castiglione's model.

LIT: Hu Jianzhong 1989, 36–41; Lang Xiuhua 1989

33

Ceremonial armour of the eight banner troops

Qianlong period (1736–95)
Jackets and skirts: satin with copper studs
Helmets: black lacquer on ox hide core
Jackets: L 73 cm
Skirts: L 78 cm
Helmets: D 23 cm, tassels H 38.5 cm

Compared with the Qianlong emperor's lavish ceremonial armour, these suits are more appealing to the modern eye because of their straightforward design and bold colours. The only adornments are the rows of copper studs on the satin. As with the emperor's armour each suit comprises several padded sections joined together by Chinese loops and toggles. Similarly the helmet is made of ox hide and covered with black lacquer.

Each banner unit was distinguished by, and called after, the colour of the banner under which it enrolled. These colours were repeated in the suits of armour: there are four monochrome suits – yellow, white, red and blue – and the same four colours with borders.

These ceremonial suits of armour were worn by the banner troops on the occasion of the emperor's military review in Beijing. According to Mark Elliot, the troops in the capital were assigned positions around the Forbidden City in accordance with their formation during the hunt: white to the east, red to the west, blue to the south, and yellow to the north.

LIT: Lang Xiuhua 1989; Elliot 2001: 102–3

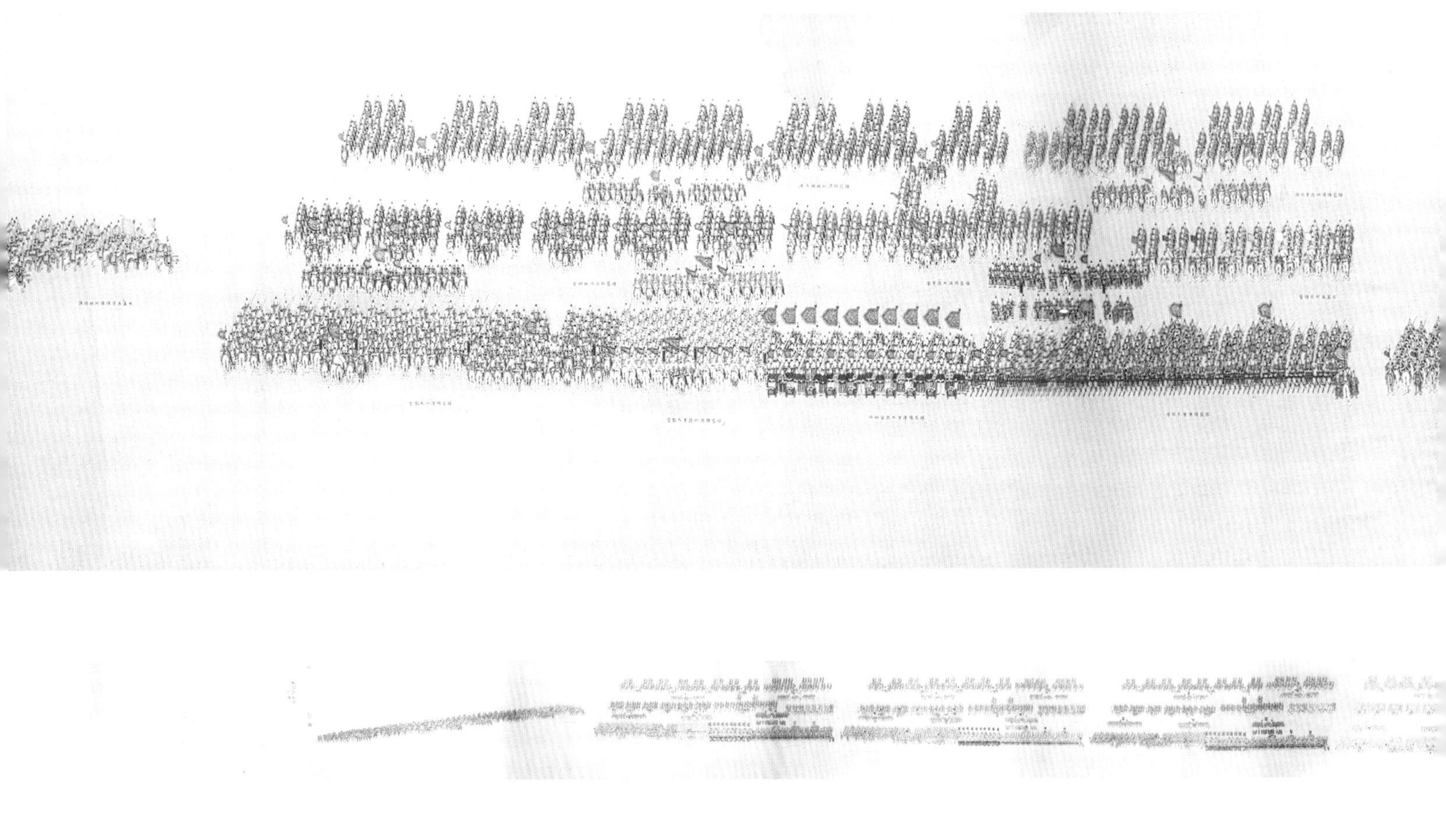

34

Parade of the eight banner troops at the grand military review

Attributed to Jin Kun

Datable to 1749

Second of set of four scrolls, ink and colour on silk

L 1757 cm, H 68 cm

Inscriptions: 88 names of the banner troops; one colophon, unsigned and undated

Seals: two of Hongli

This painting records the Qianlong emperor's first military review at the South Park on the outskirts of Beijing in 1739. Twenty thousand banner troops participated in the grand occasion, which was recorded in a set of four scrolls. This one is the second of the four and documents the disposition of the eight banner troops. According to the first sequel to the imperial catalogue *Shiqu baoji xubian*, the first scroll depicts the arrival of the emperor, the third the review of the troops, and the fourth the parade.

The scrolls were not commissioned until seven years after the event, in 1746. Upon being given the commission, the artist Jin Kun warned that he might need ten years to complete such a large documentary work as it would require careful planning and research into court records. But the impatient emperor insisted on its being completed in three years. Possibly because of the shortage of time, the artist made a mistake in the location of one of the eight banner units in this scroll,

which almost cost him his career as court artist (see Nie Chongzheng in this book, p. 167).

The troops depicted in the present scroll comprise guard brigades *(hujun ying)*, cavalry brigades *(xiaoqi ying)* and vanguard brigades *(qianfeng ying)*, complemented by dozens of companies of the same types. They are disposed according to their eight banner affiliations. On the right wing are, from right to left, plain yellow, plain red, bordered red and bordered blue; and on the left are, from left to right, bordered yellow, plain white, bordered white and plain blue.

Until recently the present scroll was the only known survivor of the set, but in October 2001 the third scroll depicting the review of the troops surfaced unexpectedly and sold at auction in Hong Kong for a high figure.

LIT: Gugong 1988: 56; Christie's sale's catalogue, 29–30 October 2001, lot 651

TRUE SELF

By all accounts the emperor was a family man. His attachment to his grandfather, mother and first wife are well documented. His unconventional marriage to his Uyghur concubine Rongfei has given rise to plays, novels and even a film (no. 36). There is ample evidence that with his family he derived immense pleasure from travelling and taking part in activities such as horse-riding and sledging.

The emperor's enjoyment of family and outdoor life went hand in hand with an intense appreciation of things that appealed to the mind. Fupeng, a courtier and school friend, wrote of him: 'Whenever he composes an essay he writes with astounding speed. He can mastermind a work of a thousand sentences within seconds.' The emperor was also an enthusiastic patron of libraries. To preserve the nation's rich literary heritage he commissioned a decade-long project to survey all surviving books, covering every branch of knowledge, and had many of them hand-copied and deposited in libraries across the country (no. 22). He also had a fascination for ancient bronzes, jades, seals and inkstones.

But it was to painting and calligraphy that he was most passionately devoted. The emperor built his collection on that of his father and grandfather and, with the assistance of well-informed courtiers who acted as agents, he avidly purchased paintings and works of calligraphy from the moment he came to the throne. For example, one of his outstanding acquisitions, the collection of An Qi, the most acclaimed collector in the field, was completed with the mediation of the emperor's brother-in-law Fuheng in 1746. The emperor also received a number of works of art as gifts. The well-known *Along the river during the Qingming Festival* by Zhang Zeduan (active early twelfth century) was given to him by Shen Deqian (see no. 41).

The emperor's love of art was not restricted to the Old Masters but extended to works by living artists as well. One of these artists, Zhang Zhao, was sentenced to death in 1736 but was saved from execution by the excellence of his calligraphy. Among the host of artists employed at court, the emperor's favourites included Ding Guanpeng, Jin Tingbiao, Yao Wenhan, Jean-Denis Attiret and above all Giuseppe Castiglione, with whom the emperor's image is inseparably associated. From the informal portraits they painted of the emperor one can imagine that the relationship between artist and emperor was one of mutual trust. Only a deep understanding of the emperor's personality would have enabled any of them to create a work such as the anonymous *One or two?* (no. 59).

Opposite:
Detail of *One or two?* (no. 59). The enigmatic relationship between the two images of the Qianlong emperor reveals his obsession with the question of self-identity.

35

Hongli (the Qianlong emperor) and the royal children on New Year's eve

Attributed to Giuseppe Castiglione and Ding Guanpeng

Possibly 1738

Hanging scroll, ink and colour on silk

L 275 cm, W 160.2 cm

Seals: three of Hongli

The Qianlong emperor had 17 sons and ten daughters. This painting has for long been entitled *The Qianlong emperor and his children on New Year's eve*. However, in the present author's opinion not all the boys in the picture are sons of the emperor. The painting has been arguably attributed, by Nie Chongzheng, to Castiglione and his Chinese collaborators and dated 1738, when the young emperor had only three sons – Yonghuang aged eleven, Yonglian aged nine, and Yongzhang aged three. If this attribution is correct, then these three sons may be the three boys wearing crowns in the painting.

EXH: Museu de Arte de Macau 2000: no. 27

LIT: Nie Chongzheng 1992: pls 50, 59; Tang and Luo 1994: 462–7

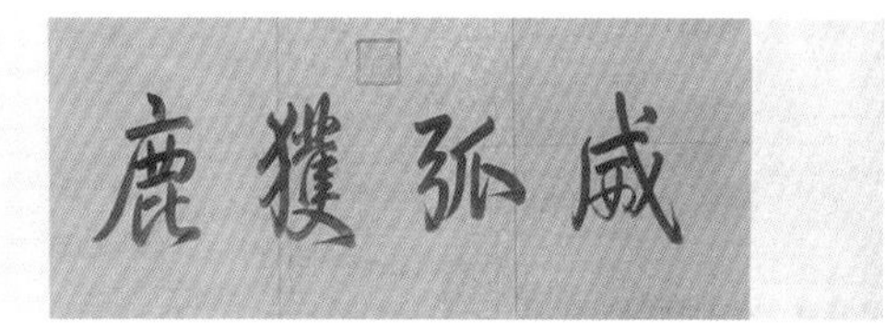

36

Taking a stag with a mighty arrow

Anonymous
Probably 1760s
Handscroll, ink and colour on paper
L 195.5 cm, H 37.4 cm
Inscriptions: frontispiece by Hongli, undated
Seals: one of Hongli on frontispiece

This painting was for the private appreciation of the emperor only, and was not intended to be shown in public. This is attested by its very personalised wrapper, on which the Qianlong emperor asked his sixth son Yongrong (see no. 52) to paint a landscape. As Yang Boda has suggested, the subject was not one for the eyes of the public: the imperial hunt was regarded as a state institution, and so it would have been considered quite improper for the emperor to be shown hunting side by side with a woman. The painting was not catalogued in the imperial collection.

The woman accompanying the emperor has been identified by Yang Boda as the emperor's legendary Uyghur concubine Rongfei on the grounds of her dress. Born to the Kiramet family in eastern Turkestan, Rongfei came into the imperial harem at the time of the Qing army's conquest of the western frontier regions from 1757 to 1759. According to the court archives, when the war began Rongfei's two uncles, Hoja Erke Husein and Parsa, and her brother Turdi refused to join the dissidents led by Khozi Khan and his brother Burhan-al-Din, in fear of the latters' domination. Then, in a fierce battle between Qing troops and Muslim dissidents at Qara Usu, near Yarkand, in 1758, the troops led by Rongfei's family helped to raise the siege on the main Qing troops by

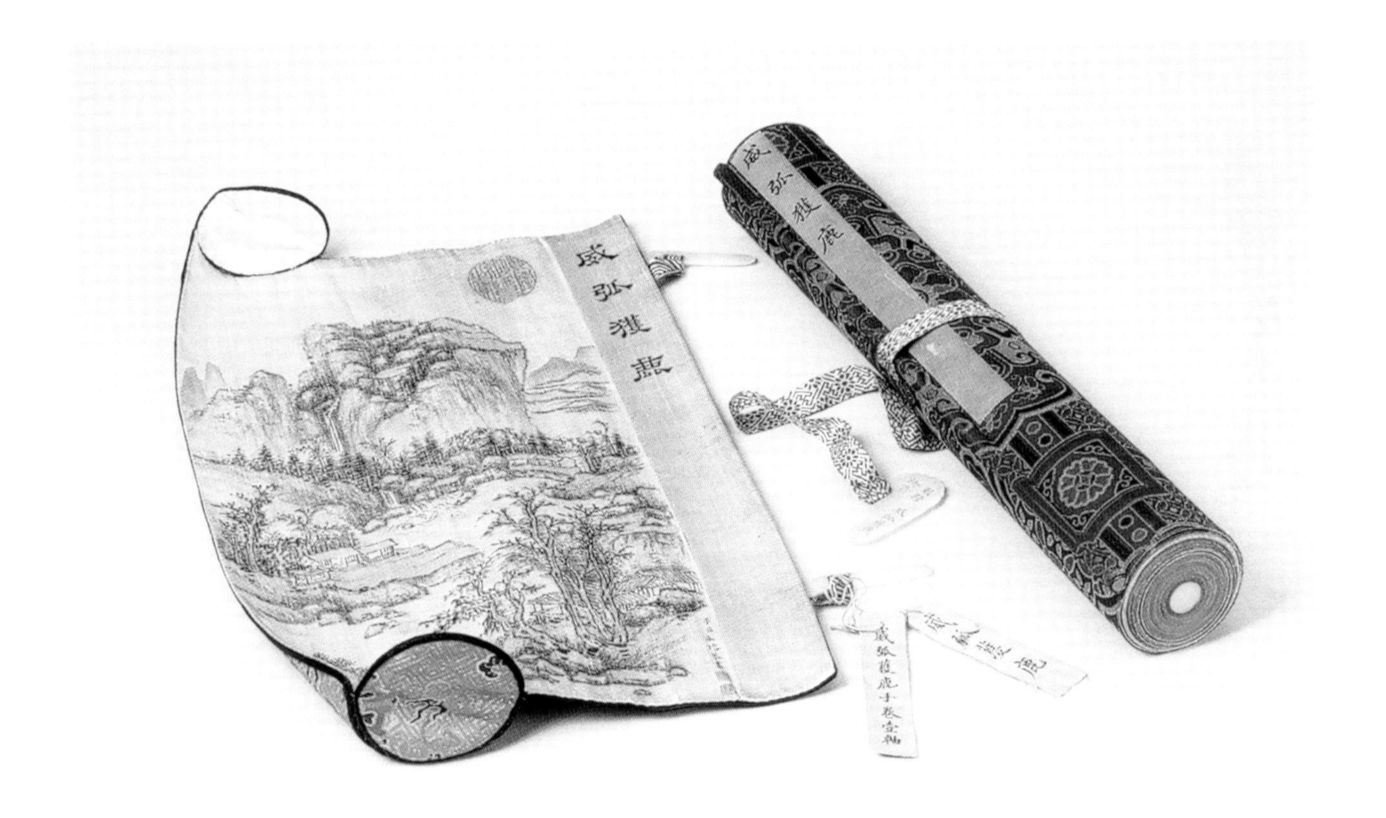

attacking the rebels' bases in Kashgar and Yengi Hissar. When the campaign was over the Kiramets were summoned to the capital where they were given high-ranking positions more commonly bestowed on members of the imperial clan, and special residences. In 1760 Rongfei became the fourth-rank concubine of the Qianlong emperor.

Rongfei seems to have enjoyed exceptional favour at the hands of the emperor. She was allowed to continue wearing Turkestani dress, and to have food prepared by her own cook to comply with Islamic dietary restrictions – it is said she ate rice pilaff, vegetables fried with onion, mutton *tatash* and sweets. The emperor even built a mosque for her at the Summer Palace near Beijing, Yiheyuan. When Rongfei died in 1788 she was buried at the Eastern Tombs near Beijing.

At the turn of the twentieth century, when anti-Manchu sentiment was at its peak among Han Chinese, many stories were fabricated about Rongfei. In some she was turned into the exotic 'fragrant consort', Xiangfei, an anti-Manchu heroine.

EXH: Museu de Arte de Macau 2000: no. 40
LIT: Yu Shanpu 1980; Millward 1994

37

Brush cabinet and brushes

Qianlong period (1736–95)
Carved red lacquer
H 36.2 cm, W 21.4 cm, L 28.2 cm

This red lacquer brush cabinet is carved all over with intricate landscapes. Inside the case are five sliding trays, each of which holds a single layer of brushes. These rabbit hair brushes were used by the Qianlong emperor to write poems.

EXH: Palace Museum 2000: no. 48

38

Ink warmer

Qianlong period (1736–95)
Gilded silver
L 21.2 cm, W 17.7 cm, H 18 cm

Ink warmers were used in winter to prevent the ink from freezing. The ground liquid ink is held in two ink slabs at the top, and underneath them is a container for hot water. The exterior of the warmer, of gilded silver, is decorated with flowers and a blue enamel dragon.

EXH: Palace Museum 2000: no. 57

39

Seal box

18th century
Black lacquer with *maki-e* and *takamaki-e* decoration, wood
L 18 cm, W 11 cm, H 12 cm

The Qianlong emperor had a taste for Japanese lacquerware. This black lacquered box, decorated with bamboo and plum blossom in gold lacquer, contains ten of the emperor's personal seals for use on paintings and calligraphy. It once also held small jade objects but these are now lost. It is not known where or when in Japan the box was made or how it came into the palace.

EXH: Palace Museum 2000: no. 71

40

Flowers and plants

Hongli (the Qianlong emperor)

Dated 1776

Set of six handscrolls, ink on paper

Each L 30.2 cm, H 18.5 cm

Inscriptions: signature on three scrolls dated 1776; title and frontispiece by the artist on each scroll

Seals: twelve of the artist on each scroll

The official account of the Qianlong emperor's life records that he rose at 6 o'clock, worked on state affairs in the morning, read, wrote or painted in the afternoon, and took only two meals a day. His court officials remarked that wherever he stayed he would try to keep to this routine.

The emperor started painting at the age of 19. His earliest recorded two paintings date from 1732, and the latest is dated to 1798 when he was 87 years old. Birds and flowers are the subjects he most frequently chose to paint, and the various flowers and plants depicted in these six handscrolls are executed with minimum brushstrokes. Of particular interest is the emperor's choice of plants: he paints not just the favourites of the scholar artist – plum blossom, old trees, bamboo, orchid – but also unusual subjects such as dandelion and calamus, showing a deep understanding of the scholarly ideals of simplicity and lack of pretension.

The emperor's taste in storage cases was lavish: the six scrolls are stored in a specially made red lacquer case.

LIT: Chou and Brown 1985: 17; Yang Danxia 2000

益壽舒芳

盎然生趣

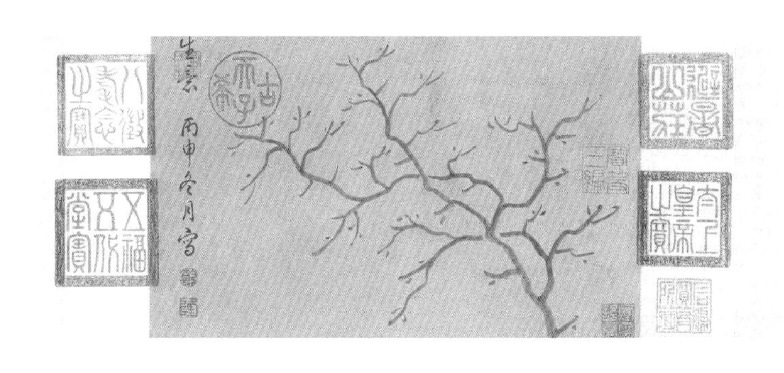

喬幹迴春

如見天心

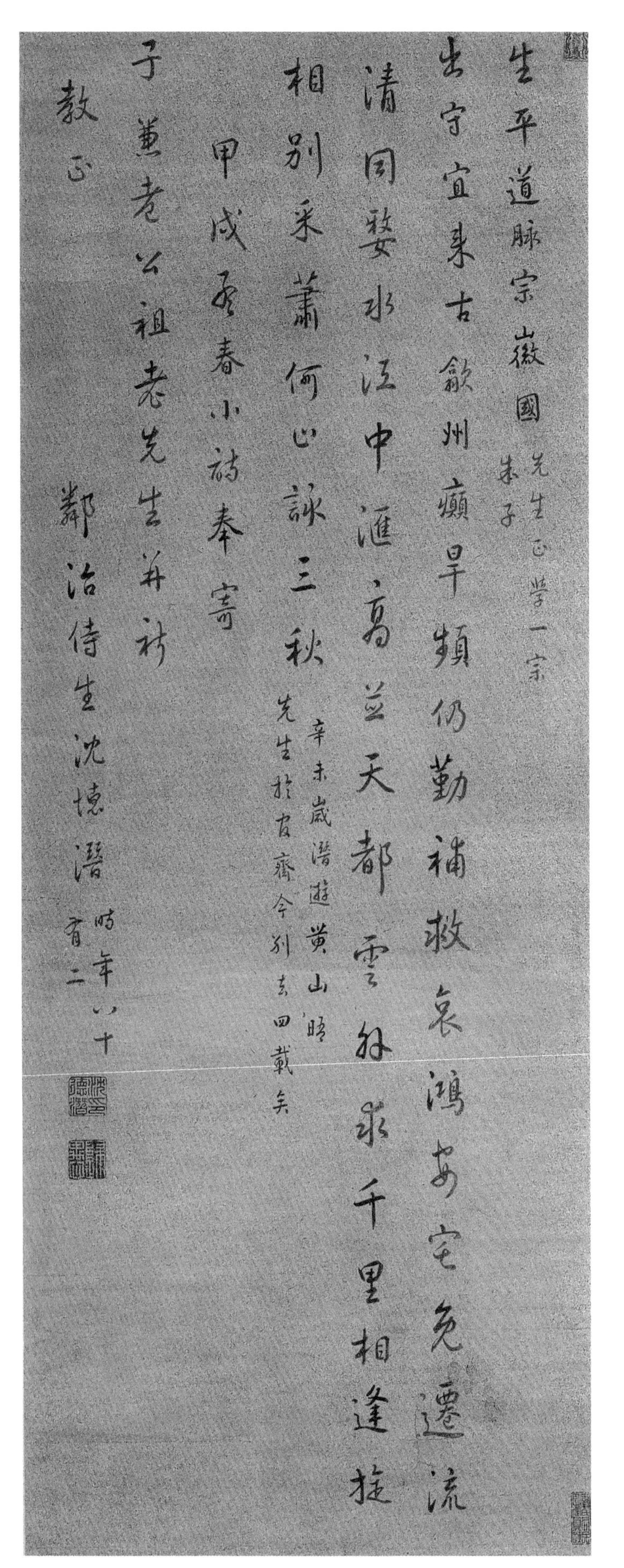

41

Poem for Mr Zu Zijian

Shen Deqian
Dated 1755
Hanging scroll, ink on paper
L 99.5 cm, W 38.2 cm
Inscription: artist's signature, dated 1755
Seals: three of the artist; one of Liu Tongming

The Qianlong emperor left behind more than 40,000 poems, a number so monumental that it has secured him the place of the most productive, though not the most gifted, poet in Chinese history. In his poetry writing he was assisted by Shen Deqian (1673–1769), a famous poet and literary critic from the lower Yangzi River valley in the south.

Born to a poor family, Shen Deqian was recognised early as a poetic genius. But he was unlucky in his pursuit of officialdom and it was not until the age of 66 that he was finally appointed a member of the Institute of Academicians in Beijing.

At this point Shen became the emperor's favourite poet, and he was to enjoy a long and unusual imperial friendship. It is said that when the emperor had composed a new poem he would give it to Shen Deqian and ask him to respond with a poem with a similar rhyme pattern. The emperor also appointed Shen as editor of his collected poems, the first edition of which was published in 1748. In fact Shen is often regarded as the major ghost writer of the emperor's poems. In this poem in calligraphy for a certain Mr Zu Zijian, Shen Deqian praises the recipient's scholarly achievements and their friendship. The verse is written in running script and in *guan'geti*, 'palace type', a style favoured by the emperor.

LIT: Hummel 1949, vol. 2: 645–6; Wu Boya 2000

42

Landscape

Dong Bangda

Qianlong period (1736–95)

Fan, ink on paper

D 16.4 cm

Inscription: artist's signature, undated

Seal: one of the artist

A native of Zhejiang province in the south, Dong Bangda (1699–1769) entered the Institute of Academicians in Beijing in 1733 after passing the official examinations in the same year. His interest in painting and calligraphy found him like-minded colleagues at the institute and together they formed a small artistic circle with which the Qianlong emperor had a long relationship. In 1743 Dong Bangda and several of his colleagues at the institute were entrusted by the emperor to catalogue the collection of paintings and works of calligraphy in the palace. This project provided an excellent opportunity for the emperor and the academicians to study old paintings and calligraphy together and to exchange ideas. The colophons added subsequently to old master paintings by both the academicians and the emperor testify to the strength of their working relationship. The emperor also became a very enthusiastic collector of works by the academicians. As the artist's signature on the present landscape is preceded by a term denoting servility, the fan must have been painted for the emperor.

LIT: Hummel 1949, vol. 2: 792; Chou and Brown 1985: 84–5

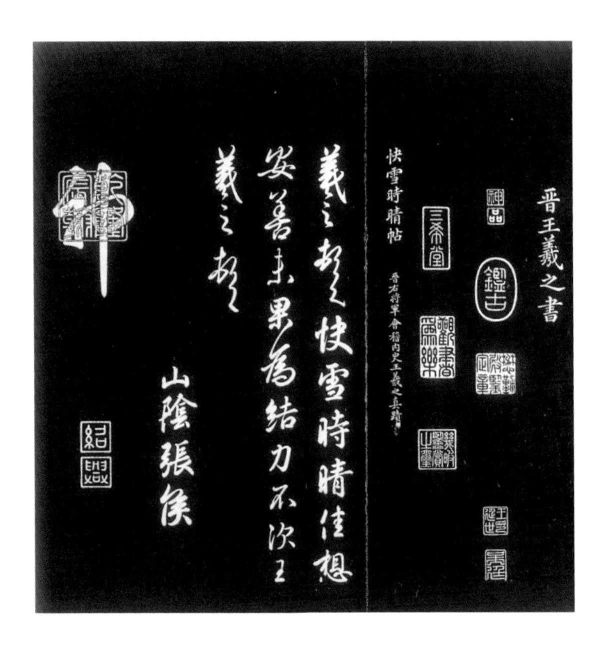

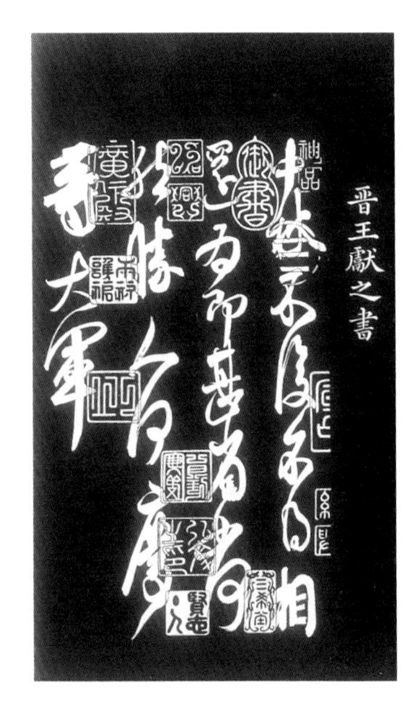

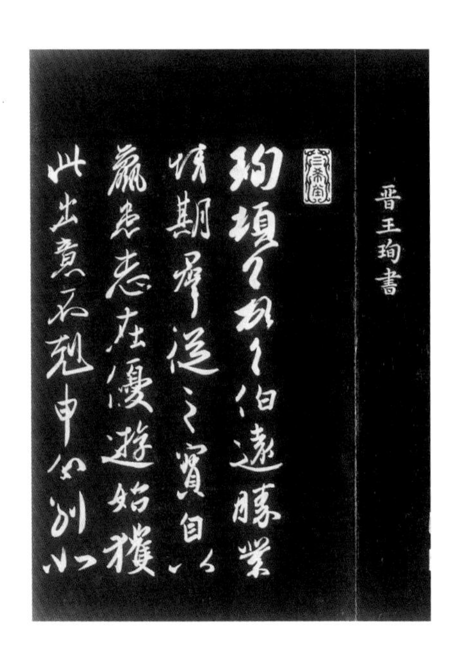

43

The Three Rarities

1749–54
Ink rubbings on paper
Each spread H 30.4 cm, W 35.5 cm

The Qianlong emperor was an avid collector of ancient calligraphy. From his massive collection, three treasures were singled out by him at an early stage. He claimed that *Clearing after snow* by Wang Xizhi (303–361), *Mid-Autumn letter* by his son Wang Xianzhi (344–386) and *Letter to Bo Yuan* by his nephew Wang Xun (350–401) were 'three rarities' among all the existing works of calligraphy, and he had them stored specially in a small room in his main residence in the Forbidden City, the Hall for the Cultivation of the Mind. The room was subsequently named after these treasures as the Hall of the Three Rarities.

These ink rubbings of the three rarities are taken from an anthology of calligraphy produced at court, called *Model works of calligraphy in the Hall of the Three Rarities*. The anthology contains rubbings of 340 works of calligraphy by 135 calligraphers from the third to the early seventeenth century. The making of this anthology involved five stages. First, a copy of the original was made by tracing the outlines of each character. This copy was then turned over and the outlines painted with vermilion on the back. By placing the copy on the prepared stone slab, right side up, and rubbing gently over it, the vermilion outlines could be transferred to the stone. The next step was for the sculptor to carve the characters, guided by the vermilion outlines. According to the court archives, 495 stone slabs were needed for this anthology alone. The Qianlong emperor ordered a special building to be constructed to house them in the Sea Palaces. Finally ink rubbings were taken of the carved works and these were bound into the present book form. The whole work took six years to complete.

EXH: Ledderose and Butz 1985: no. 79; Museu de Arte de Macau 2000: no. 60
LIT: Wan Yi 1980

44

Clearing after the night rain

Hongli (the Qianlong emperor)
Dated 1772
Hanging scroll, ink on paper
L 111 cm, W 70.7 cm
Inscriptions: artist's signature, dated 1772
Seals: three of Hongli; one of Puyi

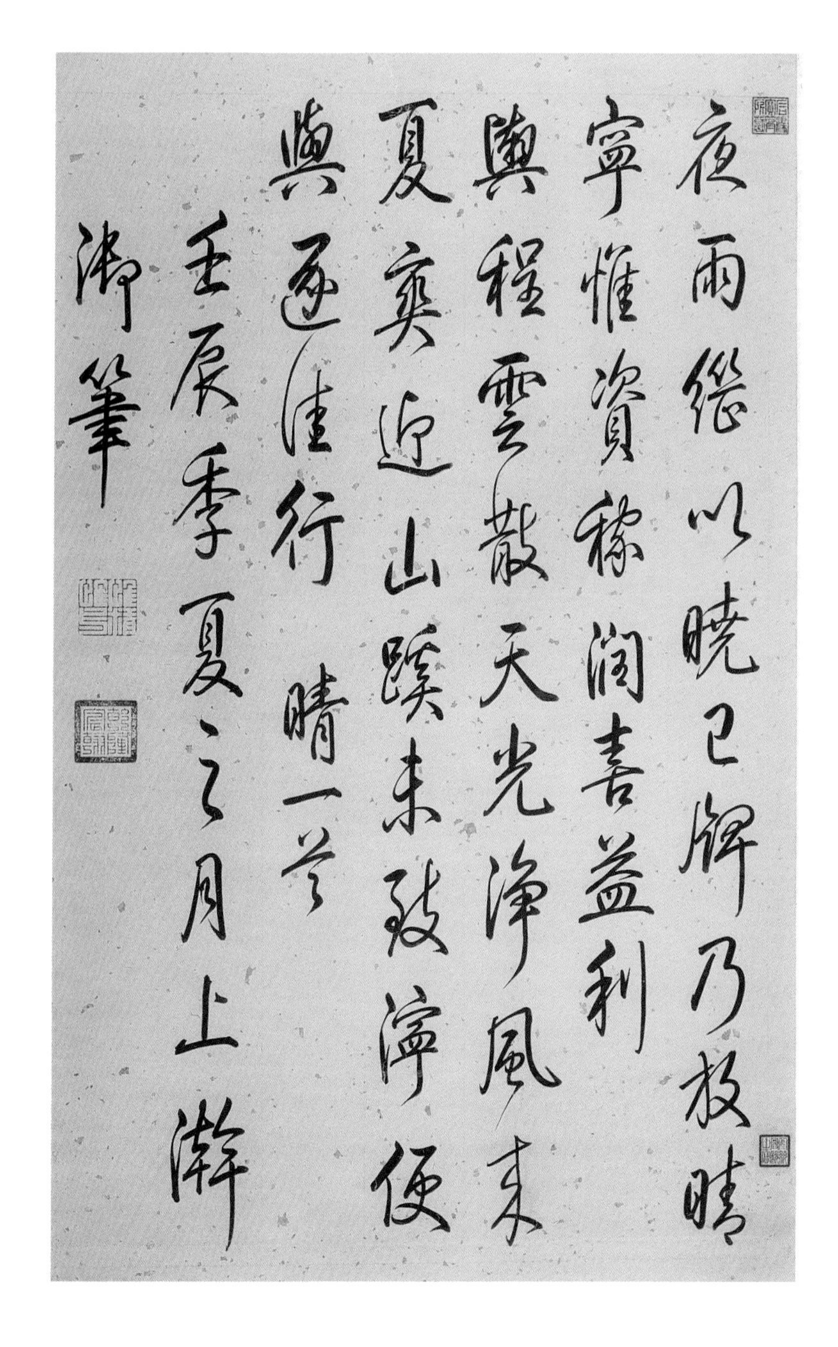

This work is a poem in calligraphy, in one stanza of eight lines, each with five characters. It was composed by the Qianlong emperor at the Summer Palace in Rehe in the late summer of 1772, when he and his court were about to set off on a journey. It may be translated as follows:

> The night rain extended to the dawn,
> And did not clear away until late morning.
> The rain moistens the crops,
> And improves the road for the journey.
> The clouds have dispersed and the sun is bright,
> The breeze greets the summer sky so crystal clear.
> The mountain path has not a trace of mud.
> It is a perfect day for an outing.

For some unknown reason the poem is not included in the published collection of the emperor's poems.

The calligraphy, in running script, is representative of the Qianlong emperor's influential style – balanced, elegant and neat. The prime source of this style is the calligraphy of Zhao Mengfu (1254–1322), a canonical scholar artist of the Yuan dynasty (1271–1368) (no. 46). Wang Menggeng has recently pointed out that the emperor's calligraphy has many similarities with Manchu script, especially the roundness of some of his individual strokes. It is very possible that his calligraphic style was influenced by his practice of Manchu calligraphy.

LIT: Wang Menggeng 1986

45

Copy of 'The Lion Grove Garden' by Ni Zan

Anonymous

Datable to before 1616

Handscroll, ink on paper

L 100 cm, H 30 cm

Inscriptions: Ni Zan's signature, dated 1373; frontispiece writing by Hongli; seven inscriptions and four colophons also by Hongli, dated 1757, 1762, 1764, 1765, 1772, 1773, 1774, 1784; one colophon co-authored by Liang Guozhi, Liu Yong, Peng Yuanrui and Cao Wenzhi, transcribed by Liang Guozhi, undated

Seals: 50 of Hongli; ten of Xiang Yuanbian; one of Dong Qichang; one of Sun Chengze; one of the Jiaqing emperor; two of Puyi; two of Liang Guozhi; two illegible; four unidentifiable

The Lion Grove Garden, one of the best-known gardens in Suzhou, is recorded as having been built by a local abbot called Tianru in his temple compound in 1342 in the Yuan dynasty. Over the centuries the garden has passed through many hands and undergone numerous changes. Its final owner, before it was turned into a tourist attraction, was the Pei family.

Despite the overcrowded landscaping of the garden its fame has never tarnished. This is largely due to its historical links with Ni Zan (1306–74), a reclusive painter and poet who is said to have designed garden rocks according to legends.

Ni Zan was born into a wealthy family in the city of Wuxi near Suzhou when China was under Mongol rule. Instead of pursuing a career in officialdom, he chose to live the life of a recluse in early adulthood. He surrounded himself with thousands of books, antiques and musical instruments, and took to painting and writing. Having planted pines, cassia trees, orchids, bamboo and chrysanthemums around his house, he named it Qingbi, the Quiet Pavilion, and called himself Yunlin, Cloudy Forest. Later in life Ni Zan abandoned

雲林清閟

his home and family and chose to live in a fishing boat on the river. He was not only greatly admired during his lifetime, but his works, which conjure up a real sense of stark isolation, were eagerly sought after by his contemporaries and later generations.

The authenticity of the present painting has been debated by connoisseurs for centuries. The painting was first recorded as a genuine work by Ni Zan by Zhang Chou (1577–1643) in 1616. His opinion was shared with some reservation by Gu Fu in 1692. Based on a study of the signature allegedly by Ni Zan and on the style of the painting, Gu concluded that most of the scroll was painted by another Yuan painter, Zhao Yuan, and that Ni Zan had painted only the bamboo. Modern scholars such as Xu Bangda and Yang Renkai, however, dismiss Zhan's and Gu's opinions outright and claim that the painting is a copy made in the Ming dynasty.

Like all connoisseurs before him, the Qianlong emperor was an admirer of Ni Zan's art and did not doubt the authenticity of the scroll. He had come to love it early in his reign, in 1739. As indicated by his inscriptions on the scroll, however, it was not until his second tour of inspection to the south, in 1757, that the emperor learned that the Lion Grove Garden was in Suzhou, whereupon he immediately paid it a special visit. Excited by his discovery, he ordered the scroll to be sent as quickly as possible from Beijing so that he might compare it with the real garden. After that he visited the Lion Grove Garden on each of his tours to the south, often taking the scroll with him.

Throughout his life the emperor's obsession with the scroll never diminished. He painted four copies of it, one of which was given to the owner of the garden to be kept there. Furthermore, he commissioned two replicas of the actual garden in his late years, one for the Summer Palace on the outskirts of Beijing, Yuanmingyuan, in 1771, and the other for the Summer Palace in Rehe four years later.

LIT: *YZSCJ* 1748: *juan* 2; *YZSEJ* 1761: *juan* 72; *YZSSJ* 1771: *juan* 21, 47; *YZSSJ* 1783: *juan* 4, 5, 10, 22; *YZSWJ* 1795: *juan* 10; Yang Danxia 2000: 6–7; Yang Renkai 1991: 389–91; Zhang Chou 1992: 351; Xu Bangda 1997: 72

46

Copy of 'Arhat in red robe' by Zhao Mengfu

Hongli (the Qianlong emperor)
Dated 1762
Handscroll, ink and colour on paper
L 50.8 cm, H 26.5 cm
Inscriptions: frontispiece writing by the artist; another inscription of the artist, dated 1762
Seals: ten of the artist

Copying has been regarded as an integral part of a painter's training in China since the late fifth century. There are three types of 'copying' in terms of the relationship between the copy and the original. *Mo* means a literal mimesis of the original work in which tracing is inevitably involved. *Lin* denotes a practice in which the original is placed in front of the painter and the painter attempts to copy it. *Fang* is not a copy *per se,* but an evocation of the style and idea of the original. Technically, the present painting falls into the first category of the Chinese concept of copying.

Zhao Mengfu, the painter of the original work now in the Liaoning Provincial Museum, was a leading proponent of the archaism movement which advocated a return to the painting styles of the Tang (618–907) and pre-Tang periods. The *Arhat in red robe,* painted in 1304, exemplifies Zhao's ideal in its very formalised and primitive treatment of the figure and the tree.

The Qianlong emperor viewed Zhao's original in 1757, and five years later made the present copy. Of particular interest are the emperor's comments on the face of the arhat. While Zhao Mengfu had been very proud of being able to capture an authentic Indian face due to his encounters with Indian monks in the capital, the emperor contended that the Yuan master's understanding of the arhat was shallow because he had concentrated on an accurate physical likeness rather than on his intrinsic qualities.

LIT: *Yiyuan duoyin* 1978: 23

47

Copy of 'Brewing tea' by Tang Yin

Hongli (the Qianlong emperor)

Dated 1754

Handscroll, ink on paper

L 107.6 cm, H 31.3 cm

Inscriptions: frontispiece writing by the artist; inscription by the artist, dated 1754; ten colophons by Jiang Pu, Wang Youdun, Qiu Rixiu, Ji Huang, Yu Minzhong, Dong Bangda, Qian Weicheng, Jin Deying, Wang Jihua and Qian Rucheng, undated

Seals: ten of the artist; 17 of the colophon writers; one of Puyi

As with two of the Qianlong emperor's other copies in this book (nos 46 and 48), this study of a work by Tang Yin (1470–1523) is a traced copy. A native of Suzhou, Tang Yin was one of the most acclaimed scholar painters of the city, renowned for his versatile styles of painting and for his colourful lifestyle. To later generations he became known as one of the 'Four Great Masters of Wumen (Suzhou)'.

Recorded in the Qianlong emperor's collected poems is a painting with a similar title by Tang Yin, which seems to have held a tremendous appeal to the emperor. To house that painting the emperor built a special tearoom in the studio of his villa on Mount Pan near Beijing (no. 50). The studio, known as Ten Thousand Feet of Snow, was itself constructed in imitation of a famous scenic spot of the same name in Hanshan, Suzhou. He had the scroll hung permanently on a wall in the tearoom and whenever he went to the villa he would take tea there and add poems to the painting. It is not yet known whether or not the painting in the tearoom was the one on which the emperor based his copy.

A comparison of this copy with the original in the Palace Museum in Beijing shows certain stylistic differences. While the general composition and details are almost identical, the painting techniques in the copy are somewhat simplified: for instance the wet ink washes of the original are represented by drier strokes with fewer nuances of tone.

LIT: *YZSEJ* 1761: *juan* 48; *YZSSJ* 1771: *juan* 55, 80; *YZSSJ* 1783: *juan* 20; *YZSWJ* 1795: *juan* 30, 46, 64; *YZSYJ* 1800: *juan* 11; Zhu Jiajin 1986: pl. 43

48

Copy of 'The study by old trees' by Wen Zhengming

Hongli (the Qianlong emperor)

Dated 1765

Hanging scroll, ink and colour on paper

L 59.2 cm, W 32.1 cm

Inscription: artist's signature and inscription, dated 1765

Seals: five of the artist; one of Puyi

A contemporary and friend of Tang Yin, Wen Zhengming (1470–1559) was another dominant figure on the art scene in Suzhou in the first half of the sixteenth century. He was known for his elegant and refined style of painting, and for transmitting the family tradition of painting through the generations. Wen Zhengming's original painting, *The study by old trees,* on which the emperor's copy is based, was painted before 1534. The work has been aptly described by Richard Edwards as 'completely unpretentious', embodying the concept of *zhuo,* loosely a sense of effortlessness and a certain naïvety, which the artist sought after. The flatness of the ink washes, the rough outlines and the limited range of shapes make the work almost like a sketch.

When the Qianlong emperor first saw Wen's painting in 1760, he inscribed on it a poem in which he expresses envy for the scholar drinking green tea in the seclusion of the mountains. On the emperor's copy, which he painted in the Garden of Clear Waves (renamed the Yiheyuan Summer Palace in the nineteenth century) in the summer of 1765, he transcribed his old poem as well as adding a new one. His new poem clearly indicates a full understanding of Wen's painting which he describes as having an air of 'archaism and solemnity'. The emperor's painting itself takes this reading of Wen's work one step further: unlike Wen, the emperor has not applied ink washes to the majestic cliffs to make them darker and more impressive, with the result that his copy is even sketchier and less pretentious than Wen's original.

LIT: *YZSSJ* 1771: *juan* 7, 51; Edwards 1976: no. XXIV

Wen Zhengming, *The study by old trees,* before 1534, hanging scroll, ink on paper, L 52.4 cm, W 31.3 cm, present whereabouts unknown

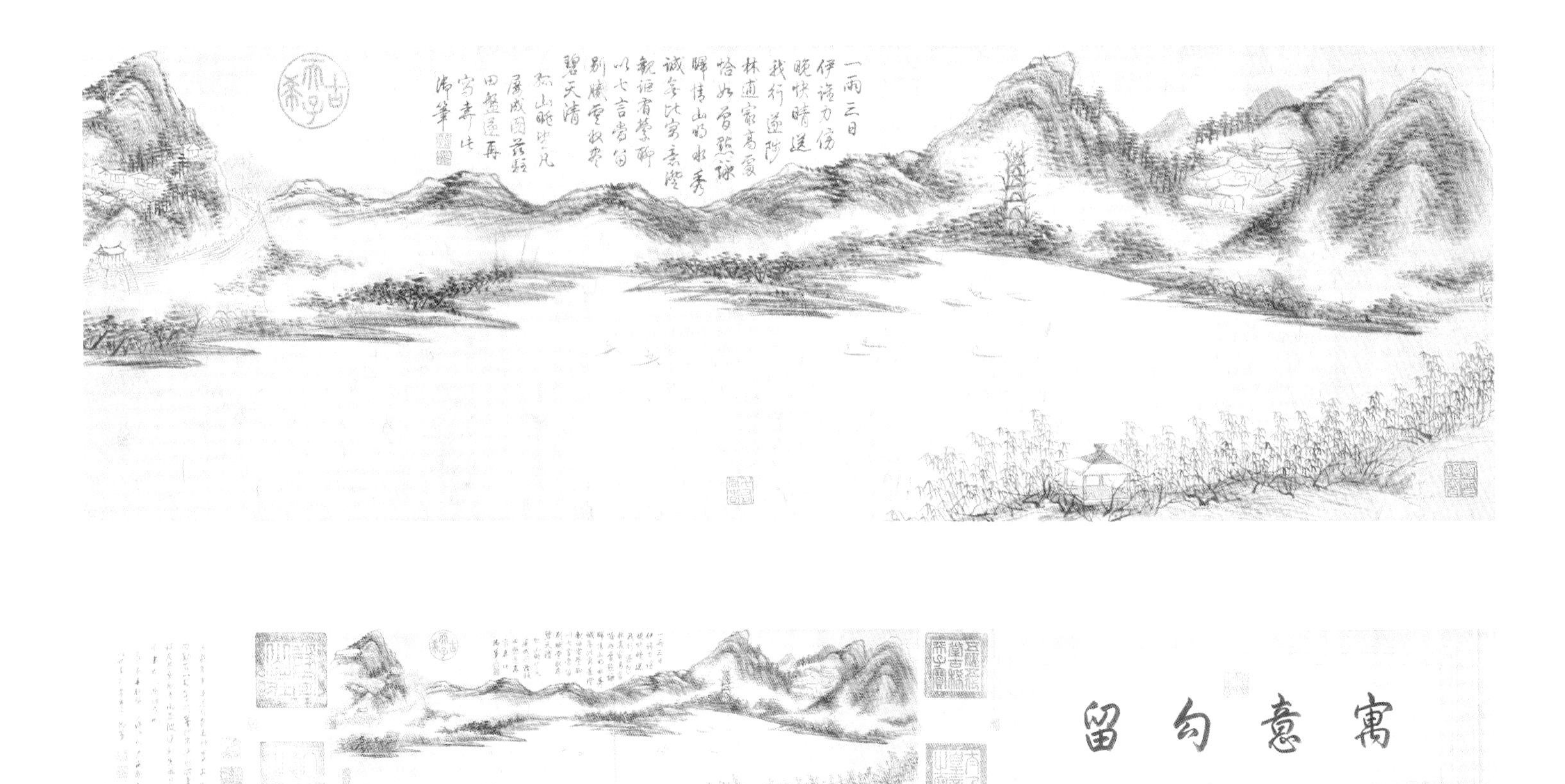

49

View of the West Lake

Hongli (the Qianlong emperor)

Dated 1789

Handscroll, ink on paper

L 91.2 cm, H 29.2 cm

Inscriptions: frontispiece title by the artist; one inscription and one colophon by the artist, dated 1789

Seals: 18 of the artist; one of Puyi

The West Lake in Hangzhou is famous for its natural beauty and its rich cultural history, and had been a favourite subject of painters since the late twelfth century. One of the earliest surviving paintings of the lake is a handscroll by Li Song (active *c.* 1190–1230), now in the Shanghai Museum.

The Qianlong emperor frequented the West Lake on his grand tours of inspection to the south, staying in the Magnolia Lodge, an imperial villa at the foot of the south side of the Hill of Solitude. On the north side of the hill was a small pavilion built in the fourteenth century to commemorate the poet Lin Pu (967–1028) who is believed to have exiled himself there. Lin Pu later became a symbol of the recluse, and is known for the poetic renderings of his solitary life in which the plum blossom is his wife and the crane his child.

As the poem inscribed on the painting indicates, the emperor had more than once painted the West Lake on previous visits. This painting was not made *in situ* but during a stay at his villa on Mount Pan (nos 47, 50) in 1789, five years after his final trip to the south. It is therefore a painting done from memory, out of nostalgia for the lake and its surrounding scenery.

LIT: *Xihu jiuzong* 1985: 48, 53

50

Mount Pan

Hongli (the Qianlong emperor)
Dated 1745
Hanging scroll, ink on paper
L 162 cm, W 93.5 cm
Inscriptions: artist's signature, dated 1745; seven place names by the artist; another 33 inscriptions by the artist, dated 1747, 1750, 1752, 1755, 1760, 1763, 1764, 1766, 1769, 1770, 1772, 1774, 1775, 1782, 1785, 1787, 1789, 1791 and 1793
Seals: 51 of the artist; one of Puyi

The Qianlong emperor paid regular visits to the Eastern Tombs near Beijing to pay homage to his ancestors. In order to have a place to stay on these trips he built a villa on Mount Pan, in the style of the Summer Palace in Rehe. It is this villa that is the subject of the emperor's painting executed in 1745, the year after the villa was built.

Cartographic in nature, the painting clearly falls within the genre of 'villa painting', a sub-genre of landscape, which began with Lu Hong (active first half of eighth century) and Wang Wei (701–761). But instead of depicting individual parts of the villa on separate leaves or sequentially, as the majority of villa painters did, the emperor chooses to contain the villa and its surroundings within a single composition. The painting is of particular importance because it records an imperial villa that no longer exists: it was destroyed some time during the revolution in the first decade of the twentieth century.

LIT: *YZSCJ* 1748: *juan* 38; *YZSEJ* 1761: *juan* 20, 32, 55; *YZSSJ* 1771: *juan* 2, 29, 42, 55, 80, 88; *YZSSJ* 1783: *juan* 3, 20, 28, 88; *YZSWJ* 1795: *juan* 14, 30, 46, 64, 79; Liu Zhenwei 1995: pl. 69; Wan Yi 1996: 101–02

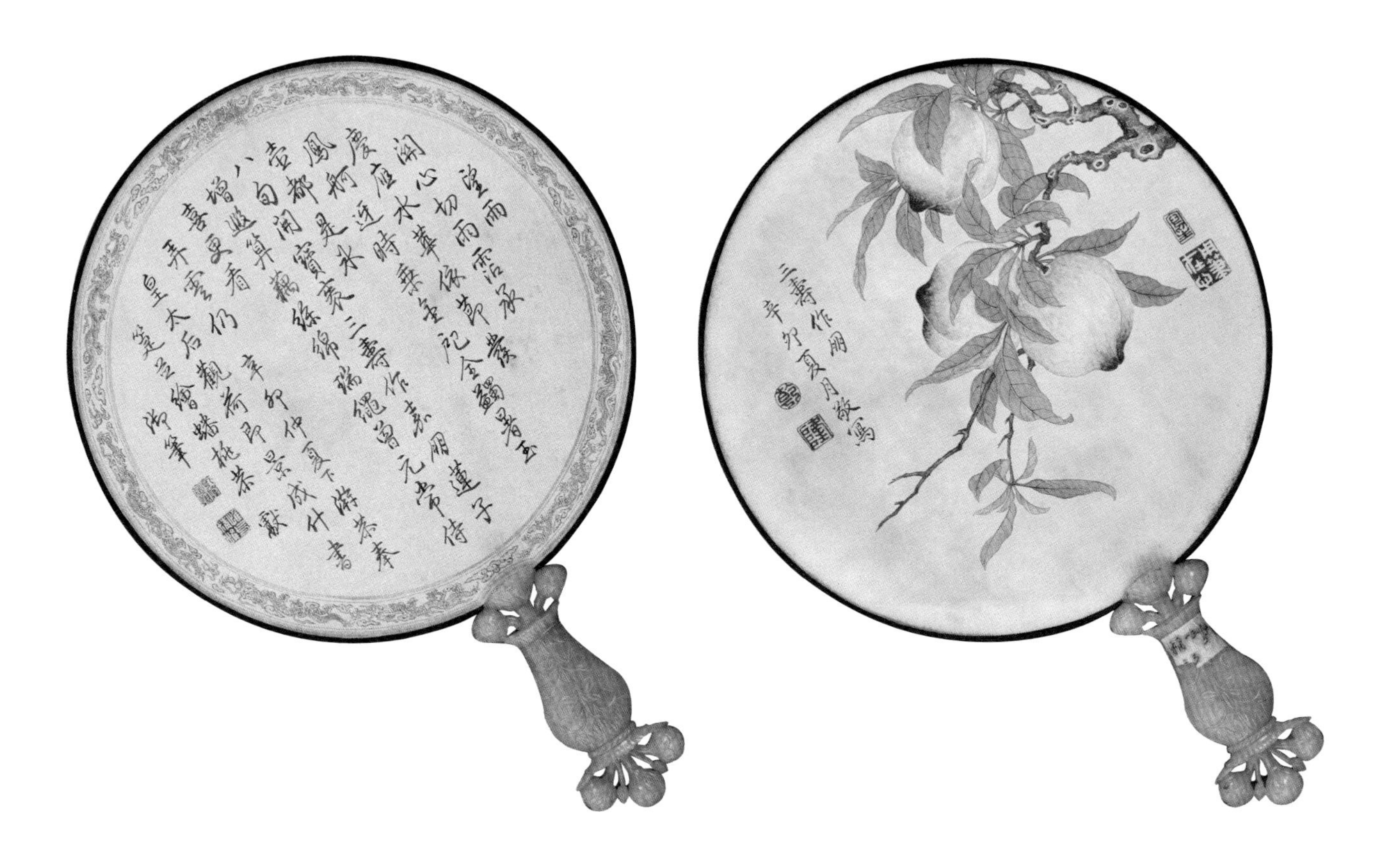

51

Three peaches

Hongli (the Qianlong emperor)

Dated 1771

Fan with jade handle, ink and colour on silk

D 26.2 cm

Inscriptions: artist's signature, dated 1771; inscription by the artist on reverse side, also dated 1771

Seals: five of the artist

Peaches are thought to have originated in China, although this is difficult to prove. There are three main kinds of Chinese peach: the cling peach from the north, the honey peach from central and southern China, and the flat peach from the south. The peach has an important place in ancient Chinese mythology. It is said that in the garden of the palace of the Queen Mother of the West grew fairy peach trees which blossomed only once every 3000 years and yielded the fruits of eternity which remained ripe for another 3000 years. Its association with longevity made the peach a popular subject for paintings to be presented as gifts.

As a filial son, the Qianlong emperor often made paintings for his mother, either for her birthday or at New Year. This small fan painting was made on a more informal occasion, when he accompanied her on a summer excursion. The rendering of the shapes and colours of the fruits is reminiscent of Song academy painting, a style seldom employed by the emperor, thereby giving this work a distinctive place in his oeuvre.

LIT: Couling 1917: 426

52

Ruyi and flowers

Yongrong

Dated 1768

Hanging scroll, ink and colour on paper

L 90.1 cm, W 34.7 cm

Inscriptions: artist's signature, undated; one inscription by Hongli, dated 1768

Seals: two of the artist; five of Hongli

Yongrong (1743–90) was the emperor's sixth son and the most accomplished painter amongst his brothers. He is said to have studied mathematics and astronomy, perhaps with the Jesuit missionaries at court, and in his later years he helped with the huge compilation of imperial manuscripts, *The Four Treasuries* (no.22). We know virtually nothing about his life, nor about his training as a painter.

Although this work was executed when Yongrong was only 24 years old it displays a very mature understanding of ink painting, with brushstrokes that are both representative and expressive. It makes an interesting comparison with the European-style representation of a similar subject by Castiglione (no. 62). The inscription written by the Qianlong emperor at the upper left corner suggests that the emperor had asked his son to paint this for the emperor to give to his mother as a New Year present.

LIT: *YZSSJ* 1771: *juan* 69; Chou and Brown 1985: 61; Tang and Luo 1994: 465

53

Reading on a snowy day

Hongli (the Qianlong emperor) and Giuseppe Castiglione

Dated 1764

Hanging scroll, ink on paper

L 87.5 cm, W 50.7 cm

Inscriptions: artist's signature, dated 1764

Seals: five of Hongli

In this self portrait the Qianlong emperor is seated on a heated bed reading a book inside a little study in the mountains. Outside the study the world is white: snow carpets the trees, the stream, the rocks, and the path on which a boy attendant approaches. At the top of the painting are a poem and a commentary by the emperor. In the latter he notes that it is the seventh day of the twelfth month of the *guiwei* year (9 January 1764) and that the timing of the deep snow is auspicious. He goes on to say that that is why he has composed this poem to add to the snowy scene he has just copied from an original by Xiang Shengmo (1597–1658), a scholar painter of the Ming dynasty (1368–1644). He confesses that, because of his lack of confidence in painting figures, he has asked Castiglione to paint them for him.

This portrait is interesting in several respects. In contrast to the formal portraits of the emperor as ruler, this one presents him as a Chinese scholar, like the artist whose painting he was copying. This artist, Xiang Shengmo, came from a renowned artistic family in the lower Yangzi River valley. His grandfather was Xiang Yuanbian (1525–90) who had amassed a vast collection of paintings, a large proportion of which came into the Qing imperial collection after the fall of the Ming dynasty in 1644. In his late years Xiang Shengmo became a recluse, whose works often evoke nostalgia for the past. In this painting the emperor identifies himself with Xiang by portraying himself as a recluse, and like a recluse he is humbled by nature.

The emperor is dressed in the robes of a Han Chinese scholar, which, considering that Han-style dress was forbidden in public at the time, is puzzling. As the well-informed ruler that he was, he must have been aware that Xiang Shengmo had remained loyal to the Ming dynasty until his death. Such an obvious contradiction can only suggest that this portrait was strictly for the emperor's private contemplation, away from the eyes of the critic.

The fact that it was not going to be seen by others may further explain why the emperor felt able to request help from Castiglione. Throughout his long years of painting, the emperor must have resorted to ghost painters on several occasions. Yang Danxia holds the view that nos 46, 47, 60 and 75 could well have been wholly or partially painted by court artists (see Yang Danxia in this book, p.179). However, a systematic authentication of the emperor's corpus has yet to be undertaken.

LIT: Chou and Brown 1985: 17; Ho 1992: 110; Wu Hung 1995: 39–40

54

Hongli, the Qianlong emperor, in Han Chinese dress

Anonymous
Qianlong period (1736–95)
Hanging scroll, ink and colour on paper
L 95.7 cm, W 101 cm
Seals: two of Hongli

In this portrait the middle-aged Qianlong emperor appears yet again as a scholar dressed in Han Chinese robes, in the act of composing a poem. The setting evokes the romanticised world of the scholar.

The similarity in size and colour scheme to the following painting of a female beauty (no. 55) suggests that the emperor is doing more than writing poetry. The paintings may have been intended to hang side by side, in which case the emperor would be gazing longingly at the seductive female, possibly a concubine, at her mirror. Although there is no signature on either painting, they would appear on stylistic grounds to be collaborative works by Castiglione and Jin Tingbiao.

55

Female beauty in Han Chinese dress

Anonymous

Qianlong period (1736–95)

Hanging scroll, ink and colour on paper

L 96 cm, W 100.2 cm

It has been suggested that this painting was for display in the imperial bedchamber. Conventional wisdom also holds that the painting portrays one of the emperor's concubines. Unlike the group portraits of court ladies engaged in leisurely pursuits (no. 60), this painting frames a single lady pinning her hair in front of a mirror. As Wu Hung has convincingly argued, such an image delivers a strong erotic message and belongs to the category of *shinuhua,* paintings of female beauties, rather than to the genre of female portraiture (no. 6).

This painting may also have a more specific reference. If, as suggested above, it was displayed in the palace alongside the portrait of the Qianlong emperor (no. 54), the pair of paintings may have alluded to the union of 'genius and beauty' which were considered ideal marriage partners in southern culture. In other words, by pairing himself with this anonymous lady, the emperor sees himself as a young genius about to have an affair with a beauty, a typical scenario in popular romances and plays.

LIT: Palace Museum 1992: 79; Wu Hung 1997: 350–1

56

The Qianlong emperor on Mid-Autumn Festival evening

Attributed to Giuseppe Castiglione
Qianlong period (1736–95)
Hanging scroll, ink and colour on silk
L 138.2 cm, W 70 cm

Among all the 'costume portraits' of the emperor, as Wu Hung has called them, this painting is perhaps the most light hearted. It shows the emperor sitting, with legs crossed casually, in a palatial garden, looking somewhat mischievously up at the moon on the evening of the Chinese Mid-Autumn Festival. That the emperor allowed himself to be depicted in such an informal pose is an unmistakable sign of the intimate relationship between him and the artist.

The portrait is unsigned, but on stylistic grounds, it is probably the joint work of Castiglione and one of his Chinese collaborators, painted around the same time as *Hongli and the royal children on New Year's eve* (no. 35).

57

Hongli, the Qianlong emperor, looking at a painting

Giuseppe Castiglione and Ding Guanpeng
Qianlong period (1736–95)
Hanging scroll, ink and colour on paper
L 136.4cm, W 62 cm
Inscriptions: artist's signature, undated
Seals: two of the artist; two of Hongli

Although this painting is signed by Castiglione, he may have been responsible for painting only the emperor's face. All the rest of the picture, including the emperor's body and the other figures, was probably painted by Ding Guanpeng (see no. 58). The work shows the typical setting of a gathering of connoisseurs, a subject common in Ming and Qing scholars' paintings. In a pleasant southern-style garden are bamboo groves and tall pine trees, and an elegant bridge leading across a winding stream. Set in the open is a table displaying a variety of antiques and scrolls. The hanging scroll that is being admired by the connoisseurs is held on a bamboo stick by young boys, while others approach merrily with more objects and a lute.

What differentiates this picture from others showing gatherings of connoisseurs is that it is not really concerned with the gathering itself. Nor is it simply a portrait of the emperor as connoisseur. In most such paintings the antiques being admired are intended to be anonymous, whereas in this painting it is the hanging scroll that is the focus of attention. Herbert Butz has identified the scroll as *Washing the elephant* painted by Ding Yunpeng (1547–after 1628) in 1588, and now in the National Palace Museum in Taipei. The painting was formerly in the emperor's collection. The present painting might be more appropriately entitled *Hongli, the Qianlong emperor, looking at 'Washing the elephant' by Ding Yunpeng* (see no. 58).

EXH: Ledderose and Butz 1985: no. 41
LIT: Kahn 1971: 83; Fong and Watt 1996: 63

58

Washing the elephant

Ding Guanpeng

1750

Hanging scroll, ink and colour on gold-flecked paper

L 132.2 cm, W 62.5 cm

Inscriptions: artist's signature, dated 1750

Seals: one of the artist; one of Hongli

The history of this painting is closely linked to the picture *Washing the elephant* by Ding Yunpeng which is the focus in *Hongli, the Qianlong emperor, looking at a painting* (no. 57) by Castiglione. The emperor's attention was first drawn to Ding Yunpeng's *Washing the elephant* in 1745 when the paintings in the palace with Buddhist and Daoist subject matter were being catalogued. The iconography of Ding Yunpeng's painting has been considered problematic, but the Qianlong emperor was convinced that the painting depicted the bodhisattva Samantabhadra (the seated figure) watching people clean a white elephant, his own mount. Struck by the deeply religious message of the work, the emperor inscribed a poem on it.

Perhaps around the same time, in order to show his special appreciation of Ding Yunpeng's work, he instructed Castiglione and Ding Guanpeng to paint *Hongli looking at a painting*. Interestingly, in *Hongli looking at a painting* the reference to Ding Yunpeng is not only literal in the sense that his *Washing the elephant* is the focus of the new work, but also stylistic. Castiglione and Ding Guanpeng adopt Ding Yunpeng's distinct brushwork – the dynamic wriggling lines – to depict the emperor. Five years later, in 1750, the emperor returned to Ding Yunpeng's work and commissioned the present painting. But instead of paying stylistic homage to Ding Yunpeng as he had done in *Hongli looking at a painting*, Ding Guanpeng, arguably with Castiglione's involvement, produced a literal copy of Ding Yunpeng's original in which the face of bodhisattva Samantabhadra is however replaced with that of the emperor.

By this time the Qianlong emperor had had himself portrayed in various guises and would continue to do so in the ensuing decades. As Harold Kahn has rightly argued these portraits exemplify the most egocentric aspect of the emperor. In the present portrait, by transforming himself into the bodhisattva Samantabhadra, the emperor intends to claim for himself the multiple manifestations of the bodhisattva – he had 32 forms – and thus his sacred qualities. Yet this painting can perhaps also be considered a philosophical critique of the Buddhist concept of multiple manifestation. Since the late Ming dynasty the subject of the painting *Washing the elephant* had been understood as the washing away of illusions, for the pronunciation of elephant, *xiang*, is the same as that for the word illusion, also *xiang*. In the context of Buddhism, phenomena of the outside world are thought to be illusions, whereas in his inscription on Ding Yunpeng's work of 1745 the emperor makes it clear that he considers the 32 forms of the bodhisattva to be an illusion as well. Therefore, instead of being a simple demonstration of the emperor as a bodhisattva, the present painting was perhaps intended to be double edged. It may serve as a reminder that the portraits of him in various guises are only façades and not his 'true self', to use his own term from his inscription on his earliest portrait (no. 3).

EXH: Ledderose and Butz 1985: no. 40; Museu de Arte de Macau 2000: no. 30

LIT: Weidner 1994: 403–04; Wu Hung 1995

59

One or two?

Anonymous
Qianlong period (1736–95)
Hanging scroll, ink and colour on paper
L 147.2 cm, H 76.5 cm
Inscriptions: one by Hongli, undated
Seals: five of Hongli

There are three versions of this portrait of the Qianlong emperor, all in the Palace Museum in Beijing. Although the present version is not signed by the artist, the museum attributes one of the other two versions to Yao Wenhan (see no. 23), one of the emperor's favourite artists in the painting workshop. It seems likely that the present painting is also by Yao Wenhan. Each of the three versions bears a poem written by the emperor, and each is identical except for the name of the place where he wrote the inscription. One was written in the emperor's study Changchun shuwu, the Eternal Spring Study in the Hall for the Cultivation of the Mind, and another was written in Naluoyanku, the Cave of Narayana, the whereabouts of which in the palaces has yet to be identified. The present version was also written in the Hall for the Cultivation of the Mind. According to the curator of the Palace Museum all three versions were originally mounted on screens, probably at least two of them, including the present one, in the Hall for the Cultivation of the Mind.

The fascination of this portrait lies first of all in the portrait-within-a-portrait device it employs. The main figure, the Qianlong emperor, sits on a couch holding a scroll in his left hand and a brush in his right, and there is another image of him in a hanging scroll on the screen, seemingly turning his head to communicate with the main seated figure. Herbert Butz has traced the source of this device, and indeed of the entire composition, to an anonymous Ming painting, now in the National Palace Museum in Taipei, that was once in the emperor's collection. The use of this device shows that the emperor and his painters were interested in questions to do with mimesis, such as surface and depth, mirroring and doubling, illusion and reality.

However, the painting is more than just an illustration of the problems of pictorial representation. In the painting the emperor is surrounded by objects from his collection, including two vessels, one on each side of the couch. The sizes and locations of these indicate their importance.

As Chang Lin-sheng has pointed out, the bronze vessel on a high wooden stand to the left of the couch is a standard measure made by the government in the year CE 9 during the flamboyant, despotic and short-lived rule of Wang Mang (CE 9–23) of the Han dynasty (206 BCE – CE 220). It is now in the National Palace Museum in Taipei, but was once in the emperor's collection. The bronze measure is of prime importance in the history of China's weights and measures as it sets the standard measure for a foot and an inch. It is also a measure of volume, and one that is remarkably close to π. The emperor had one of his ministers, Zhang Ruoai (1713–46), transcribe the inscription from the vessel to be stored in a drawer of the stand on which the object stood.

Equally important is the vessel to the right of the couch which Geng Baochang has identified as being identical to a blue and white porcelain jar made in the Xuande period (1426–35) of the Ming dynasty (1368–1644), now in the Palace Museum in Beijing. The mandala shape of its cover and the seed syllables in Nagari script on the body suggest that the jar was used in tantric rituals at the court of the Xuande emperor.

If we accept that the assembling of objects is the material expression of one's self, then these two vessels may have been used deliberately by the emperor as symbols of his desire to set standards and to patronise Tibetan Buddhism. If he was attempting to compare himself with either or both of the rulers in whose reigns the two vessels were made, the Qianlong emperor certainly had much in common with the Xuande emperor. Both men were fond of hunting, both had close ties with Tibetan Buddhism, and both were the greatest patrons of court art in their respective dynasties. In fact in 1746 the Qianlong emperor had copied a New Year picture by the Xuande emperor, himself a distinguished amateur emperor-painter.

The emperor's poem on the painting adds a further problem to the reading of the portrait. The poem may be rendered as follows:

> Is there one or are there two?
> They are neither identical nor dissimilar.
> One may be Confucian, the other Moist,
> Why should I worry, why even bother to ask myself?

While the first half of the verse seemingly refers to the double-portrait device and to the issue of representation, the second half makes it clear that the emperor is using the device to question his identity. Wu Hung argues that the emperor leaves the question unanswered, thereby intensifying the mystery. Given the private nature of the portrait, however, we can perhaps say that the emperor both mystifies and de-mystifies, because he reveals to himself that which he would have concealed in public.

EXH: Ledderose and Butz 1985: no. 42
LIT: Kahn 1971: 183; Wang Yao-ting 1989; Geng Baochang 1993: 44–6; Chang Lin-Sheng 1996: 16, 18, 93–4; Lachman 1996; Wu Hung 1996: 231–6; Zito 1997: 40

EMPEROR SAGE

Our experience of time is conditioned by our constant referral to the calendar. The Chinese had used a *yin-yang li*, a lunar-solar calendar, since the Shang dynasty (*c.* sixteenth–eleventh century BCE), and it was only in 1912 that they adopted the Gregorian calendar. The distinguishing features of the lunar-solar calendar are its 24 climatic points in the year cycle, and the system of naming the months according to seasonal flowers. Both features derive from the ancient Chinese observation of the cycles existing in the environment, which in turn gave rise to the dominant Chinese view of time as a cyclic flow.

No one in eighteenth-century China would have been more aware of the cyclic nature of time than the Qianlong emperor. As son of heaven he would lead the important annual rituals and celebrations that marked the major climatic points such as the beginning of spring (no. 71), the summer solstice (no. 72) and the winter solstice. He would also celebrate the three main festivals of the year: the Lunar New Year (nos 35 and 69), the Dragon Boat Festival (no. 62) and the Mid-Autumn Moon Festival (nos 56 and 61).

To the emperor time was not simply a series of recurring events but was also a one-way path ending in death. The emperor's awareness of this was accentuated by the unexpected death of his first wife, the Xiaoxian empress, in 1748, and reinforced in the late 1760s and early 1770s by the deaths of most of his favourite courtiers and many of the major court artists who had been active for decades: Castiglione died in 1766, followed by Jin Tingbiao in 1767, Attiret in 1768, Shen Deqian and Dong Bangda in 1769, Fuheng in 1770 and Qian Chenqun in 1774. The emperor's acceptance of the irreversibility of time is graphically illustrated by the verses he added during this period to earlier paintings (no. 30). In one of these he poignantly notes the decaying of his own body (no. 2).

Perhaps to mitigate the anxiety of being annihilated, the elderly emperor began passionately to commission and collect jades, and to have his names carved into many of these immortal stones. He also adopted the Buddhist view of life as illusion. On the first and fifteenth day of each month he would copy out the *Heart Sutra*, an important Mahayana text.

The Qianlong emperor abdicated in 1796 after 60 years on the throne. His own explanation was that he was acting out of respect for his grandfather whose reign had lasted for 61 years. Modern historians interpret it, however, as a symbolic claim for uniqueness, for there had been very few cases of abdication in previous dynasties and none had been voluntary. Another explanation might be that he abdicated after consulting the ancient *Book of changes* and the *ganzhi* year-counting system. According to this time-honoured system the greater time cycle is completed every 60 years. Hence, the emperor's abdication could be regarded as an instance of cosmic timing.

Opposite:
Surging waves. Detail from *Copy of 'Studies of water' by Ma Yuan* (no. 72). The seal reads: 'Son of heaven, who is of an age seldom reached since antiquity'.

60

Ladies enjoying antiques in a winter boudoir

Cheng Zuzhang and assistants

Datable to 1741

Album of 12 leaves, ivory, gold, mother-of-pearl, lacquer

Each L 32.9 cm, W 3.2 cm, H 39.1 cm

Of all the art works produced at court, the seasonal picture was one of the major types. As pictures of this kind were for display in the relevant month, the subject of each had to accord with the seasonal activities described in the monthly calendar developed in pre-dynastic China. In this calendar the seasons are identified by natural cyclic phenomena such as the hibernation of animals, the migration of birds and the blooming of plants.

This picture, made of ivory and other precious materials, is one of a set of twelve representing the activities of court ladies throughout the twelve months of the year. Each picture is accompanied by a poem by the Qianlong emperor, carved from mother-of-pearl and inlaid into lacquer. The present scene shows ladies enjoying antiques in the eleventh month when their year-long needlework draws to a close. While this particular picture does not make a specific reference to a season, it is unusual as most of the others show seasonal flowers in bloom.

These seasonal pictures usually had a purpose: this set was placed in the Hall of Abstinence for the emperor to refer to as he prepared for the sacrifice to heaven at the winter solstice.

Many of the carvings made during the Qianlong reign are copies of paintings in the palace collection. This set imitates an album by the court painter Chen Mei, and according to the court archives was made in 1741 by the ivory craftsman Chen Zuzhang and his four assistants.

LIT: Palace Museum 1994: vol. 4, 1826

61

Pair of rabbits under a wutong tree

Leng Mei
Early 18th century
Hanging scroll, ink and colour on silk
L 175.9 cm, W 95 cm
Inscription: artist's signature, undated
Seal: one of the artist

Like the previous work (no. 60) this painting has a seasonal subject, with two types of flower and a tree: osmanthus and chrysanthemum, and the *wutong* tree. From the Chinese system of naming each month according to a plant, we know that this painting represents the seventh, eighth and ninth months, hence autumn. As the most important autumn festival is the Mid-Autumn Festival (the fifteenth day of the eighth month), the painter adds the pair of jade-white rabbits that, according to legend, lives on the moon.

We know little about the life of the court painter Leng Mei (active 1696–1745). A native of Shandong province, he entered the court of the Kangxi emperor as a student of Jiao Binzheng (active second half of the seventeenth century) who was a well-known painter at that time working with the Jesuit missionary artists. The obvious traces of European influence in the present painting can probably be explained by Leng's apprenticeship under Jiao. Towards the end of the Kangxi reign Leng Mei became a key figure in the palace painting workshop, producing many fine pieces of work. By the time the Qianlong emperor came to the throne Leng Mei was an old man. He served the emperor for only ten years before his death.

EXH: Ledderose and Butz 1985: no. 113; Museu de Arte de Macau 2000: no. 45
LIT: Yang Boda 1993: 109–15

62

Still life for the Dragon Boat Festival

Giuseppe Castiglione
Early 18th century
Hanging scroll, ink and colour on silk
L 140 cm, W 84 cm
Inscription: artist's signature, undated
Seal: one of Hongli

If Leng Mei belonged to the older generation of court painters at the beginning of the Qianlong reign, Giuseppe Castiglione represents the middle-aged artists. During his long and distinguished service in the palace painting workshop, he was responsible for many projects of great importance to the emperor, such as the works depicting the emperor's early years and the military campaigns of the 1750s (nos 2, 3, 16, 21, 30, 31, 35, 56). Although not a trained architect, Castiglione was responsible for the creation of the European buildings in the summer palace near Beijing, Yuanmingyuan. He died in Beijing in 1766 at the age of 78 and was buried in the graveyard of the Catholic church to the south of the city.

Judging from the strongly European style of this painting, it was possibly painted not long after Castiglione entered court, some time in the Yongzheng reign. Like Leng Mei's work (no. 61) it is a seasonal picture but, unlike Leng's painting, it does not represent a complete season but rather a specific moment in that season: the Dragon Boat Festival, held on the fifth day of the fifth month. On that day dragon boat races take place to commemorate the famous poet Qu Yuan (*c.* 340–278 BCE) who drowned himself in protest against the corrupt government of the time. The boat race symbolises people setting out to the spot where the tragedy took place, and in the past they would throw rushes and glutinous rice dumplings wrapped in leaves into the water to feed any fish who might have had designs on the poet's corpse. To indicate this special time of the year, Castiglione includes a few rushes amongst the flowers in the vase and places several dumplings beside it. Otherwise the painting would appear to be no more than a still life.

EXH: *Die Verbotene Stadt* 1997: no. 124; Museu de Arte de Macau 2000: no. 47
LIT: Yang Boda 1993: 131–77

63

Travellers crossing a stream

Jin Tingbiao

Datable to before 1759

Hanging scroll, ink on paper

L 191 cm, W 96 cm

Inscriptions: artist's signature, undated; one by Hongli, dated 1759

Seals: one of the artist; twelve of Hongli

Jin Tingbiao (d. 1767), a native of Wucheng in Zhejiang province, belonged to the same generation of court painters as Castiglione. Little is known about his life. His entry to the palace atelier was connected with the Qianlong emperor's tour of inspection to the south in 1757 when he presented a painting album to the emperor and was subsequently invited to court. Jin probably died around the time of the New Year in 1767 as in a poem written in the first month of that year the emperor laments Jin's recent death. In the heyday of his service at court Jin Tingbiao produced numerous fine works. He was also one of the key artists responsible for the important commission, the *Illustrated tributaries of the Qing empire* (no. 25), but he died well before its completion in 1775. Over 70 paintings by him bear poems by the emperor, testifying to his position as one of the emperor's most favoured painters and one of the most distinguished among his fellow artists. When Jin died the Qianlong emperor expressed deep sadness.

This painting was kept by the emperor in his mountain villa on Jade Spring Hill on the western outskirts of Beijing. It bears a poem by the emperor in the upper right corner. The two large imperial seals towards the top centre suggest that the emperor unrolled and examined the scroll in his late years.

LIT: *YZSEJ* 1761: *juan* 88

64

Huang pendant

Neolithic period, Liangzhu culture (c. 3200–2000 BCE)

Nephrite, L 20.8 cm, H 8.3 cm, D 0.6 cm

Inscription: poem by Hongli on wooden support, undated

The Chinese *yu* and the English jade are umbrella terms referring to two distinct minerals, nephrite and jadeite. Nephrite has been the favoured stone in China since the neolithic period. *Huang* pendants made of nephrite and semi-annular in shape had a number of different functions. Some were used in rituals: according to a pre-Qin text it was the key object in the sacrifice to the spirits of land and grain, and it could also be used in the ritual of official appointments. Some *huang* were worn as bodily accessories.

This jade is yellowish brown in colour with surface cracks that suggest it may have been burned at some point. Both sides have incised decoration. Superimposed on this on one side in relief are, at the centre, the head of a beast with open eyes, and in the upper corners two small birds in profile.

A poem, dated 1748, on the wooden container for the jade suggests that the Qianlong emperor's interest in jade began early. The poem recounts that the jade had been recently presented to him as a *qin* or stone chime, showing the ignorance of the gift-giver as the emperor believed that it had originally been intended for wear on the body. The date of the poem indicates that the jade entered the imperial collection in the summer of 1748, the very time when the emperor was in the depths of mourning for the death of his first wife, the Xiaoxian empress. Writing about this jade may have provided a temporary diversion from his sadness.

LIT: *YZSEJ* 1761: *juan* 4; Li Xueqin 1989; Palace Museum 1995: pl. 27

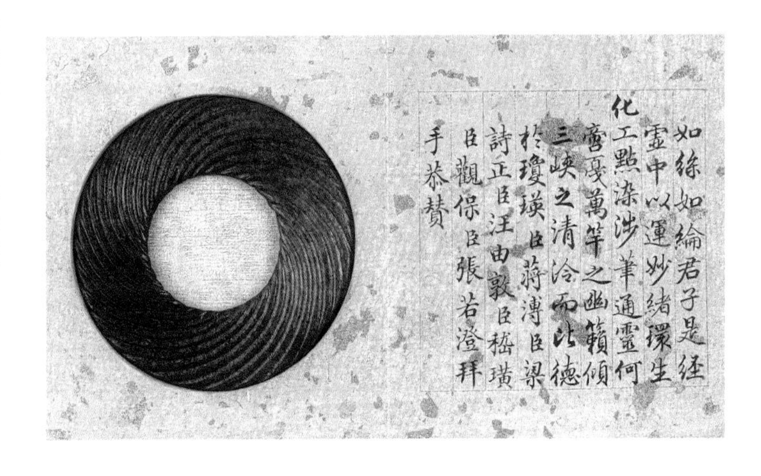

65

Finding order amongst ten thousand threads

Hongli (the Qianlong emperor) and others

1749

Album of three leaves, with jade disc on colophon leaf

Each leaf L 20 cm, H 10.5 cm

Inscriptions: artist's signature, dated 1749; frontispiece writing by the artist; colophon co-authored by Jiang Pu, Liang Shizheng, Wang Youdun, Ji Huang, Guanbao and Zhang Ruocheng, undated

Seals: four of the artist

This album is an example of composite art of a most unusual format. It consists of three leaves: one with an ink painting by the Qianlong emperor of a veranda overlooking water; one frontispiece leaf written by the emperor; and one leaf with a colophon composed collaboratively by six ministers. The most distinctive feature of the album is the inclusion of a brown jade ring set deep in the left hand page of the leaf with the colophon. The jade is decorated with a whirling-ripple pattern on the circular band.

Why did the emperor place a piece of jade alongside his landscape painting? What is the connection between the jade and the painting? The colophon by the emperor's ministers tells us that it was not simply for the purpose of decoration:

> With silken threads and silken cords,
> A gentleman weaves a length of cloth.
> Springing from an absent mind,
> Endless patterns of stunning beauty.
> Dots and washes without design,
> Lines endowed with the power of the divine.
> This is more than the swishing of
> ten thousand bamboo stems,
> More than the pure water of the Three Gorges.
> This is the sign of a mind of jade.

The writers seem to be saying that the jade ring and the painting express the emperor's desire to create a sense of calm and stability out of the many events troubling his mind. In the previous year he had lost his wife, the Xiaoxian empress, and her death was followed by several crises at court.

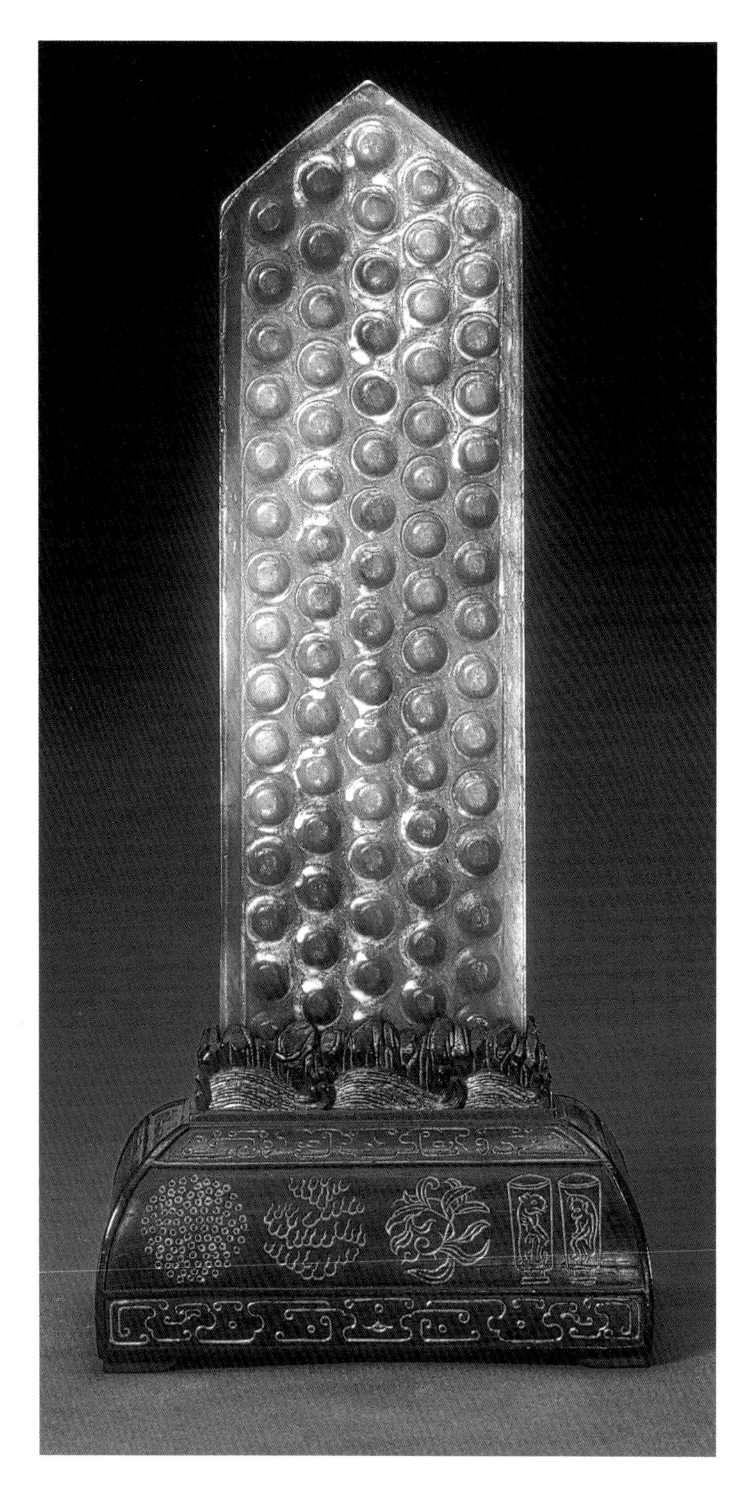

66

Gui tablet

Ming dynasty (1368–1644)
Nephrite
H 21.3 cm, W 6.3 cm, D 0.9 cm
Inscriptions: reign mark of Hongli on wooden stand

The brownish patina on this green jade tablet is not natural but the result of its having been subjected to a high temperature. This was probably an attempt on the part of the maker to give the jade an antique appearance. The shape and decoration of the tablet point to a date within the Ming dynasty as the distinctive nipple pattern made its first appearance during this period.

Many of the Ming jade tablets in the Qing palace collection were probably inherited from the Ming court when it was overthrown in the mid-seventeenth century. The wooden stand for the piece was added in the Qianlong period. The four sides of the stand bear the twelve imperial insignia, incised and filled with gold. On the stand is a six-character inscription in regular script: 'Made in the Qianlong reign of the Great Qing', which may indicate a desire to appropriate this piece as a product of the Qianlong reign.

In the Qing dynasty jade tablets were important ritual objects. This tablet may have been used when making sacrifices to the earth and grain spirits.

LIT: Zhang Guangwen 1991.1: 30–1; Palace Museum 1995: pl. 155

67

Jade cabbage

Qianlong period (1736–95)
Feicui jade
H 24.3 cm

The Qianlong emperor loved not only to collect ancient jades but also to commission new pieces. There had been a jade workshop at court before his time, but it was the Qianlong emperor who was responsible for the rapid growth of the palace jade collection. Yang Boda has estimated that in the collections of the Palace Museum there are several tens of thousands of jades, most of which were collected or made during the Qianlong period.

One of the factors that contributed to this jade boom was the conquest in the late 1750s of eastern Turkestan and the subsequent re-opening of the jade route between China proper and Khotan, one of the major sources of the stone. Vast quantities of jade flooded into China, prompting imperial commissions of a monumental scale that were to last for more than two decades. One such commission was the gigantic carved jade boulder known as 'Yu the Great taming the flood' which was completed in 1788 (see Craig Clunas in this book, p. 14).

The elderly emperor's passion for jade was unprecedented, but it may have had something to do with the stone's association with immortality. Objects of jade made their appearance throughout the palace: as ritual objects, as bodily accessories, as combs, as bowls, chopsticks, spoons, writing brush handles, and even miniature potted landscapes.

This jade cabbage served as a decorative flower vase. The jade from which it is made is described as *feicui*, a word which means literally the emerald-green colour of a kingfisher's neck feathers, but which is often applied to jadeite of a similar colour. Presumably the Qing court was well aware of the discovery of a source of jadeite in northern Burma (present-day Myanmar) in the late Qianlong period, but it would be almost impossible to determine the source of this *feicui* jade.

LIT: Yang Boda 1982; Zhang Guangwen 1990; Yang Boda 1993.4

68

Bi disc

1st–2nd century CE

Jade

H 18.6 cm, W 12.5 cm, D 2.6 cm

Inscription: poem by Hongli on the rim, dated 1788

The term *bi* was first employed by specialists in the rituals of the Zhou (eleventh century–221 BCE) and Han (206 BCE–CE 220) to categorise jade discs with a small hole at the centre. Such discs were commonly used in court rituals, especially when making sacrifices to heaven as heaven was believed to be round. Archaeological evidence discovered over the last century has revealed that jade discs predate even the Zhou dynasty, and that they have performed diverse functions throughout their history.

The present disc was probably a bodily accessory. It is decorated on both sides with grain pattern, and extending beyond the disc is an openwork design of rampant dragons. Both features are typical of Warring States (475–221 BCE) and Han jades. The unusual feature of this disc is the carved inscription reading *changle,* eternal happiness, supported by the dragons. So far only two other jade discs of this period with openwork characters are known.

The disc seems to have stimulated the elderly Qianlong emperor's imagination, prompting him to compose a poem to be inscribed on the rim. It reads:

> The *changle* disc is a supreme example of jade carving,
> The majestic spirit of the Han spans the sky like a rainbow.
> It is similar to the type of disc inscribed *yizisun,* suitable for sons and grandsons,
> Its beauty is a match for pieces made in the Xia, the Shang and the Zhou.
> Some are inclined to envy the owner,
> And the owner should no longer feel poor.
> Stories fabricated in the inner court
> Tell it was once worn by the lady who courageously confronted a bear.

The emperor appears to date the piece correctly and further imagines that it might have belonged to Lady Feng who is said to have saved the Yuan emperor's (48–33 BCE) life by shielding him from a ferocious bear.

LIT: *YZSWJ* 1795: *juan* 35; Zhang Guangwen 1990: 49; Zhou Nanquan 1991: 83; Palace Museum 1995: pl. 217

69

Spring plants and fruit

Hongli (the Qianlong emperor)

Dated 1763

Hanging scroll, ink and colour on paper

L 95.8 cm, W 57.4 cm

Inscriptions: frontispiece writing by the artist; one inscription also by the artist, dated 1763; collaborative inscription by Fuheng, Laibao, Liu Tongxun, Liang Shizheng, Chen Dehua, Liu Lun, Dong Bangda, Peng Qifeng, Guanbao, Yu Minzhong, Zhang Taikai, Wang Jihua, Dou Guangding, Jin Shen, Wang Huifen, Ni Chengkuan, Jiang Ding, Lu Wenchao, Bian Jizu, undated

Seals: ten of the artist; one of Puyi; two of Yu Minzhong

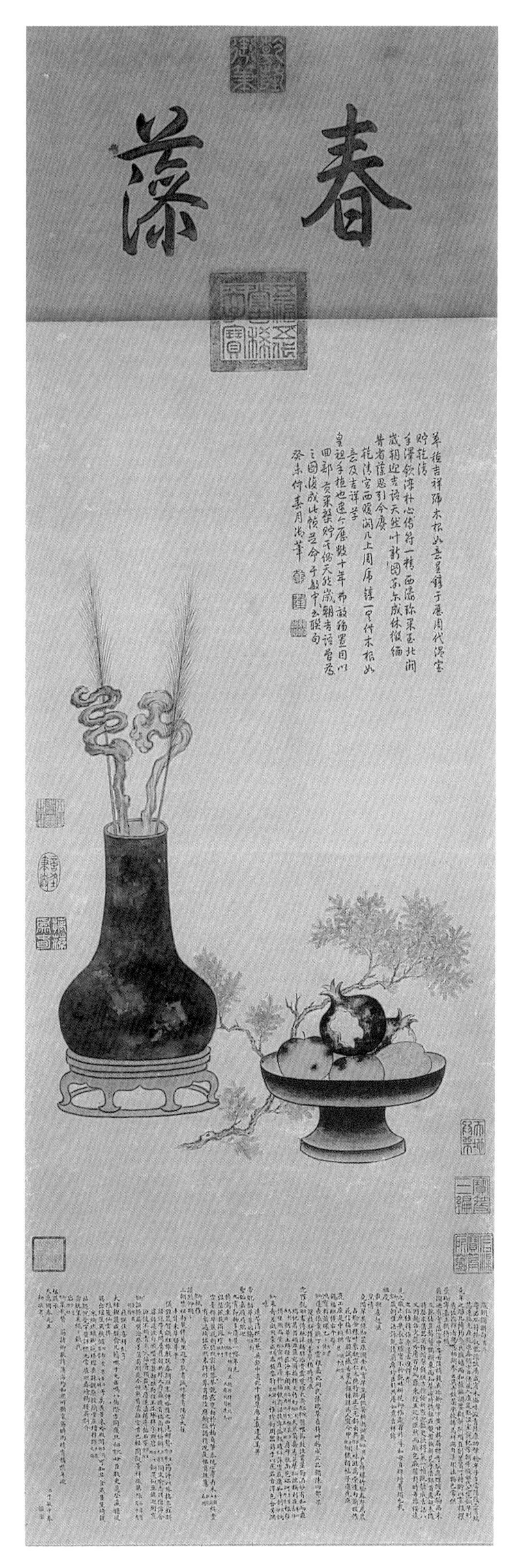

Of all the seasonal festivals the Lunar New Year is the most important indicator of the passage of time. New Year's day marks the start of the new seasonal cycle and is when the emperor, from 1742, renewed his tally with heaven in the most awe-inspiring of the grand sacrifices, the worship of heaven. It was customary for the ruler to paint or write something to commemorate this significant moment.

The present painting is unusual among the emperor's New Year pictures. According to his inscription the subject matter is not the normal assemblage of seasonal fruits, plants, dried grasses and twigs. Instead, the grasses and twigs in the bronze vessel came from plants grown personally by the Qianlong emperor's grandfather the Kangxi emperor, and the pomegranates on the plate were New Year tributes from the Uyghur Muslims in eastern Turkestan. Placing the plate of pomegranates from eastern Turkestan beside his grandfather's grasses and twigs, the emperor exclaims: 'These are the best greetings for the New Year!' The painting thus subtly alludes to the completion by the emperor of the enterprise begun by his grandfather. It was not until his fiftieth birthday that the emperor began to pray that he would live long enough to be able to abdicate after a reign of 60 years like his grandfather. The painting may therefore also be a sign that the emperor had begun to view his reign in relation to those of previous rulers and to that of his grandfather in particular.

LIT: *YZSSJ* 1771: *juan* 27; *YZSWJ* 1795: *juan* 100

怡神

70

Silent night on Mount Pan

Anonymous

Datable to 1763

Hanging scroll, ink on paper

L 120.2 cm, W 65.4 cm

Inscriptions: frontispiece writing by Hongli
14 poems also by Hongli, dated 1763, 1766, 1769, 1770, 1772, 1774, 1775, 1782, 1785, 1787, 1789, 1791, 1793 and 1797

Seals: 24 of Hongli

This portrait of the Qianlong emperor shows him as a scholar recluse nestling in his studio surrounded by misty trees and fantastical rocks. The blurred contours suggest a moment deep in the night. The elongated composition is reminiscent of a work by the famous Suzhou scholar artist Shen Zhou (1427–1509) which depicts the artist holding a philosophical vigil in his mountain studio. It is not known however if the painter of the present picture had Shen's work in mind. At the top of the painting are two characters written by the emperor reading 'To delight the spirit'.

The painting was kept not in the Forbidden City but in the emperor's villa on Mount Pan near Beijing (nos 47 and 50). Whenever the emperor went to the Eastern Tombs to pay homage to his ancestors he would stay there for several weeks. Over these weeks he would lead the life of a scholar, visiting scenic spots and the cultural sites dotted about the mountain, drinking tea, playing the lute, and holding vigils to cleanse the mind.

Of interest in this painting are the 14 poems inscribed on it by the emperor. These were added on his visits to the villa over a period of more than 30 years from 1763 to 1797. Thus in a sense one must not take 1763 as the date of the completion of the painting but as the starting point of the process towards its completion. Each time the emperor added a poem he was changing the appearance of the work.

None of the poems is a simple self-contained entity recording the thoughts of a specific moment. The first poem was composed with a series of rhyming words that were to be used in any future poem: *shen* (deep), *yin* (shadow), *qin* (lute), *yin* (sound) and *xin* (heart or mind) in lines 1, 2, 4, 6 and 8 respectively. By creating poems in this vein the emperor was transforming his painting into a work that he could imbue with his deepest thoughts, into something that would serve as an anchor throughout his life, and into a tapestry that would weave together the threads of his life past and present.

The poems also allowed the emperor to mark the passage of time in a meaningful way. By regulating the rhyming words he was setting himself a target for the number of poems he must write. That number was ten, symbolic of perfection. Thus every time he added a new poem to the painting the emperor would be reminded not only that time had elapsed, but also that he was one step closer to perfection.

LIT: *YZSSJ* 1771: *juan* 29, 55, 80, 88; *YZSSJ* 1783: *juan* 3, 20, 28, 88; *YZSWJ* 1795: *juan* 14, 30, 46, 64; *YZSYJ* 1800: *juan* 10

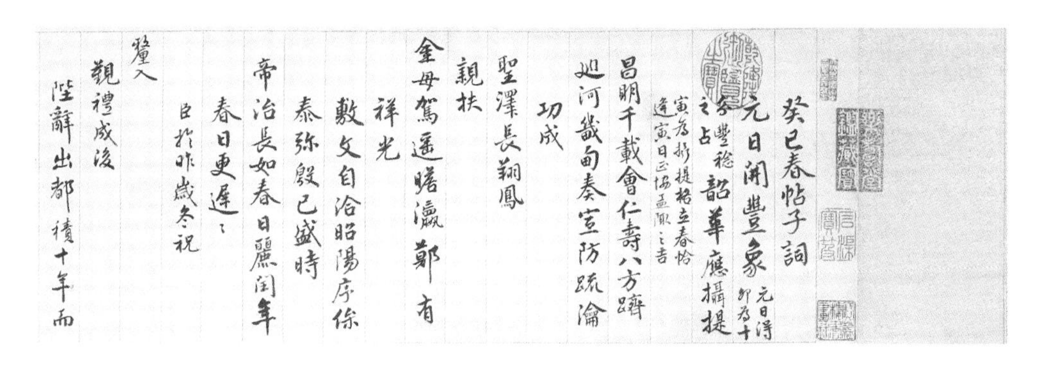

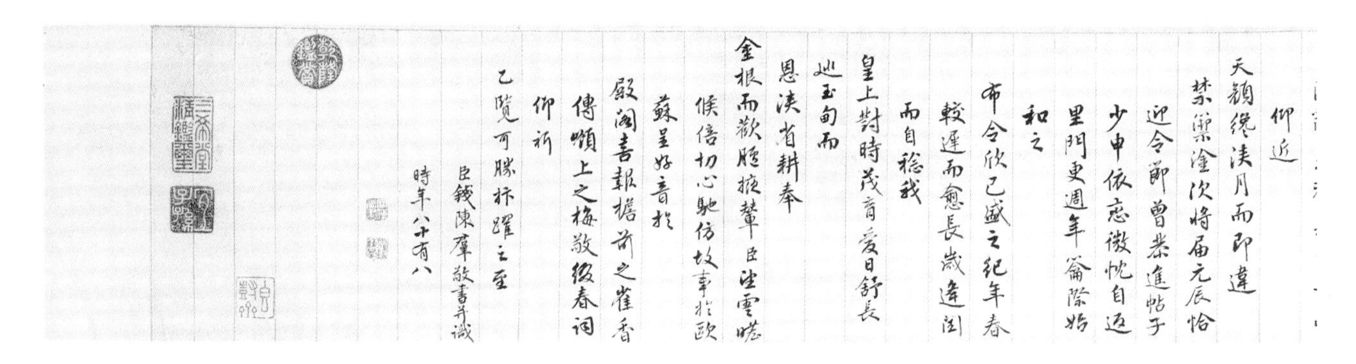

71

Ode to spring

Qian Chenqun
Dated 1773
Handscroll, ink on paper
L 107.6 cm, H 17.2 cm
Inscription: artist's signature, dated 1773
Seals: three of the artist; eight of Hongli

Qian Chenqun (1686–1774) was one of the Qianlong emperor's two favourite official poets, the other being Shen Deqian (no. 41). A native of Jiaxing in Zhejiang province, Qian was born to a scholar official family. His mother Chen Shu (1660–1736) was a celebrated painter to whom he owed his early education. Qian entered court in 1721 as an official scholar at the Institute of Academicians and retired in 1752, thus serving three generations of emperor.

This poem in calligraphy is an ode to spring, *chuntiezi,* or more accurately an ode to the beginning of spring which in China is considered to be the first or second week of February in the western calendar. This genre of seasonal poetry was invented by the court of the Song dynasty (960–1279). Qian's poem comprises two stanzas and a commentary. The poem is no clichéd praise of spring but an ingenious exploitation of his calendrical knowledge. According to him the coinciding of New Year's day and the day *mao* in the *ganzhi* counting system was an auspicious sign, as was the coinciding of the beginning of spring and the day *yin*. 1773 was an especially auspicious year because both coinciding days occurred.

LIT: Hummel 1949, vol. 1: 146–7

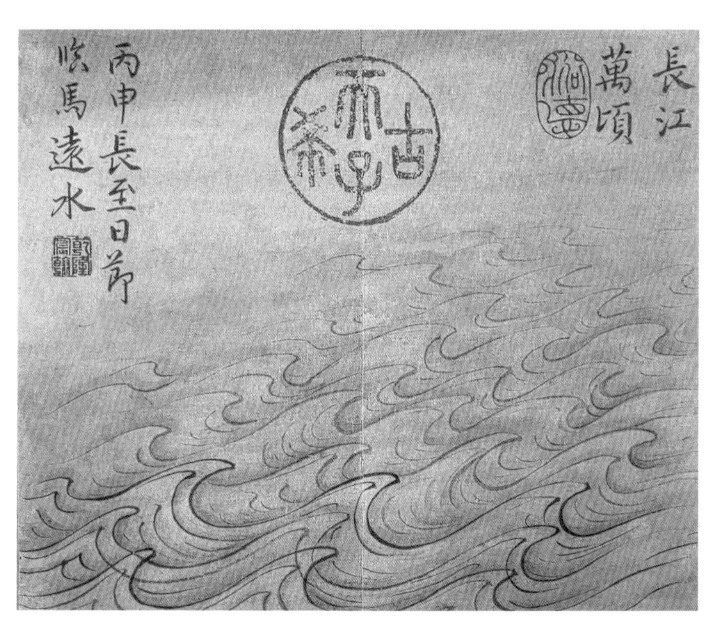

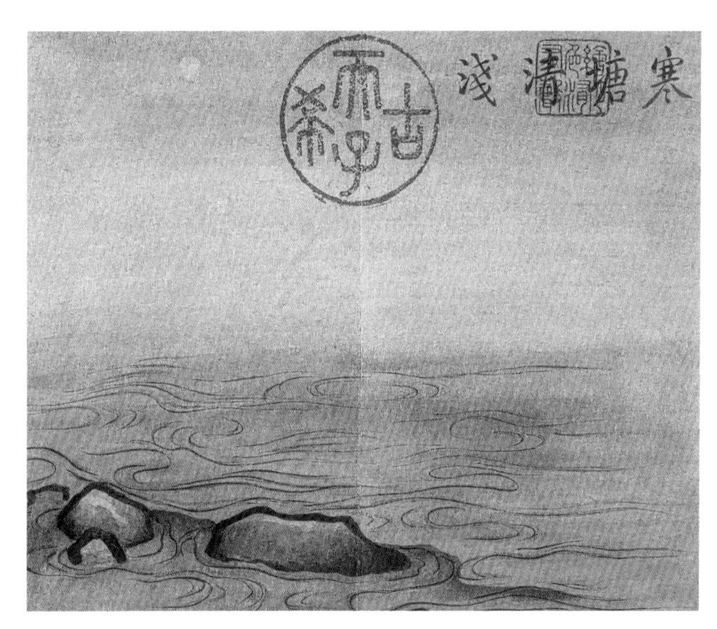

72

Copy of 'Studies of water' by Ma Yuan

Hongli (the Qianlong emperor)

Dated 1776

Album of four leaves, ink and colour on paper

Each H 16.3 cm, W 19.5 cm

Inscriptions: title on each leaf by the artist, dated 1776

Seals: nine of the artist

At the summer solstice every year the Qianlong emperor made great sacrifices to earth at dawn in the north of the capital. On the day of the sacrifice in 1776, 23 June, just prior to the ritual, it rained heavily, an auspicious sign for a good harvest. This album of four leaves was painted just after the grand ritual and can thus be considered as a visual expression of gratitude for the earth's abundant sources of water. The four leaves are exact copies of studies of water in various states by the famous Southern Song painter Ma Yuan (1190–1224) now in the Palace Museum in Beijing. The four poetic titles read: *Breeze-stroked ripples on Lake Dongting, Surging waves, Boundless the Yangzi River* and *Cold pool clear and shallow.*

LIT: *YZSSJ* 1771: *juan* 38; Zhu Jiajin 1986: pl. 33

73

The Tower of Mist and Rain

Dong Gao

1781

Hanging scroll, ink on paper

L 185.5 cm, W 89 cm

Inscriptions: artist's signature, undated; two inscriptions by Hongli, dated 1781 and 1795; artist's inscription, undated

Seals: two of the artist; six of Hongli

A son of Dong Bangda (no. 42), Dong Gao (1740–1818) was one of the few younger scholar officials at court capable of pleasing the wise and knowledgeable elderly Qianlong emperor. As a young man Dong Gao was admitted to the Institute of Academicians after passing the highest level of the official examinations in the capital. He participated in some of the emperor's projects of the late 1750s, such as the compilation of *Illustrated regulations for ceremonial paraphernalia* (1759), yet he did not become a favourite of the emperor until the 1770s. In that decade the most important commissions entrusted to Dong Gao and others included the ambitious compilation of Manchu history, *Research into the origins of the Manchu*, and *The Four Treasuries* (no. 22).

Like his father, Dong Gao was a well-trained scholar artist. He liked to paint bamboo groves, misty scenes and water and his style is typical of the so-called Southern School of painting. The emperor must have felt that Dong's style would be particularly suitable for the subject of this painting, the Tower of Mist and Rain in its lakeside setting by the Summer Palace in Rehe, for the building itself was the recreation of a building of the same name in southern China, in Jiaxing in Zhejiang province. To the emperor this painting by Dong, himself a native of Zhejiang, was proof of the success of his transplantation of southern garden culture to the northern frontier.

The emperor inscribed two poems on the painting in which he voices two very different thoughts. In the first he praises the artist's accurate observation of the mist and drizzle and his ability to capture them with ink and brush. However, in the second poem, written some 14 years later when the elderly emperor revisited this Tower of Mist and Rain in the summer, his former optimism has turned to melancholy.

LIT: *YZSSJ* 1783: *juan* 83; Hummel 1949, vol. 2: 791–2; Du Jiang 1998: 45

74

Pair of the Qianlong emperor's seals commemorating his seventieth and eightieth birthdays

1781, 1791

Jade

Each H 11 cm, W 12.9 cm

The closer his abdication came to realisation the more anxious the elderly Qianlong emperor became. In the last two decades of his life he was obsessed with the idea of longevity. To mark his seventieth birthday he commissioned a large jade seal with an inscription reading 'Treasure of the son of heaven, who is of an age seldom reached since antiquity'. The words derive from a poem by the famous Tang poet Du Fu (712–770): 'Seventy is an age seldom reached since antiquity.' At eighty the emperor had a matching seal carved to create a pair. Its inscription reads: 'Treasure commemorating the advanced age of eighty.' On each occasion the emperor composed an essay, in the first expressing his gratitude to heaven for its benevolence and in the second restating his desire to abdicate. Each is carved into the sides of the seal and filled with gold.

LIT: Tian Xiu 1992; Guo Fuxiang 1993; Xu Qixian 1995

會心艱食

75

Copy of 'Chicks waiting to be fed' by Li Di

Hongli (the Qianlong emperor)
Dated 1788
Handscroll, ink and colour on paper
L 69.3 cm, H 24.8 cm
Inscriptions: frontispiece by the artist, undated; colophon by the artist, dated 1788
Seals: 15 of the artist; one of Puyi

This painting of two chickens is a copy of a work by the Southern Song painter Li Di (active late twelfth to early thirteenth century), now in the Palace Museum in Beijing. The inscription suggests that the emperor attempted his copy not simply because he appreciated the skills of the Song master but because he saw a moral in the subject matter. On Li Di's original the elderly emperor had inscribed:

> The two chicks look up,
> Where is their mother?
> They have not yet learned to feed themselves.
> Who does not pity their hunger?
> Holding the painting is like clutching a carpenter's square,
> Looking at the image makes me deeply aware:
> Hundreds of disaster-struck areas are waiting for food.
> Beware of those in office!

As the real subject of Li's painting was thought to be people's livelihoods, the emperor copied it with great care. He went even further and had it made available for others to copy: he had his own copy, with a new poem, transferred to a stone slab so that multiple reproductions could be made and distributed to every provincial governor. The present painting is the second copy to be made, and it was kept in the Summer Palace in Rehe as a permanent record of the project.

The Qianlong emperor's moralistic treatment of Li Di's work is understandable when we consider that, as a ruler, he was expected to place moral values on a higher plane than aesthetics. The acutely moralistic overtones of much of his later writing may also reflect the growing problems in the later years of his reign. As well as retaining his ritual relationship with heaven, earth and his ancestors, the emperor was aware that the realisation of his dream for a 60-year reign depended above all on his carrying out his official duties as diligently as possible and continuing to care for his subjects.

LIT: *YZSWJ* 1795: *juan* 41; Palace Museum 1991: pl. 770

76

The elderly Qianlong emperor in formal court robe

Anonymous
Datable to 1792
Hanging scroll, ink and colour on silk
L 253 cm, W 149.2 cm
Seals: three of Hongli

Contemporary accounts of the elderly Qianlong emperor describe him as being of extraordinary good health and stamina. Lord Macartney, Britain's first ambassador to China, noted in his diary after his audience with him on 14 September 1793 that he was 'a very fine old gentleman, still healthy and vigorous, not having the appearance of a man of more than sixty'. Later that year, on 16 December, Lord Macartney added that he 'is naturally of a healthy constitution and of great bodily strength, and though upwards of eight-three years old, is as yet but little afflicted with the infirmities of age'.

However, this extraordinary portrait, painted by an anonymous court artist a year before Lord Macartney's meeting with him, exhibits a different view. His 'bodily strength' may still be visible in the majestic posture, but the impression of old age predominates. A comparison with the 'inauguration' portrait of the emperor at the age of 24 in 1735 (no. 5) shows how the painter successfully manages to record the emperor's decline while not violating the rules of ancestral portraiture. The two compositions are identical, both conforming to the formula of imperial ancestral portraiture: the figure is dressed in formal court attire and seated on the throne in a rigidly frontal and symmetrical pose. The only trace of asymmetry is in the position of the arms.

Here the two portraits start to show seemingly minor differences: whereas the young emperor raises his left hand to hold his necklace, the elderly emperor raises his right arm to do so instead. In a sense the two portraits form a pair of mirror images, although this may not have been intentional on the part of the artist. However, the artist did have to make a conscious decision as to how to position the emperor's head in relation to his shoulders. In most ancestral portraits of the Qing period both old and young are portrayed with their head held high – a sign of good health. In the present portrait, however, the artist places the elderly emperor's chin well below his shoulders, thereby indicating his advancing years. To further accentuate the emperor's decline the artist makes minor alterations to his dress. A telling detail is the way in which the shoulder lappets are rendered. In the portrait of the emperor as a young man the lappets bend outwards and upwards forming a shape almost like upheld wings. In contrast, the elderly emperor's lappets point downwards, conveying a sense of exhaustion.

Although he may never have admitted to his exhaustion – indeed he was still carrying out official duties five days before his death – the Qianlong emperor died a realist. Not long after his abdication ceremony he briefed his emperor son as to how his portrait should be displayed in the imperial family ancestral hall in Beijing after his death. The portrait of his grandfather, the Kangxi emperor, was to be hung in the centre of the hall, with that of his father, the Yongzheng emperor, on the left and his own on the right. In the Qing dynasty there were two imperial ancestral halls – one in Beijing, the other in the Summer Palace in Rehe. It is unclear in which one the present portrait was hung and worshipped.

LIT: Kahn 1971: 249–50; Tang and Luo 1994: 439

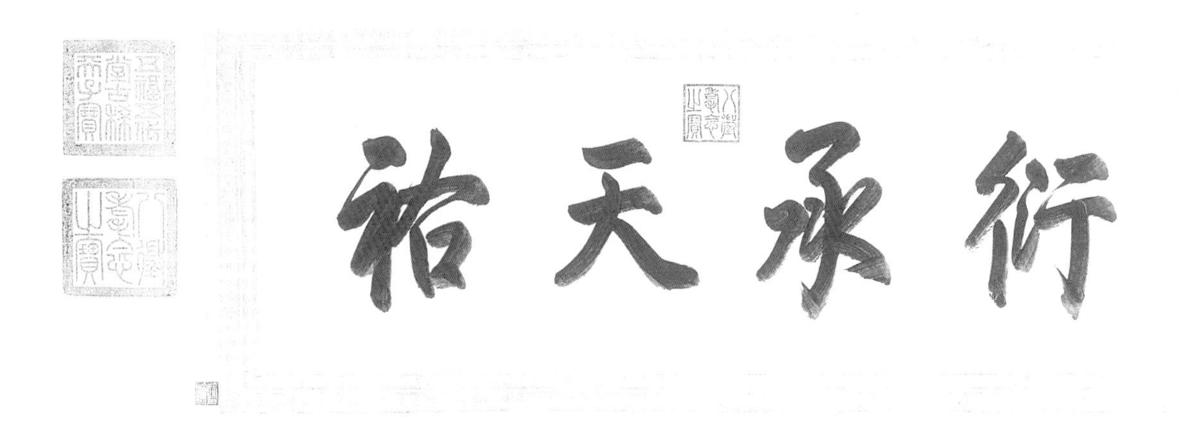

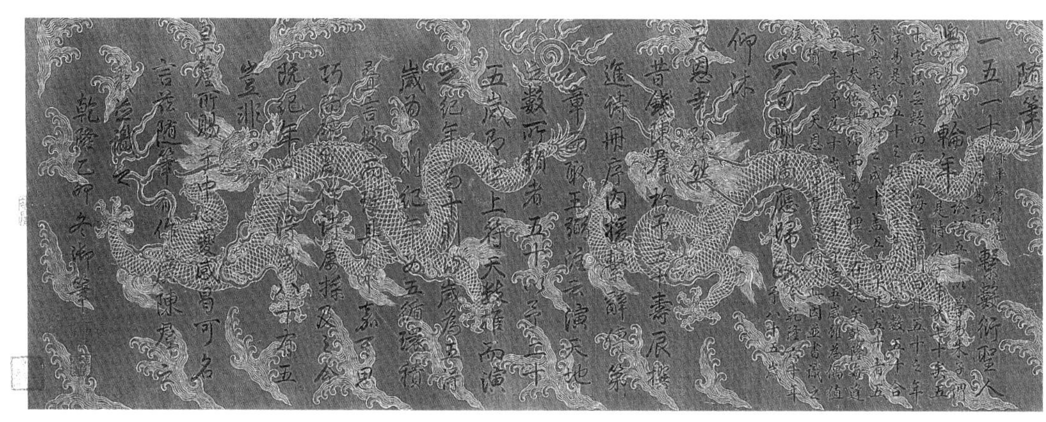

77

Heaven's beneficence

Hongli (the Qianlong emperor)

Dated 1795

Handscroll, ink on decorated paper

L 91 cm, H 35.5 cm

Inscriptions: artist's signature, dated 1795; frontispiece writing by the artist

Seals: six of the artist; one of Puyi

This poem and commentary in regular script were written by the Qianlong emperor in the winter of 1795. The poem on the numerological significance of his reign provides an insight into the emperor's state of mind shortly before his abdication:

> Fifty is the root number on which the generation of the hexagrams is based.
> While sages study the *Book of changes* I calculate my age.
> The sixtieth year of my reign is drawing to a close,
> I am fortunate to be the recipient of heaven's beneficence.

The commentary on the poem runs: 'On my fiftieth birthday Qian Chenqun [no. 71] elaborated on the numerological meaning of my reign. He started with a quotation from Wang Bi's (CE 226–249) commentary on the eighth appendix of the *Book of changes*: "The root number for the changes of heaven and earth is fifty." He then explained that my age at the time of accession, that is 25 [by Chinese reckoning], is a heavenly number. Comparing my age with the number of years of my reign he wrote that whenever the regnal year is a multiple of ten (an even and therefore a *yin* number), my age is a multiple of five (an odd and therefore a *yang* number), and vice versa. This pattern of *yin* and *yang* moves in circles and tallies with the principles of the changes. ... This year counts as the sixtieth of my reign, and my age is eighty-five. Alas! Isn't this computation a gift from heaven!' It is clear from this that the elderly emperor was attempting to apply to his life and reign the concept of time as expounded in the *Book of changes*.

LIT: *YZSWJ* 1795: *juan* 100; Legge 1882: 365

78

New Year wine cup

Datable to 1797
Gold, rubies, sapphires, pearls
H 12.5 cm, D 8 cm, weight 733 g
Inscription: one near the rim

Although this cup was made in 1797, the year after the abdication of the Qianlong emperor, it still bears the inscription 'Made in the Qianlong reign'. The reason for this discrepancy is that although the new calendar of the Jiaqing reign was proclaimed in 1796, within the Forbidden City the Qianlong calendar continued to be used until the former emperor's death.

The handles of the gold cup are modelled in the shape of baby dragons, with a pearl inserted in the mouth of each, and the three feet are in the form of elephant trunks bordered with ivory and gold filigree. The main body of the cup is decorated with *boaxianghua,* lotus flower pattern, inlaid with rubies and sapphires. On the rim are four raised characters which read 'A gold cup lasts for ever'.

The cup was used only once a year, on the first day of the New Year, in a ritual known as the First Brushstroke that was held in the Hall for the Cultivation of the Mind. On this occasion a table would be laid with the gold cup, a white candle and a brush with the name Ten Thousand Years of Green. The emperor would fill the cup with a red wine known as *tusu,* light the candle and write with the special brush in vermilion the words 'Let there be great peace under heaven'.

LIT: Zhang Shiyun 1980; Palace Museum 1994: 855

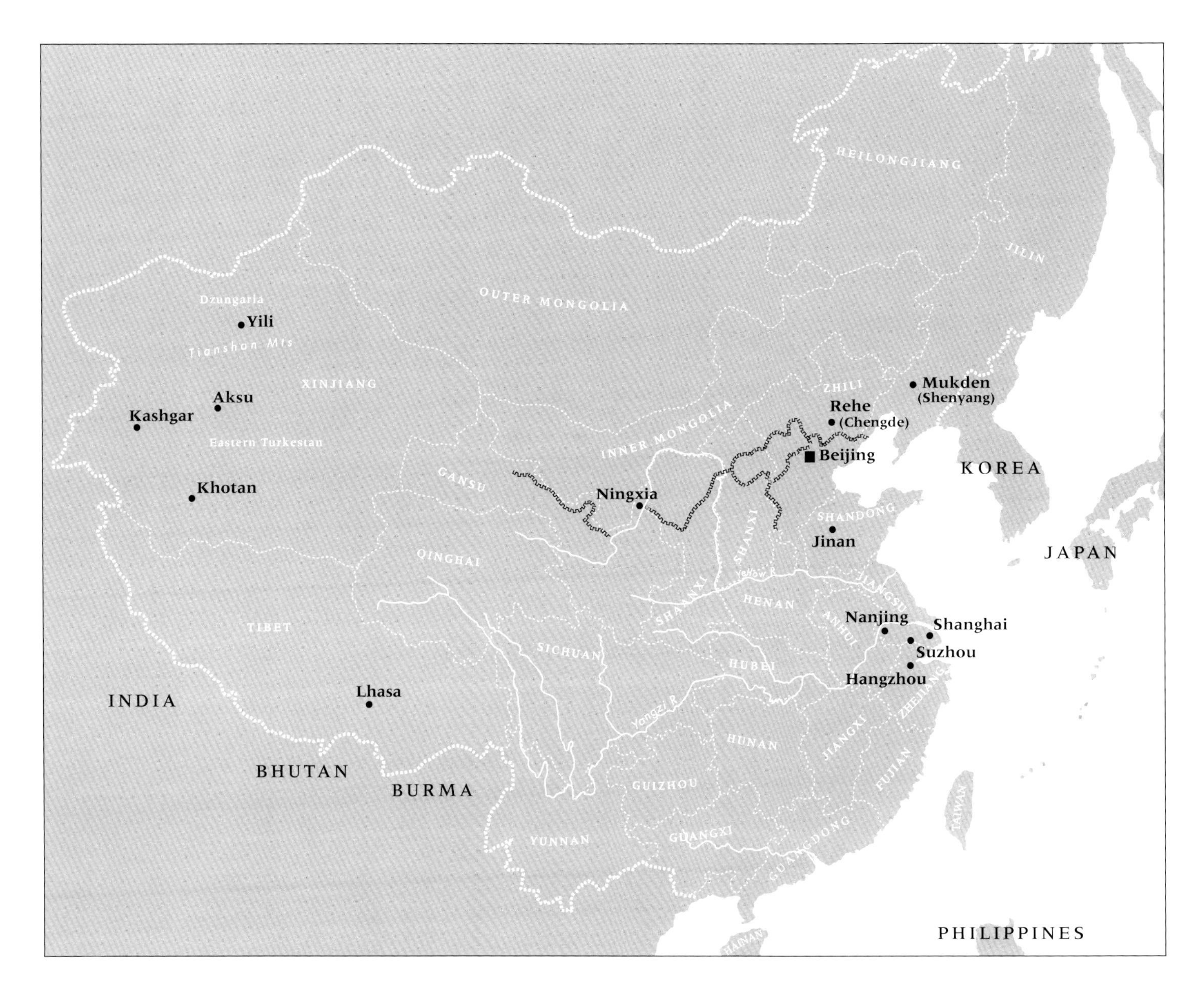
HEILONGJIANG
JILIN
OUTER MONGOLIA
Dzungaria
Yili
Tianshan Mts
XINJIANG
Aksu
Kashgar
Eastern Turkestan
Khotan
GANSU
INNER MONGOLIA
ZHILI
Mukden
(Shenyang)
Rehe
(Chengde)
Beijing
KOREA
Ningxia
SHANXI
SHANDONG
Jinan
JAPAN
QINGHAI
Yellow R.
SHAANXI
HENAN
JIANGSU
ANHUI
Nanjing
Shanghai
Suzhou
Hangzhou
TIBET
SICHUAN
HUBEI
INDIA
Lhasa
Yangzi R.
HUNAN
JIANGXI
ZHEJIANG
FUJIAN
BHUTAN
BURMA
GUIZHOU
YUNNAN
GUANGXI
GUANGDONG
TAIWAN
HAINAN
PHILIPPINES

Map of the Qing Empire, *c.* 1820

Aisin Gioro Rulers

Regnal names and dates are in bold

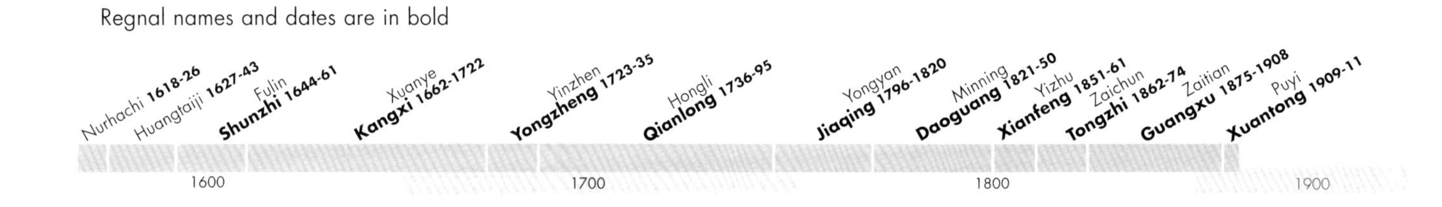
Nurhachi **1618-26**
Huangtaiji **1627-43**
Fulin **Shunzhi 1644-61**
Xuanye **Kangxi 1662-1722**
Yinzhen **Yongzheng 1723-35**
Hongli **Qianlong 1736-95**
Yongyan **Jiaqing 1796-1820**
Minning **Daoguang 1821-50**
Yizhu **Xianfeng 1851-61**
Zaichun **Tongzhi 1862-74**
Zaitian **Guangxu 1875-1908**
Puyi **Xuantong 1909-11**
1600
1700
1800
1900

Chinese Historical Periods and Dynasties

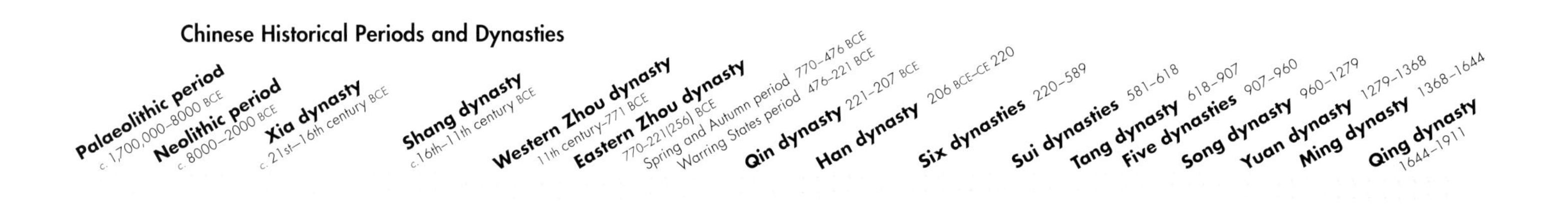
Palaeolithic period c. 1,700,000–8000 BCE
Neolithic period c. 8000–2000 BCE
Xia dynasty c. 21st–16th century BCE
Shang dynasty c.16th–11th century BCE
Western Zhou dynasty 11th century–771 BCE
Eastern Zhou dynasty 770–221(256) BCE
Spring and Autumn period 770–476 BCE
Warring States period 476–221 BCE
Qin dynasty 221–207 BCE
Han dynasty 206 BCE–CE 220
Six dynasties 220–589
Sui dynasties 581–618
Tang dynasty 618–907
Five dynasties 907–960
Song dynasty 960–1279
Yuan dynasty 1279–1368
Ming dynasty 1368–1644
Qing dynasty 1644–1911

ESSAYS

三壽作朋

THE QIANLONG EMPEROR AND HIS REIGN

Zhu Chengru

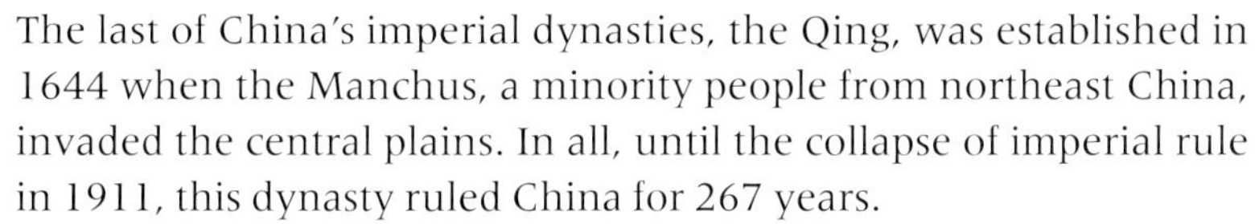

The last of China's imperial dynasties, the Qing, was established in 1644 when the Manchus, a minority people from northeast China, invaded the central plains. In all, until the collapse of imperial rule in 1911, this dynasty ruled China for 267 years.

The Qianlong emperor was the fourth to take the throne after the arrival of the Manchu armies and the establishment of a multi-racial empire, the Great Qing. China had assumed a position of stability during the reigns of the Shunzhi emperor and of the Kangxi and Yongzheng emperors in particular. The country's political and economic situation was showing signs of recovery and growth, and the scars left from the final rebellious years of the Ming had mostly healed. The ethnic conflicts of the early years of the dynasty, especially between the Han and the Manchu, had begun to subside, and government infighting was being resolved. The foundations were in place for the building of a powerful nation.

This so-called Kang-Qian period, encompassing the reigns of the Kangxi, Yongzheng and Qianlong emperors, is generally recognised as China's final golden age. The first two reign periods saw a growth in prosperity that reached its peak in the Qianlong reign, although the final decades of his rule were to witness a steady decline. The Qianlong emperor held power for longer than any other emperor in Chinese history, being on the throne for 60 years, and then holding the reins of power for a further three years as father of the young Jiaqing emperor. Living to the age of 89, he was also the longest living of all Chinese emperors. His expertise in both cultural matters and military skills marks his reign as one of China's most glorious.

The Qianlong emperor was not only a careful strategist but also a man of action. Building on the foundations laid by the Kangxi and Yongzheng emperors, he helped China to become one of the most powerful empires in the world at that time. By the final years of his reign, however, corruption had erupted and the economy had ground to a standstill. Ultimate responsibility for the decline of the once wealthy Qing dynasty rested with the Qianlong emperor himself.

On the morning of the 23rd day of the eighth month of the thirteenth year of the Yongzheng reign (8 October 1735), the Yongzheng emperor died, after 13 years on the throne. In accordance with the emperor's last wishes, his fourth son Hongli inherited the throne. In the same month Hongli made the required sacrifices to his ancestors and to heaven, and the following year, 1736, became the first year of the Qianlong reign period.

After the Qianlong emperor came to power he relaxed many of the harsh administrative policies of his father's government. He began by reopening the cases of the royal princes Yinsi (1681–1726) and Yintang (1683–1726) who had been involved in the struggle for succession in the early years of the Yongzheng reign. He decided to restore their lineage, readmitted them to the imperial clan and gave them

Opposite:
Detail of *Three peaches* (no. 51)

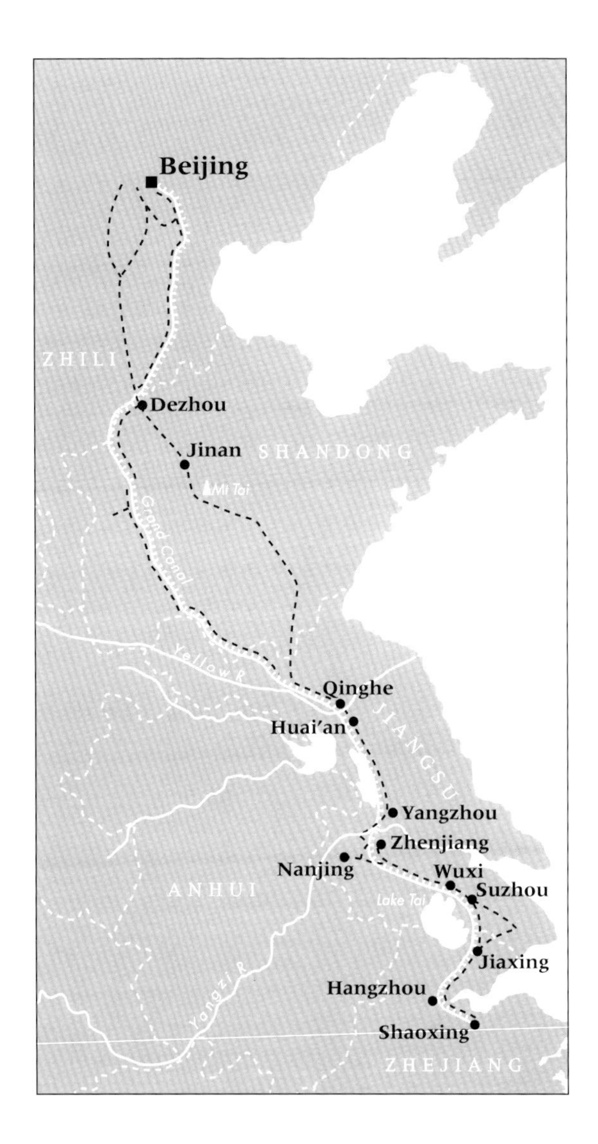

Route of the Qianlong emperor's southern tours

high official posts. He ordered the release of Yin'e (1683–1741) and Yinti (1688–1755) who had been detained for several years, and appointed them as 'bulwark dukes' (the sixth of the twelve ranks of imperial nobility); when Yin'e died he received the funeral rites of a Manchu Bele prince (fourth rank), and Yinti was promoted to commandery prince (second rank) of Xun. At the same time, verdicts on those involved with or affected by other major cases were re-examined and many talented people were re-employed. By regulating the internal affairs of the government the emperor was hoping to create a more stable political situation in general.

The emperor was of the firm belief that 'the people are the cornerstone of the country; there is no better way to rule all under heaven than to love the people. The best means by which to love the people is first to lessen the burdens of taxation and land rent.'[1] He therefore adopted a series of measures such as doing away with corvée labour and reducing both financial and grain taxes in order to relieve people's hardship. In his 63 years of rule he implemented general tax reductions on five occasions, a reduction of 20,000 taels of silver in all. He also established a reward system to encourage agricultural development, implemented various aid programmes in the wake of natural disasters, and released many servants and slaves of the imperial household and related families. All these measures helped to increase productivity, which was one of the contributing factors to the success of the Qianlong era.

Extensive tours throughout China were another means by which the emperor consolidated his rule. In fact he was to conduct more tours during his reign than any other emperor in China's history. Totalling over 150, an average of more than two per year, these included autumn hunting expeditions in the north, visits to the imperial tombs to the east, and tours of inspection to Jiangsu and Zhejiang provinces to the south.

Of these, the six southern tours of inspection, carried out between 1751 and 1784, were the most productive. As the Jiangnan region south of the Yangzi River was an important source of grain and taxes, its prosperity was essential to the stability of the empire. On these southern tours the emperor saw for himself the dam construction projects on the Yellow and Huai rivers and the repair of existing dams in Zhejiang and coastal areas. He met with local officials, intellectuals and members of the landlord classes. He abolished accumulated debts to demonstrate the lavishness of imperial favour and the dynasty's hold over the country, and to buy the affection of the people. Without doubt the southern tours helped to strengthen ties between central and local levels of government, to quell the Jiangnan gentry's dissatisfaction with the Qing rulers, and to stabilise taxation. On the other hand, these six tours consumed vast amounts of human and material resources, an extravagance that only added to the burden of the ordinary people.

Khan Badashan asking to surrender, drawn by Damascene and engraved by Pierre-Philippe Choffard, 1772, H 55.4 cm, W 90.8 cm. From *The Conquests of the Qianlong Emperor*, set of 16 copper engravings, 1769–74, Palace Museum, Beijing.

As well as his concern with the prosperous southern region, the Qianlong emperor was anxious to strengthen his control of the border regions and create a large multiracial empire. In the face of opposition on the frontiers, he resolutely fought to suppress it. This reinforcement of Qing rule over the border regions not only added to the wealth and stability of the empire but it was also a contributing factor to the empire's final delineation of China's current national borders.

On his succession to the throne, the Qianlong emperor's first priority was to resolve the problems in the southwest border region. During the Yongzheng period this region, and in particular the area inhabited by the Miao tribes, had been continually at war. The emperor attempted to reform tribal organisations in the area and deployed troops to suppress any uprisings. After almost a year, in 1736, the rebels were finally pacified, prompting the emperor to implement a series of economic policies to promote the development of the area.

Almost 20 years later, in 1755, the emperor sent troops to the far northwest (present-day Xinjiang province) to campaign against the Dzungars in the northern part of Tianshan. The Dzungar tribal leaders had long established anti-imperial strongholds. It was only after 67 years of resistance, years that spanned the reigns of the Kangxi, Yongzheng and Qianlong emperors, that the region was subjugated to the Qing court. Following this, the Hodja brothers, leaders of the Muslims in the southern part of Tianshan, rallied against the Qing. In 1758 the Qing court once again deployed troops and defeated their rivals, thus rounding off their control of the whole northwest border region.

Another priority of the Qing was to strengthen its ties with Tibet. In 1747 Sonam Stobgyal, the minister who presided over Tibetan governmental affairs, died. Power was assumed by his second son Jurmet Namjar who refused to comply with the Qing imperial representative in Tibet, and plotted with the Dzungar tribe to instigate unrest. In his capacity as sovereign leader of Tibet, the Qianlong emperor ordered the abolition of the Tibetan monarchy in 1750. He replaced it with a Tibetan office with the right to give orders. Power and the affairs of government were in the hands of four people: three laymen and one monk, who were subordinate to the Dalai Lama and the imperial representative. The status of the Qing imperial representative was raised and his powers increased. In 1793 the Qing court issued the Regulations for Tibetan Domestic Reconstruction, which stipulated that the imperial representative was to be in charge of internal Tibetan affairs, and was to be of equal status to the Dalai Lama and the Panchen Lama. Officials in the newly appointed Tibetan office were all under the authority of the imperial representative, and had to act in accordance with his commands.

The Qing court also created a new lottery system for selecting the child heir to the Dalai Lama, a process known as 'drawing lots from the golden urn'. Both the Dalai Lama's and the Panchen Lama's reincarnations had to be selected in the presence of the imperial representative. Moreover, all Tibetan local officials and all ranks of military official stationed in Tibet were to be chosen by the representative with the aid of the Dalai Lama. The representative also had power of jurisdiction over foreign and religious affairs, and legislative cases, as well as control of Tibet's finances. Taxes and revenue collected in the Tibetan region belonged to Tibet, whereas the expenses of the imperial representative, the imperial troops and the salaries of all the major local Tibetan officials were paid by the Qing court. These regulations all helped to consolidate Qing suzerainty in Tibet.

Further dealings with the Tibetans took place in the northwest, in present-day Sichuan province, in the Jinchuan area, so called because of the local gold mines (*jin* is the Chinese for gold). This region was inhabited by Tibetans. In 1666, during the reign of the Kangzi emperor, the local tribal chieftain Jialeba had pledged allegiance to the Qing court. Proclaiming him a convert, the Qing court permitted him to continue governing the local Tibetans. Jialeba's grandson Solobun, who had supplied local troops to assist the Qing general Yue Zhongqi (1686–1754) during his deployment in Tibet, was given charge of the Minority Pacification Commission of the Jinchuan region in 1723. From 1746 Solobun and his nephew Langka sought ever greater power, and unrest ensued. The Qing court twice deployed troops to Jinchuan, over a period of five years, with several changes of command. In total the court recruited several tens of thousands of soldiers from all over China, and spent 70 million taels of silver,

Round tower in Putuozongcheng Temple or Lesser Potala in Rehe. The map shows the location of Rehe.

before finally subduing the rebellion in 1776. To prevent further uprisings by tribal chiefs, the Qianlong emperor abolished the system of tribal chiefdoms, replacing them with administrative divisions of sub-prefectures, departments and districts.

Alongside its forcible suppression of uprisings in the northwest, the Qing court adopted policies of appeasement towards those tribes eager to submit to the Qing. One such tribe was the Turguts, one of the four Eleuths, the Western Mongols. Originally a nomadic tribe from the Tarbagatai region, they left their homeland and migrated to the lower Volga River valley when under pressure from the rising Dzungar tribe in the early years of the Chongzhen emperor (1628–44) of the Ming dynasty. A century and a half later, the majority of the Turguts, along with some of the Derbets, Khoits and Khoshotes who later had also moved to the Volga River region, almost 170,000 people in all, embarked on the long journey home to their motherland. In midwinter they travelled on foot over snow and ice, in the severest of temperatures, broke through the Russian blockades and re-entered China. The journey took over seven months, and totalled almost 5000 km. By the time they reached China, only 70,000 migrants were left.

As soon as news of the Turguts' return to China reached the Qing court, it became a matter of extreme importance. As the Turguts approached the border, two commanders of the Qing army, Yichanga and Suotong, went out to greet the tribal leader Ubasi (d. 1774) and his subordinates on the banks of the Yili River. The Grand Minister Consultant Shuhede (1711–77) read the Qianlong emperor's decree, namely that 'it is right and proper that you should be henceforth

Section of one of the four scrolls making up the catalogue of *The Four Treasuries* (no. 22)

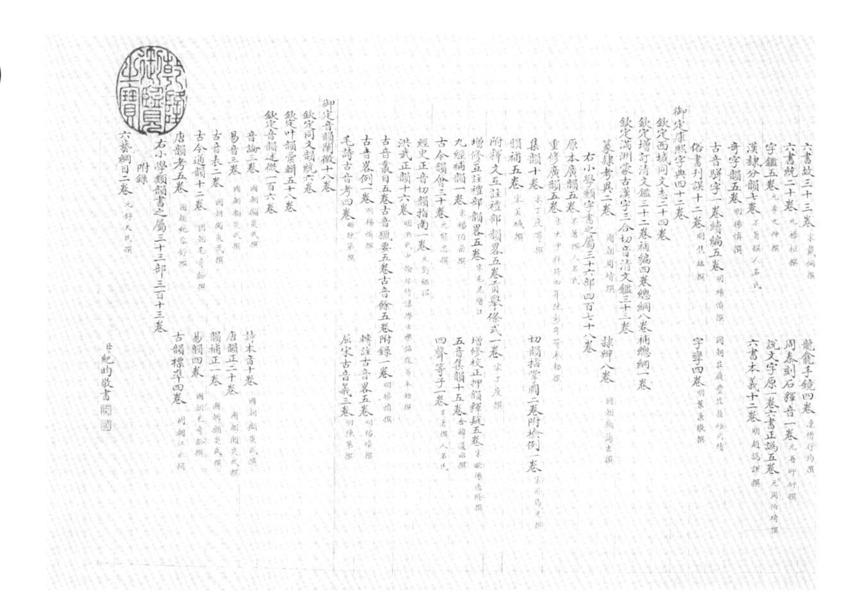

accepted into the land and should receive appropriate settlements'. The court immediately provided aid for the Turguts from Xinjiang, Gansu, Shaanxi, Ningxia and Inner Mongolia and made arrangements for their resettlement. When the court learned that Ubasi had set off from Yili to Rehe to pay tribute, local officials along the route were instructed to offer him lavish hospitality. On 15 October 1771 Ubasi arrived at the Mulan hunting grounds for an audience with the Qianlong emperor, presenting him with bejewelled swords, bows and arrows, clocks and watches. The following day the emperor held a huge banquet to entertain Ubasi and his entourage. On the seventeenth day of the ninth month, in the Summer Palace in Rehe, the Qianlong emperor conferred on him and his men ranks of nobility and presented them with gifts. Afterwards he held a private meeting with Ubasi to enquire about his experiences on the journey to China. To commemorate this, the emperor wrote two essays entitled 'Record of the Turguts' return' and 'Record of the generous appeasement of the Turguts' and had them inscribed in four languages, Manchu, Chinese, Mongolian and Tibetan, on two large stone tablets. These were erected in the Putuozongcheng Temple in Rehe.

During the reign of the Qianlong emperor imperial expansion was matched by cultural enterprise, funded by a healthy and growing economy. Scholars were assigned the tasks of collating, editing and cataloguing classical texts, on a monumental scale. According to the incomplete statistics available, the Qianlong emperor presided over the editing and compilation of 110 works, comprising a total of 7000 *juan*. If we add to this the massive compilations of ancient texts such as *The Four Treasuries* (see no. 22) and *The Essentials of the Four Treasuries*, the total number of *juan* would be in the vicinity of 100,000. Of these, the most influential is *The Four Treasuries*, an enterprise which, it could be argued, consumed the energies of the entire empire at the time, and involved the compilation of every major classical work published to date. The total number of volumes in *The Four Treasuries* is 3461, made up of 79,309 *juan*. This was an outstanding achievement in the history of Chinese librarianship.

As a Manchu, the Qianlong emperor was particularly sensitive to any disrespectful references to the Manchu in *The Four Treasuries.* To expunge any racial bias he implemented strict censorship of the written word and imposed restrictions on cultural activities, to a degree as yet unprecedented in the dynasty. A single word out of turn could be incriminating, which led to petty criticism and groundless inferences being made from texts. At least 80 such cases of criticism were recorded in the Qianlong reign, although, of these, very few were the result of intentional opposition to the Qing. The vast majority concerned writers breaking the taboos, or, in some cases, writers being accused of making intentionally slanderous remarks or having their words twisted to make them appear so. Sometimes even attempts to flatter were considered incriminating due to an author's unfortunate choice of words. The literary censorship that was exercised throughout the reigns of the Kangxi, Yongzheng and Qianlong emperors was targeted not only at scholars, but also upwards to government officials and downwards to the commoners. Within this strict net of control, every educated person felt threatened, daring neither to express an opinion on the government nor to concern himself with the conduct of state affairs.

When the Qianlong emperor first came to power at the age of 24, he would offer prayers to heaven to the effect: 'If you are gracious enough to protect me, and to bestow upon me a 60-year reign, then I will pass on the throne to my son. I would never presume to exceed the length of my grandfather's reign.'[2] For his reign to have lasted longer than the 60 years of that of his grandfather the Kangxi emperor, he knew he would have to live to the great age of 85, a feat which, in the light of contemporary living conditions and the state of medical science, he must have considered impossible. However, he did just this. He therefore had no choice but to fulfil his promise and to pass on his throne to one of his sons, Yongyan, who became the Jiaqing emperor.

On 9 February 1796, the first day of the first month of the Chinese year, the Qianlong emperor held a formal abdication ceremony. The 86-year-old emperor became the father of the new Jiaqing emperor, the first of the Qing emperors to assume the throne as the result of an abdication. However, the elderly emperor was not about to relinquish his power, and so just as the formal inauguration of the new emperor was taking place he proclaimed: 'After this transferral of power, how could I possibly take no interest in military or state affairs, government policy or in the choice of personnel? I will still be a personal adviser to my son.'[3] During the three months between his abdication of power and the inauguration ceremony, the Qianlong emperor instructed his son on the ways of government. So, although power had been nominally transferred to the new emperor, it was still very much in the hands of the retired emperor. His position as 'father of the emperor' was different from that of fathers previously in this situation: he was in both name and actuality the 'father of the emperor', a status higher than that of his son. After the lavish inauguration of his son, the Qianlong emperor began his period of 'political tutelage'. This he treated little differently from the actual exercise of power, except that he now had a young emperor at his side, following his every move.

From the very day he ascended the throne, the Jiaqing emperor was aware of the extremely awkward and intolerable position he was in. Emperor in name alone, he was unable to wield the power expected of him, and for three years he was little more than a puppet emperor. As if his having to cope with his father's unwillingness to relinquish power was not enough, the young Jiaqing emperor also had to contend with an arrogant and irrepressible 'second emperor', Heshen (1750–99), a palace guard who had been manipulating imperial rule for almost 15 years, and who did not give the young emperor a second glance. In order to maintain his status as emperor, Jiaqing had to bide his time, and his tongue: 'In his daily life and in his dealings at court, he remained silent and composed, showing neither pleasure nor anger.' Towards his father he was always deferential and submissive, 'every day serving the sacred imperial father, respectfully listening to his words of instruction ... his appearance was peaceful and expressionless whatever he was doing, be it attending a banquet or watching a play. He sat and served his father: when his father was happy, he was happy, and when his father laughed, he laughed.'[4] In his dealings with Heshen he was prudent also, refusing to allow Heshen to gain any hold over him. In order to put Heshen off his guard, the young emperor would use Heshen to pass on any messages to his father concerning matters that they needed to discuss. Moreover, he asked as few questions as possible about governmental matters: 'Ever since he came to the throne in 1796, he has shown no interest in administration. Whenever Heshen asks for his opinion on a governmental matter, he always says without a second thought, "The imperial father alone can deal with it, how dare I interfere?"'[5] By concealing his abilities the young emperor achieved the desired results. He was praised by his father for his obedience: 'Ever since the emperor came to power, day and night he respectfully understands my wishes, and is agreeably filial.' The Jiaqing emperor's caution and flattery in his dealings with Heshen eventually paid off and Heshen and his corrupt clique were eventually put down.

On the third day of the first month of the fourth year of the Jiaqing reign, 7 February 1799, the Qianlong emperor, having ruled China for a period of 63 years, passed away in the Hall for the Cultivation of the Mind, at the age of 89. The Jiaqing emperor was finally able to grasp the reins of power. However, from the middle of the Qianlong period, the once strong Qing dynasty had begun to show signs of decline: land was owned by an ever decreasing number of people, the economy was weakening by the day, the treasury was empty, the civil service was rife with corruption and the armouries were in a state of neglect. Conflicts erupted and the empire descended into chaos. China's former golden age had tarnished and the Jiaqing emperor inherited a dynasty on the brink of collapse.

Translation: Frances Weightman

Notes

1 *QSL-GZ: juan* 4
2 *Idem: juan* 1486
3 *Ibid.*
4 *CXSL* 1980: vol. 12
5 *QSL-GZ: juan* 1496

THE FORBIDDEN CITY DURING THE QIANLONG REIGN

乾象

Liu Lu

The imperial palace of the Ming and Qing dynasties, known as the Forbidden City, was designed by the Yongle emperor (1403–24) of the Ming. Various principles are followed in the design, such as the stipulation that 'court affairs should be to the front, sleeping quarters to the rear' as outlined in the *Book of rites* (*Li ji*). The layout also adheres to the theories of *yin* and *yang* and the five phases. The emperor and his ministers therefore conducted the affairs of government to the fore of the city, while the imperial family lived their daily lives to the rear. There were also theoretical reasons for the division of the living quarters. The emperor and his children lived on the east side, east being governed by the element wood, implying the vitality of spring; and the empress and the imperial concubines lived on the west side, west being governed by the element metal and associated with the bounty of autumn.

The present-day layout of the numerous palaces of the Forbidden City is considerably different from the original design of the Ming emperors. Some of the most significant changes were made by the Qianlong emperor. For example, in the northwest corner lies the Palace of Double Glory, which was built for the Qianlong emperor to live in as a young prince. At that time it was called the Abode of the Hiding Dragon, suggesting that it harboured the heir apparent, or future dragon, whose role in life had not yet been revealed. This palace complex incorporated a ceremonial hall to the front and a palace to the rear, as well as the Studio of Delicate Fragrance, a theatre, and the garden of the Palace for the Establishment of Happiness. In the eastern section of the city is the Palace of Peaceful Longevity which was built for the emperor in his retirement. This complex incorporates offices, sleeping quarters, studies, a garden, and buildings for making sacrifices to the gods and performing Buddhist rituals.

The Qianlong emperor spared no expense in his extensive programme of rebuilding and refurbishment within the Forbidden City. In many ways his building projects can be seen as reflecting aspects of the time, such as political infighting at court and the attempt to create a fusion of Manchu and Han Chinese cultures. These aspects are exemplified by three of the Qianlong emperor's main buildings: the Palace of Double Glory, the Hall for the Cultivation of the Mind and the Palace of Peaceful Longevity.

The first of these, the Palace of Double Glory, was created for reasons which reflect the political struggles at court at the time. According to Ming regulations the heir apparent's palace had to be situated on the eastern side of the Forbidden City. At the beginning of the Qing dynasty there was indeed a palace for the heir apparent on the eastern side, known as the Palace of Blessing, which had been built for Prince Yinreng (1674-1725), heir apparent at the start of the reign of the Kangxi emperor.[1] For a few years after the Yongzheng emperor ascended the throne this palace was occupied by Hongli, the young Qianlong emperor,

Opposite:
Detail of *The Qianlong emperor on his first inspection tour of the south* (no. 26)

Main hall of the Hall of Delight in Doing Good

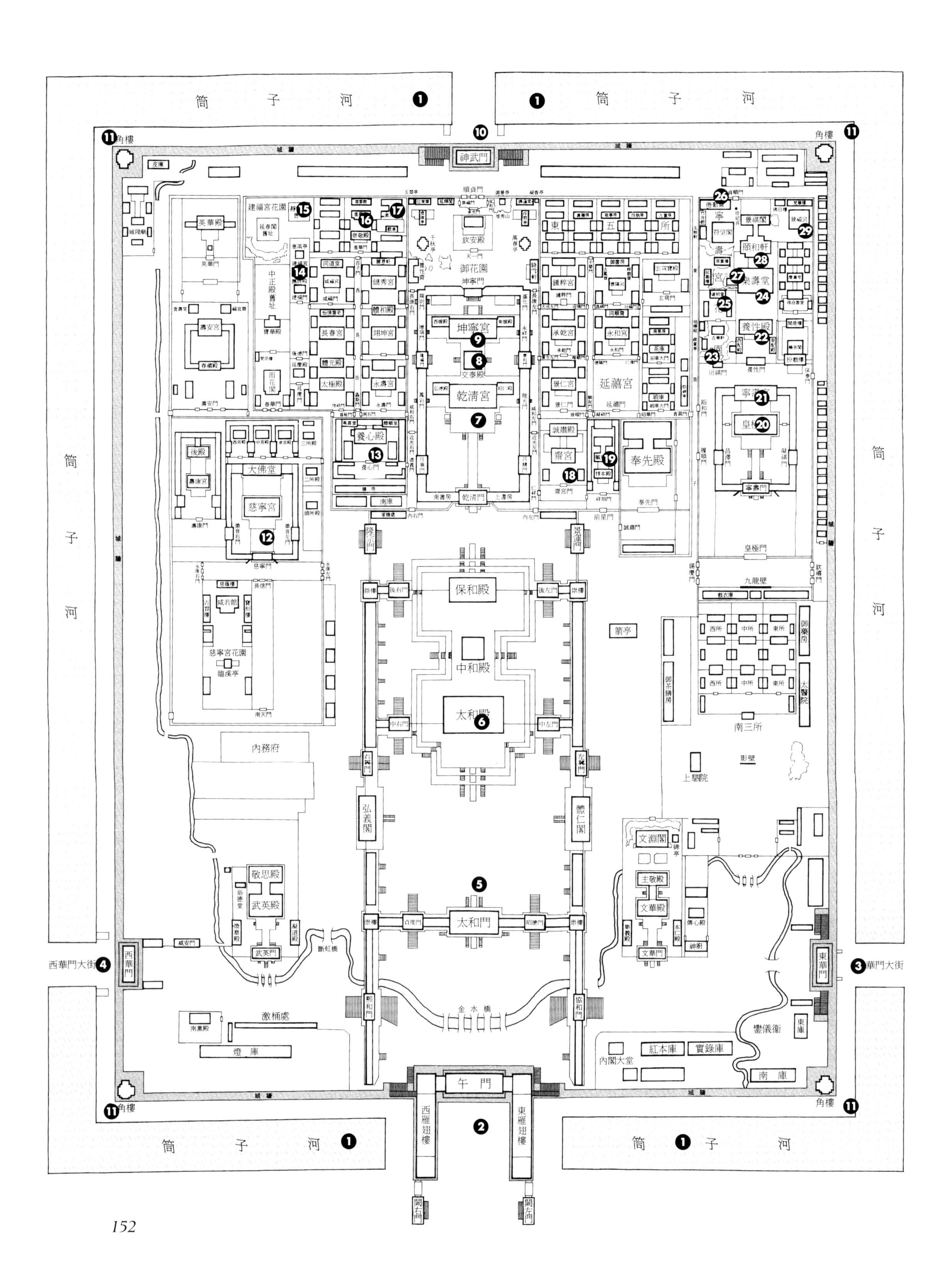

筒子河
角樓
城牆
神武門
順貞門
欽安殿
御花園
坤寧門
坤寧宮
交泰殿
乾清宮
乾清門
南書房
上書房
養心殿
英華殿
英華門
壽安宮
城隍廟
皮庫
建福宮花園
延春閣舊址
中正殿舊址
寶華殿
雨花閣
長春宮
體元殿
太極殿
儲秀宮
體和殿
翊坤宮
永壽宮
東五所
鍾粹宮
承乾宮
景仁宮
永和宮
延禧宮
奉先殿
誠肅殿
齋宮
景祺閣
符望閣
頤和軒
樂壽堂
養性殿
寧壽宮
皇極殿
寧壽門
皇極門
九龍壁
大佛堂
慈寧宮
慈寧門
咸若館
慈寧宮花園
臨溪亭
隆宗門
景運門
保和殿
中和殿
太和殿
箭亭
西所
中所
東所
南三所
御藥房
太醫院
御茶膳房
上駟院
影壁
內務府
弘義閣
體仁閣
敬思殿
武英殿
武英門
斷虹橋
太和門
文淵閣
主敬殿
文華殿
文華門
傳心殿
西華門
西華門大街
東華門
華門大街
金水橋
激桶處
南薰殿
燈庫
鑾儀衛
東庫
內閣大堂
紅本庫
實錄庫
南庫
午門
西雁翅樓
東雁翅樓

Plan of the Forbidden City

1 Moat
2 Meridian Gate
3 East Flowery Gate
4 West Flowery Gate
5 Gate of Supreme Harmony
6 Hall of Supreme Harmony
7 Palace of Heavenly Purity
8 Hall of Union
9 Palace of Earthly Peace
10 Gate of Divine Martial Spirit
11 Watchtower
12 Palace of Compassion and Peace
13 Hall for the Cultivation of the Mind
14 Palace for the Establishment of Happiness
15 Veranda of Serene Tranquillity
16 Palace of Double Glory
17 Studio of Delicate Fragrance
18 Hall of Abstinence
19 Palace of Blessing
20 Hall of Imperial Supremacy
21 Palace of Peaceful Longevity
22 Hall for the Cultivation of the Spirit
23 Orchid Pavilion
24 Hall for Enjoying Longevity
25 Hall for the Fulfilment of Promises
26 Lodge for Retiring from Hard Work
27 Veranda for Three Friends
28 Veranda for Nourishing Harmony
29 Palace of Great Happiness

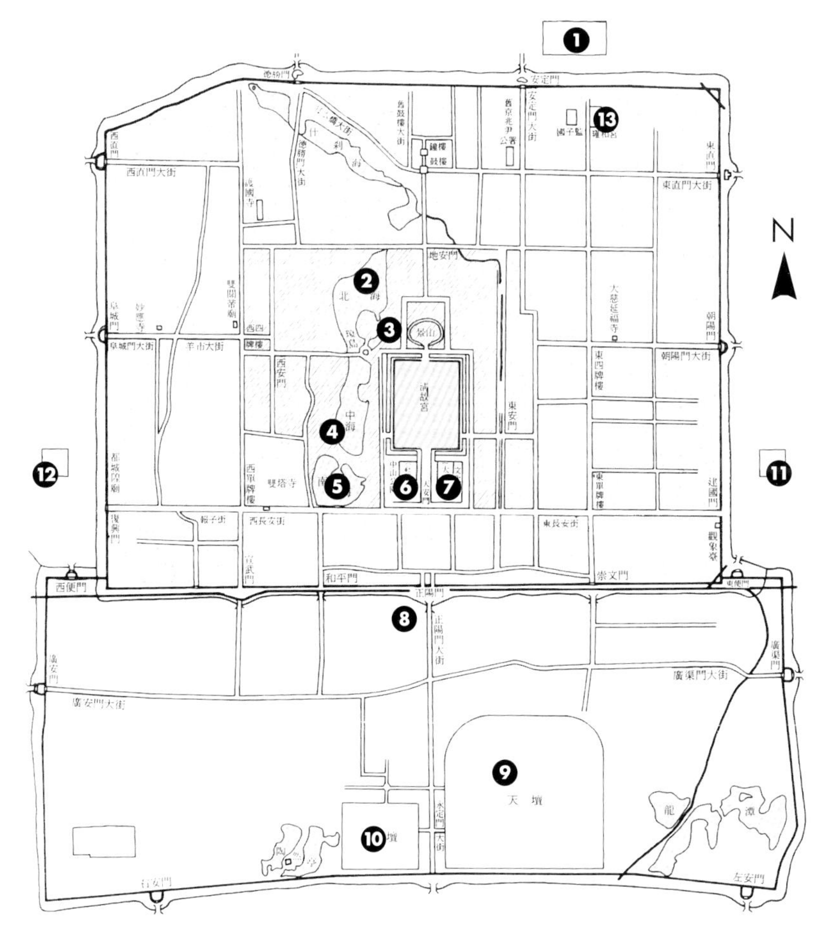

Plan of the City of Beijing

Chinese City
Manchu City
Imperial City
Forbidden City

1 Altar of Earth
2 North Sea
3 Prospect or Coal Hill
4 Middle Sea
5 South Sea
6 Altar of Land and Grain
7 Great Imperial Ancestral Temple
8 Gate of Positive Yang
9 Altar of Heaven
10 Altar of Agriculture
11 Altar of the Sun
12 Altar of the Moon
13 Palace of Complete Harmony

and his brothers.[2] But Hongli was soon to move into the Palace of Double Glory, for reasons related to the question of succession.

The choice of successor to the throne had seldom been easy. Towards the end of the reign of the Kangxi emperor there had been such a bitter struggle for succession that, as soon as the Yongzheng emperor came to the throne, he decided it was necessary that the choice of heir apparent should remain a closely held secret. Hongli, the future Qianlong emperor, was his secret choice. According to Hongli's own account he was selected as heir apparent because, at the age of twelve, he had won the heart of his grandfather, the Kangxi emperor. Although there may be some truth in this story, the iron-fisted Yongzheng emperor was not one to obey his father's wishes wholeheartedly. Hongli must have met his father's requirements.

The political climate at the start of the reign of the Yongzheng emperor was tense. The opponents with whom the Yongzheng emperor had been disputing the succession were still causing trouble both openly and behind his back, and in order to consolidate his power the emperor demoted and imprisoned some of them and had others put to death. Even one of his own sons was not spared: in 1727 Hongshi, the 23-three-year-old elder brother of Hongli, was put to death on account of being 'overindulged and prone to unsuitable behaviour'.[3] Whether or not this was the real reason, it serves at least to demonstrate that the Yongzheng emperor would not tolerate misbehaviour in a son.

Hongli was different. Although capable of voicing his own political opinions, he understood the need to comply with the Confucian ethic of fitting in to one's social environment. He even applied this philosophy to the naming of his study in the Palace of Double Glory: 'In my princedom I choose the name Sui'an for my study to convey the idea of *suiyu eran*, the ability to adapt oneself to different circumstances.'[4] Of another room he said: 'I used to stay in the Palace of Double Glory. When I set up my study in the western side of the building, I called it the Studio of Restraint.'[5] The names suggest that the prince felt somewhat unsettled at the time. The Yongzheng emperor, not wishing Hongli to be too gentle, 'repeatedly warned him against being soft'.[6] However, it was no doubt precisely because Hongli was capable of holding his tongue that he was chosen as heir apparent.

The Yongzheng emperor seemed intent on keeping a careful watch over the young Hongli. In 1723 he moved his centre of government to the Hall for the Cultivation of the Mind. Four years later, in 1727, the year in which Hongshi was put to death, Yongzheng granted the newly married Hongli a private residence, the Abode of the Hiding Dragon, thereby indicating a promising future for his son. The reason for siting the residence close to the Hall for the Cultivation of the Mind may have been so that the emperor and his ministers could keep an eye on the activities of the heir apparent.

Gate of the Hall for the Cultivation of the Mind, viewed from the south

At the start of the Qing dynasty, when a new emperor came to the throne, the mansion in which he had been brought up was not automatically upgraded to the status of a palace. While still just a prince, the future Kangxi emperor had been sent to live beyond the West Flowery Gate to avoid catching smallpox, but when he became emperor his previous residence was not upgraded. However, when the Yongzheng emperor ascended the throne he upgraded his previous residence outside the Forbidden City to the Palace of Complete Harmony, with the intention of demonstrating his hold on imperial power.[7] Thirteen years later, when Hongli became the Qianlong emperor, Grand Secretaries Oertai (1680–1745) and Zhang Tingyu (1672–1755), both of whom had been favoured ministers of the Yongzheng emperor, immediately proposed that Hongli's princely residence be upgraded to a palace. In their choice of name for the palace, the ministers compared the young Qianlong emperor with the legendary sage ruler Shun who is said to have redoubled the glory of the reign of his predecessor Yao. With this story in mind they renamed the Abode of the Hiding Dragon the Palace of Double Glory. Although Hongli is said to have insisted that his ministers' comparison of him with Shun was mere flattery, he accepted the proposal on the grounds that 'that is what the rules say'.[8]

Upgrading a mansion to a palace did not just involve a change of name. It also entailed the start of a major building project. To begin with the reason for the name of the Palace of Double Glory was not divulged. Only seven years later, when the Palace for the Establishment of Happiness and the Western Garden were constructed to its west, was the meaning clarified. In his rhapsody 'On the Palace for the

Establishment of Happiness' the Qianlong emperor wrote: 'Places like the Study for the Respect of Excellence in the Palace for the Establishment of Happiness are built as places for the pursuit of leisure. Being located to the right [when facing south]of the Palace of Double Glory suggests comparisons with the Palace of Splendour.'[9] As the Palace of Splendour had been the heir apparent's palace during the Yuan dynasty (1279–1368), Hongli's reference to it made it very clear that from then on the Palace of Double Glory was to be the new palace for the crown prince in the Forbidden City.

The second major building to undergo change at the hands of the Qianlong emperor was the Hall for the Cultivation of the Mind. From the early years of the reign of the Yongzheng emperor this hall, located among the six western palaces of the Forbidden City, was the one used for the affairs of government. During the Ming dynasty political affairs had been discussed in the Hall of Supreme Harmony and in the Gate of Supreme Harmony (known in the Ming dynasty as the Hall for Serving Heaven and the Hall of Imperial Supremacy respectively). At the beginning of the reign of the Kangxi emperor the political centre was moved to the Palace of Heavenly Purity which had been used by the Ming emperors as sleeping quarters. That one palace should serve both for the discussion of political matters and as sleeping quarters was a reflection of the traditional Manchu way of life whereby the lifestyles of ordinary people and court officials differed little, and working and sleeping quarters were not separated.[10] To perpetuate such a tradition suited the more traditional members of the family such as the Kangxi emperor's elderly mother. Moreover, at a time when court finances were tight and much of the Forbidden City was somewhat run down, it made sense to combine office and home under the one roof.

But the Palace of Heavenly Purity was not to remain the seat of government. When the Yongzheng emperor came to power he had no desire to use his father's palace because of his indignant words: 'When the time of my own death comes, you will start your bloodthirsty fights while my body is still lying in the Palace of Heavenly Purity'.[11] The Kangxi emperor was referring to the bitter power struggle for succession that was being played out amongst his sons. The Yongzheng emperor therefore moved to the Hall for the Cultivation of the Mind.

The moving of the seat of government to the Hall for the Cultivation of the Mind can be seen as a transfer of the heart of government further towards the inner court. This again was a statement of adherence to Manchu traditions. The Yongzheng emperor would later build a Hall of Abstinence for offering sacrifices to heaven (these were previously made in the southern outskirts of the city) within the six palaces of the eastern section of the Forbidden City. He also built the palace school within the Palace of Complete Peace in the western

Hall of the Three Rarities in the Hall for the Cultivation of the Mind

section of the six palaces for educating children of the eight banner armies. Neither building was in accordance with Ming dynasty practice.[12] However, as Manchu traditions held that both the right hand and the western side be held in high esteem, there was every reason why the seat of government should be moved to the western side of the Forbidden City.[13]

In his redesign of the Hall for the Cultivation of the Mind, the Yongzheng emperor combined Han and Manchu traditions by creating an audience hall with a Han-style central bay and a Manchu-style bay to west. The style of some of the furnishings in the central partitioned room of the west bay, such as the *kang* or heated bed and the table on it, can be traced back to similar examples in the palace in Shenyang (Mukden), the former Manchu capital beyond the Great Wall.

In 1735, the year in which his father died, Hongli moved into the Hall for the Cultivation of the Mind where he was to live for the following 63 years. Many changes took place in those years, the most noteworthy of which being the establishment of the Hall of the Three Rarities. Although its furnishings display elements of Manchu style, the very contents and purpose of the room point to the Qianlong emperor's passion for Confucian culture. This room displays three rare calligraphic treasures: Wang Xizhi's *Clearing after snow*, Wang Xianzhi's *Mid-autumn letter* and Wang Xun's *Letter to Bo Yuan*, which the emperor could admire at his leisure (no. 43).

The pursuit of culture was essential to the Qianlong emperor. By the time he came to the throne in 1736, almost a century had passed since the Manchus first entered China. Already the sons of the eight banner armies 'read Han books, were immersed in Han customs and were gradually forgetting old Manchu customs'.[14] It was in such an atmosphere that Hongli, together with his younger brother Hongzhou (1712–70), 'studied ancient poetry and prose, eating and sleeping by the great historical texts, [his] mind not in the least bit bothered by affairs of commonplace'.[15]

By the age of six Hongli could recite the essay 'Affection for the lotus flower' by the Song neo-Confucian scholar Zhou Dunyi (1017–73), and by the age of 13 he knew by heart the *Book of odes (Shijing)*, the *Book of documents (Shujing)* and the works of the four great philosophers.[16] Such a model education ensured that Hongli, despite his Manchu origins, was completely versed in Confucian ideology. After moving in to his Abode of the Hiding Dragon he chose the name Hall of Delight in Doing Good for his principal study, alluding to the legendary sage ruler Shun.[17]

On his succession to the throne the Qianlong emperor was to say of himself: 'I learned to read when I was very young. Books have been with me ever since, so in my heart of hearts I am a scholar.'[18] The Confucian notion of combining the virtues of private scholar with those of public ruler became his lifelong goal. In his 'Record of the Hall of the Three Rarities' he makes clear this twofold aim: he so treasured his three rare works of calligraphy that 'even a sword from Fengcheng and pearls from Hepu could not match them'. But the real reason why he coveted them was that they symbolised the three aspirations of a scholar and ruler.[19] Throughout his life the emperor spent many an hour in his cramped study appreciating his three calligraphic treasures to remind himself of these aspirations. So although his palace may have displayed Manchu elements in its design and decoration, its very heart, the Hall of the Three Rarities, paid homage not only to Han Chinese culture but also to the emperor's Confucian upbringing and aspirations.

If the Palace of Double Glory represents the solution to political infighting, and the Hall for the Cultivation of the Mind reflects the fusion of Manchu and Han traditions, the Palace of Peaceful Longevity can be seen as a microcosm of the Qianlong emperor's journey through life. Of all the construction work carried out in the Forbidden City during the Qianlong period, none was a match, in terms of either scale or exuberance, for the complex of the Palace of Peaceful Longevity built in 1771. This complex, which occupies approximately one sixth of the total area of the Forbidden City and incorporates the Hall of Imperial Supremacy and the Palace of Peaceful Longevity itself, is situated in the northeastern corner and is almost a miniature city within a city. It incorporates the Hall of Imperial Supremacy and the Palace of Peaceful Longevity itself. The emperor repeatedly stressed that the complex was for his retirement[20] which is reflected in some of the names within it, such as the Veranda for Nourishing Harmony,

Hall of Imperial Supremacy in the Palace of Peaceful Longevity, viewed from the south

the Hall for the Fulfilment of Promises, the Room for the Pursuit of Leisure and the Lodge for Retiring from Hard Work.

Some scholars believe that the siting of the palace in the eastern part of the Forbidden City is connected with the Qianlong emperor's quest for immortality.[21] However, the reason may have been a purely practical one: when the emperor began to plan a palace for his retirement, his mother, who had just celebrated her eightieth birthday, was living in the Palace of Compassion and Peace in the west of the Forbidden City. The fact that he could not demolish her palace to make space for his own may have forced him to build on the eastern side.

Despite all the effort and expense that went into the building of the Palace of Peaceful Longevity, the Qianlong emperor never really lived there. Even after his abdication in 1795 he continued to live in the Hall for the Cultivation of the Mind until his death, although he regularly conducted activities in his newly built palace complex. In many ways the palace complex can be seen as a microcosm of the Qianlong emperor's life from prince to emperor and then to emperor in retirement.

Harking back to his early years in the Palace of Double Glory where he had spent so much time studying, the emperor reused the names of his early studies, the Sui'an Room and the Eternal Spring Study. Moreover, he incorporated within the Palace of Peaceful Longevity copies of many of the towers and pavilions of the Palace for the Establishment of Happiness where he had lived when he was young.[22]

Some buildings within the complex of the Palace of Peaceful Longevity were built as copies of existing buildings and later given new names: for example, the Palace of Great Happiness and the Lodge for Retiring from Hard Work were replicas of the Veranda of Serene Tranquillity and the Study of Respect for Excellence in the Palace

Stream on which to float cups of wine, in the garden of the Palace of Peaceful Longevity

for the Establishment of Happiness. In some cases identical buildings, such as the Veranda for Three Friends, appear in both locations with the same name, showing his lifelong attachment to the Western Garden of his youth.

The emphasis placed by the emperor on combining the display of imperial power with the worship of heaven and his ancestors is apparent in both the Hall of Imperial Supremacy and the Palace of Peaceful Longevity. Both in name and form the Hall of Imperial Supremacy reflects the highest level of imperial power. The roof has double eaves in imitation of those on the Hall of Supreme Harmony, the most revered building in the Forbidden City. The Hall of Imperial Supremacy was the emperor's way of saying that in his hands imperial power had attained its zenith.

The Palace of Peaceful Longevity was used by the elderly emperor for the worship of his ancestors and for shamanistic rituals. From the very beginning of the Qing dynasty in 1644, one of the ways in which the Qing court had asserted its Manchu origins was to perpetuate its own religious practices. The Palace of Earthly Peace, which had been used by the Ming empresses as sleeping quarters, was converted into a hall for the worship of shamans and then continued to be the place where shamanistic sacrifices were carried out for over 200 years. This palace therefore performed similar functions to the Palace of Earthly Peace.

The Hall for the Cultivation of the Spirit, the dimensions and construction of which are almost identical to those of the Hall for the Cultivation of the Mind, was the clearest expression of the Qianlong emperor's enthusiasm for self-cultivation. The later hall however has no Hall of the Three Rarities, for the treasured works of calligraphy could not be moved. Nevertheless the emperor went to the lengths of obtaining ink made in the Tang dynasty (618–907) as a sign of respect for his three Tang calligraphic treasures, and he established the so-called Room of Flowing Ink where he could appreciate antique objects and cultivate his mind as he had done in the Hall of the Three Rarities.[23] He made a further reference to the three rarities by constructing a stream on which to float cups of wine, an allusion to the Orchid Pavilion terrace where the calligrapher Wang Xizhi (author of one of the rarities) had held a literary gathering in the fourth century. Similarly the colossal jade boulder carved with the scene of the legendary emperor Yu the Great taming the primeval flood, which stands in the Hall for Enjoying Longevity, serves as a visual reminder of the emperor's desire to stress the importance of military activities.

The Palace of Peaceful Longevity draws together elements from every stage of the Qianlong emperor's long life and in this respect can be appreciated as a microcosm of his life and reign. As a city within a city the palace complex can also be regarded as a microcosm of the whole Forbidden City, which is a testimony not just to the life and work of one emperor but to the many who made up the Ming and Qing dynasties.

Translation: Julian Ward

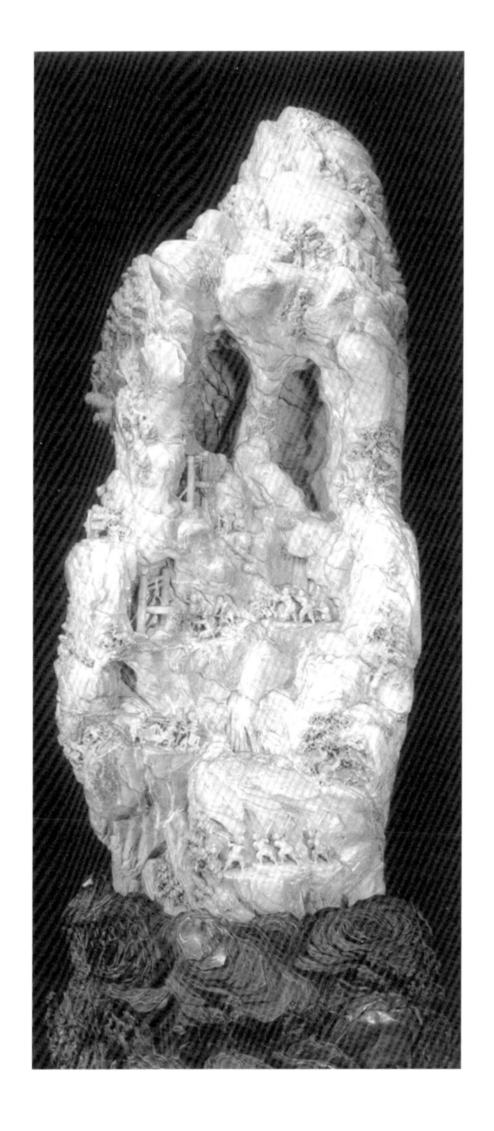

Yu the Great taming the flood, 1787, H 224 cm, W 96 cm, weight 5330 kg, Palace Museum, Beijing

Notes

1 Zhang Tangrong 1985: *juan* 5
2 The Jiaqing emperor said: 'During the reign of the Yongzheng emperor my father and Prince He lived in the Palace of Blessing', *GCGSXB* 1932: *juan* 39
3 Tang Bangzhi 1923: ch. 3
4 *RXJWK* 1774: *juan* 17
5 *GCGSXB* 1932: *juan* 56
6 Tang Bangzhi 1923: *juan* 3
7 *RXJWK* 1774: *juan* 20
8 Hongli, 'Record of the Palace of Double Glory', *GCGSXB* 1932: *juan* 56
9 Hongli, 'On the Palace for the Establishment of Happiness', *GCGS* 1769: *juan* 13
10 Liu Lu 1996
11 *QSL-SZ*: *juan* 261
12 Zhang Tangrong 1985: *juan* 21
13 Liu Lu 1996
14 *QSL-GZ*: *juan* 181
15 Hongli, 'Preface to the collection of prose from the Jigu studio' in *Qing Gaozong yuzhi shiwen chuji* (imper ial publication): *juan* 10
16 Zhaolian 1980: *juan* 1; Zhu Shi, preface in *LSTQJ* 1758: *juan* 8
17 Hongli, 'Account of the Hall of Delight in Doing Good', *LSTQJ* 1758
18 *QSL-GZ*: juan 5
19 *GCGSXB* 1932: *juan* 59
20 *GCGSXB* 1932: *juan* 2
21 Zhu Jie 1999
22 Hongli, 'On the Palace for the Establishment of Happiness', *GCGS* 1769: *juan* 13
23 Hongli, 'Account of the Room of Flowing Ink' in Zhang Tangrong 1985: *juan* 6

THE STATUS OF ARTISTS AT THE QIANLONG COURT

Nie Chongzheng

Histories of Qing dynasty painting tell us little about the workings and organisation of court painters. Fortunately the archives of the Department of the Imperial Household at the Palace Museum in Beijing contain sufficient, although fragmentary, material to piece together information on the subject. From this documentary material we can begin to understand a little about how court artists were selected, how they were graded, and how they were rewarded or punished.

The first thing that becomes clear from surviving documents is that in order to become an artist at court a prospective candidate had to paint an assigned subject and have his work scrutinised by the emperor. In 1749 Xu Zhang (1694–?), a little-known portrait painter, went to Beijing to take part in the painting examination. The archives record: 'On 10 July 1749, following the recommendation of Tula, Bai Shixiu, storekeeper, presented the portrait painter Xu Zhang, a 55-year-old from Luo county in Songjiang prefecture. A memorial was written to be transmitted to the emperor by Hu Shijie. The emperor ordered Xu to present a painting.' On the same day a reply came from the emperor: 'Today, after a small unfinished landscape on silk by Xu Zhang was presented by Hu Shijie for the emperor's inspection, a decree was issued that Xu Zhang be sent to assist Chunyu and Shuhe.' What is clear from these two documents is that the selection of artists in the Qing dynasty, as in previous dynasties, involved a process of recommendation and approval.

As can be seen from the case of Xu Zhang, the first step for a person from an ordinary background who aspired to enter the court as an artist was to seek the recommendation of someone in a position of power and influence. Xu Zhang was recommended by Tula, superintendent of the Imperial Silk Manufactory in Suzhou. It would appear that, as well as being responsible for producing goods for the imperial family, the superintendent was also expected to recommend artists for the court.

Such a responsibility also lay in the hands of both court and local officials, as evidenced by the case of two brothers, Yu Sheng and Yu Zhi, who had studied painting under Grand Secretary Jiang Tingxi (1669–1732) and resided for more than 20 years in the home of Haiwang (?–1755), Minister of the Board of Revenue and Grand Minister of the Department of the Imperial Household. The two brothers were recommended for consideration as court painters by Haiwang and Jiang Tingxi. In a similar case the artist Wang Cen, while spending some time in the capital, had become associated with high officials such as Zhang Zhao (1691–1745), Dong Bangda (1699–1769) (see no. 42) and Zhang Ruoai (1713–46), and he eventually entered court on the recommendation of Li Zongwan (1705–59), Vice Minister of the Board of Justice. Another example is the landscape artist Yuan Ying, who was recommended in 1756 by Li Yinpei, Vice Minister of the Board of Revenue, and who went on to hold a post at court for

Opposite:
Detail of *Pair of rabbits under a* wutong *tree* (no. 61)

more than 20 years. The portrait painter Chen Shijun had dealings with Zhang Zhao and Zhang Ruoai, and on the latter's recommendation Chen entered court where he worked as an artist for many years. In all these cases, however, a recommendation was only the prelude to an examination.

There were of course alternative paths to court. An aspiring painter could seek entry to court by 'presenting a painting in order to recommend himself', although this path was open only to those with a certain degree of power and who were smart enough to take advantage of a suitable opportunity. Xu Yang (*c.* 1751–76) and Jin Tingbiao (d. 1767) serve as good examples. In 1751 the Qianlong emperor embarked on his first tour of the south. On the emperor's arrival in Suzhou, Xu Yang, an accomplished artist skilled in a variety of subjects including landscape, the painting of birds and flowers, grasses, insects and architecture, presented the emperor with an album of paintings. His work met with imperial approval and, before long, he was sent to Beijing to take up a position at court (see no. 26). Similarly, when the Qianlong emperor went on his second tour of the south in 1757, Jin Tingbiao (see no. 63), another highly versatile artist, presented an album entitled *Arhats*. He promptly received the approval of the emperor and followed him north to serve at court.

Succession was another way in which a painter could assume a position at court. A substantial number of Qing court artists inherited their positions from their fathers, and many apprentices succeeded their teachers. Hierarchies of grandfather, father, son, and of master, apprentice were not uncommon. During the reign of the Kangxi emperor, Leng Mei (*c.* 1677–1742 or later) (no. 61), pupil of Jiao Bingzhen, succeeded his master as court artist; and Zhang Weibang, son of the artist Zhang Zhen who had served at court during the reigns of the Kangxi and Yongzheng emperors, became a court artist during the reign of the Yongzheng emperor. Zhang Weibang's period at court continued into the reign of the Qianlong emperor. In his old age, Zhang in turn recommended his own son Zhang Tingyan as his successor. In another case, Sun Weifeng, the son of Sun Fu, a court artist of the Kangxi period, entered court as a painter during the reign of the Yongzheng emperor, while Wang Youxue, who became a court painter in 1751, was the son of Wang Jie, who had been an official painter during the reign of the Kangxi emperor. Another of Wang Jie's sons, Wang Ruxue, later also took up an appointment at court.

Archival evidence shows that, once admitted to court, painters were graded and given a rank. These are described in the 1741 Inventory of the Workshops of the Department of the Imperial Household: 'The storekeeper Bai Shixiu announced a proclamation, issued through eunuch Gao Yu, that the following artists are hereby graded. The first rank comprises the following six artists: Jin Kun, Sun Hu, Ding Guanpeng, Zhang Yusen, Yu Sheng and Zhou Kun; each will receive a monthly allowance of eight *liang* of silver for food and three *liang* for other expenses. The second rank is made up of the following four artists: Wu Gui, Yu Zhi, Cheng Zhidao and Zhang Weibang; each will receive a monthly allowance of six *liang* of silver for food and three *liang* for other expenses. The third rank is made up of the following five artists: Dai Hong, Lu Zhan, Wu Yu, Dai Zheng and Xu Dao; each will receive a monthly allowance of four *liang* of silver for food and three *liang* for other expenses.' This grading of 15 artists in the early years of the Qianlong period shows that, as in earlier dynasties, Qing court painters were graded according to three ranks. Expenses issued for food were dependent on rank, but ancillary expenses were the same throughout.

When the Qianlong emperor went to Suzhou in 1751 on his first southern tour, he was presented with paintings by the artists Zhang Zongcang and Xu Yang; the two men were later summoned to court to paint. In the seventh month of the same year the records of the Department of the Imperial Household state: 'From the start of the sixth month, the painters Zhang Zongcang and Xu Yang are to be awarded the same monthly eating and living expenses as Yu Sheng and Ding Guanpeng.' According to the proclamation of 1741 cited above, Yu Sheng and Ding Guanpeng belonged to the first rank. For Zhang and Xu to receive the treatment reserved for the highest rank as soon as they entered the court is testimony to the high esteem in which the emperor held them.

No clear evidence of artists' ranks before the reign of the Qianlong emperor has been found in the archives, although there appear to have been rules governing artists' salaries. In 1726, in the reign of the Yongzheng emperor, the Inventory of the Workshops states: 'Sixth rank officer Alantai received the decree: The artists Ding Yu, Zhan Xi, Ding Guanpeng, Cheng Zhidao and He Yongqing will each receive a monthly allowance of eight *liang* of silver for food and three *liang* for other expenses.' These allowances equate with those of the highest rank in the reign of the Qianlong emperor. It seems then that Ding Guanpeng was treated as a first rank artist in the reigns of both the Yongzheng and Qianlong emperors, whereas Cheng Zhidao, a first rank artist during the reign of the Yongzheng emperor, was demoted to the second rank by the Qianlong reign. This suggests that grading was by no means permanent. An artist's rank depended not only on his diligence and creative development but also on the taste of each individual emperor. In other words, there was no 'iron rice bowl' and court painters could be promoted, demoted or, at worst, dismissed.

On arrival at court each painter had to undergo a period of probation, during which he received no pay other than an allowance for food. The position of an artist under probation was therefore similar to that of an art student in the past at the Song dynasty Academy of Painting. A document dated 1726 records how Prince Yinxiang

(1686–1730), responsible for the Department of the Imperial Household, issued an order that Zhang Lin, Wu Gui, Wu Yu, Chen Min, Peng He, Wang Jun and Ye Lüfeng, seven new artists at the Palace of Peace and Tranquillity, should be put on probation and awarded a monthly allowance of three *liang* of silver for food. Of these seven, Wu Gui became a first rank artist and Wu Yu a second.

The documents quoted so far mention only remuneration in the form of expenses. However, the archives reveal two further kinds of reward for court artists: luxury goods and leave of absence.

In 1736 the Qianlong emperor decreed that the court artists Tangdai (1673–1752), Giuseppe Castiglione and Castiglione's pupil Wang Youxue should be rewarded for their outstanding work. Tangdai and Castiglione were each presented with two catties (*jin*, each approximately 500g) of ginseng and four catties of silk, while Wang Youxue was given two bolts of imperial satin. The same year Castiglione and other artists were given a variety of precious goods, including imperial satin and marten fur. As a reward for his many years of hard work at court, the elderly master Leng Mei (no. 61), who had entered court during the Kangxi reign, was given the substantial sum of fifty *liang* of silver in 1742. In the same year Castiglione, Wang Zhicheng, Zhang Weibang, Sun Hu, Ding Guanpeng and Shen Yuan were each awarded a gold ingot and a bolt of satin.

Another kind of reward was special leave of absence. In 1763, on the death of his father Jin Hong, the artist Jin Tingbiao was permitted by the emperor to return to his home village in southern China to attend the funeral; he continued to receive his salary. When the southerner Zhou Kun first went to Beijing as a court artist, he struggled to acclimatise himself. After a lengthy illness he requested the emperor's permission to return home for a period of recuperation, expressing his desire to resume his duties once he had recovered. Because the Qianlong emperor admired his artistic skills he agreed to Zhou's request and within three years Zhou returned to court.

Rewards to artists in the form of birthday treats were exceptional but not unheard of. In 1777, on the occasion of his seventieth birthday, the European missionary artist Ignatius Sickelbart (Ai Qimeng, 1708–80), was summoned to the Summer Palace near Beijing, Yuanmingyuan, by the emperor to be presented with a court robe and a plaque inscribed in his own hand 'Venerable old man from a kingdom over the sea'. Other western missionaries resident in Beijing attended the celebrations and Sickelbart was honoured by being taken for a tour of the capital on a palanquin supported by eight men and accompanied by a troupe of musicians.

Artists particularly admired by the emperor were not only rewarded in their lifetime but were also glorified after their death. For example, after his death in 1766, Castiglione was posthumously appointed Vice Minister and three hundred *liang* of silver were presented to help with funeral expenses. Such instances of posthumous rewards to artists are, however, rare.

Rewards such as the above provided an incentive to court painters, just as the threat of punishment acted as a warning to those whose work was careless or slipshod. The archives of the Department of the Imperial Household for the eleventh month of 1728 state: 'Sixth rank officer Alantai announced: Because of the negligent and indolent work of the artists in the Palace of Compassion and Peace, Yinxiang has ordered Shen Yu to subject these artists to daily inspection by Tang Ying.' Shen Yu subsequently took to overseeing the artists in the Palace of Peace and Tranquillity, and as a result Wang Jun was removed in the fourth month of the following year. This constituted the most serious punishment for a Qing court artist.

Other artists suffered similar humiliation. In the eleventh month of 1746 Jin Kun was commissioned to paint a documentary record of the grand military review that had been held in Beijing in 1739 (no. 34). In this work Jin inadvertently painted one of the eight banners in the wrong position, an error that he later tried to cover up. When the Qianlong emperor discovered the mistake, he was extremely angry and ordered Grand Minister Haiwang to punish Jin: his salary was halted and he was dismissed from his post. At the same time it was decided that, as a result of the inadequate supervision by Huashan, foreman of the inspectorate of court painters, his salary should also be halted. Jin Kun lost no time in rectifying his mistakes and found someone to plead for mercy on his behalf. For one month both Jin and Huashan had their salaries cut by half. In the end Jin Kun had a long career at court, but it was only because his artistic talents were so exceptional that the emperor allowed him to remain in his post.

Translation: Julian Ward

COLLABORATIVE PAINTING AT THE QIANLONG COURT

Yu Hui

The intermarriage of Chinese and European painting techniques began when a handful of European missionary artists were accepted into the Qing court of the Kangxi emperor. Throughout his reign and those of the Yongzheng and Qianlong emperors, these artists collaborated with Chinese painters and a new style of court art emerged. The most famous of the Jesuit missionary painters is the Italian Giuseppe Castiglione (1688–1766), who arrived at the court of the Kangxi emperor in 1715 and went on to serve both his son and grandson.

First and foremost the Jesuit missionaries were clergymen, although some of them had undergone extensive training in the arts and the sciences and had carried out work in these fields in their native countries. However, these pursuits remained secondary to their religious interests; their primary aim in going to China was to undertake missionary work. When the Kangxi emperor learned that some of these missionaries were also painters practised in the European techniques of naturalistic representation, he realised that this might be something worth taking advantage of: paintings in a new style might be used to glorify his rule and embellish his palaces. Missionaries were therefore invited to work in the palace workshops as full-time artists, thereby relinquishing their religious duties. The fact that the lives of many missionaries did not turn out as they had expected caused a number of them to feel embittered. Yet, living in the repressive imperial court, they had little choice but to direct their energy and talents to painting, and in turn they were treated favourably. Some worked at court until their deaths, when they were buried in the Catholic cemetery in the south of Beijing.

These missionary artists not only executed paintings but were also willing to teach Chinese and Manchu court artists about European painting conventions. Thus court artists learned about the depiction of light and shade to suggest volume, theories of colour, the anatomy of the human body, and scientific perspective. The assimilation of these techniques was neither instant nor ubiquitous as the gulf between Chinese and European aesthetics was still enormous in the eighteenth century.

The first area of disagreement was the depiction of colour and light. In his approach to colour the Chinese artist advocated 'conformity to kind in the application of colour'. The aim of the artist was to depict primarily local colour, that is to present the actual colour of an object in ordinary daylight. By contrast, the European painter was trained to modify the colour of an object according to the amount of light shining on different parts of it. This conceptual clash meant that the western technique of *chiaroscuro*, the depiction of light and shade, had a fateful reception at the Chinese court. The missionary painters' realistic portrayal of the light and shade on the folds of garments was accepted with reluctance. But when painters attempted to capture the effect of light and shade on the human face, they were confronted

Opposite:
Detail of *Ten imperial horses* (no. 29)

with blunt rejection, since to a Chinese the colours in the shaded areas of the painted face simply did not exist in 'reality'. Should a missionary painter have used this method to portray the face of the emperor, he might have met with great misfortune, for the verbal phrase used to describe the application of dark colour to a face is an insult in Chinese meaning to bring shame on someone. As a result the missionary painters had to devise a method of painting that would be acceptable to the Chinese, while still giving play to their skills. They came up with a technique that could be called 'diffused light': the figure looks as if it is placed against a white background in clear diffused daylight. To prevent the face from appearing too two-dimensional, a faint degree of shading was applied to small areas of the face with great care. The treatment of light and shade on a person's clothing was then modified to harmonise with that on the face.

This method is employed most successfully in *The Qianlong emperor in ceremonial armour on horseback* (no. 16) attributed to Giuseppe Castiglione. Painting on silk, Castiglione used Chinese brushes to apply a thin coat of oil pigments. Although the 'diffused light' technique is used to the render the figure, the stronger contrast between light and shade in the depiction of the horse, and of its head in particular, suggests that Castiglione was not prepared to compromise his skills at every turn.

This new style of figure painting was fully endorsed by the Qianlong emperor. However, contemporary Chinese court painters were not shy to voice their own opinions, the most famous being Zou Yigui (1686–1772), Vice Minister of the Board of Rites, who commented in his *Painting Manual of Xiaoshan* that European painting showed no skill in brushwork, and although 'it is carried out with meticulous care, in the end it is but the work of a mere artisan'. His lack of sympathy for European brushwork techniques stems from the fact that Chinese painting, unlike its European counterpart, is almost entirely dependent on line. To a Chinese painter, his personality, his feelings and his skill can all be embodied in a single line. There is no limit to what the line can represent, and even ink washes and dots are considered as extended lines. By contrast, the missionary painter sought to depict structural form through light and shade and modified colour, rather than through line. To the Chinese painter this disregard for line was tantamount to depriving painting of its spiritual quality.

The missionary painter paled at the thought of depicting structural form through a few simple brushstrokes. He knew that the Chinese painter's facility with the brush stemmed from his daily practice of calligraphy. How could a European painter who was not trained in wielding a brush to write Chinese characters be expected to produce such lines? An ingenious solution to the problem was soon found: the missionary artists and the Chinese court artists collaborated to produce figure paintings in which each displayed his own particular skill.

The missionary artists rendered the faces and hands of the figures, and took responsibility for the composition and for the use of scientific perspective, while the Chinese artists worked on areas of the painting best suited to treatment with line, such as draperies, trees, rocks and distant mountains. The Chinese artists even wrote the missionary artists' Chinese names on the paintings for them. Such collaboration on the one painting by Chinese and European artists led to a new style of court figure painting, of which numerous examples were produced. A typical such work is the painting entitled *Hongli (the Qianlong emperor) and the royal children on New Year's eve* (no. 35). The use of scientific perspective to depict the buildings in the painting suggests the hand of Castiglione; he was also responsible for all the faces in the painting while the Chinese artist Ding Guanpeng took care of the clothing, trees and rocks.

The concept of perspective is closely linked to that of proportion. European artists were well versed in the proportions of the human body, having learned how to paint the human figure through the anatomical study of the body. The Chinese artist had no such access to studies of human anatomy, and treated the human figure in a different light. His aim was to capture a person's inner being and personality through his command of line, and often a simplification of form, with less regard to exact proportions.

At the start of the Kangxi reign in the mid-seventeenth century, Chinese court artists still adhered to the principle of treating figures according to their social status: the higher the rank of a person in a picture, the larger he would appear. For example, the painter of *The Kangxi emperor in military attire* (no. 1) pays no heed to the relative positions of the figures in the landscape. The seated figure of the emperor is clearly set back some distance behind the two pairs of ministers in the foreground, but, rather than appearing smaller, the emperor is rendered the same size as his ministers as convention would not have tolerated an emperor smaller than his subordinates. The Kangxi emperor was later to develop a keen interest in European science and technology, including mathematics, cartography and medical anatomy. This interest was passed on to the Yongzheng and Qianlong emperors, creating a climate ripe for the acceptance of naturalistic means of representation and some of the scientific theories of European painting brought to court by the likes of Castiglione and other missionary artists.

The naturalistic treatment of subject matter was introduced only gradually by the missionary artists. Towards the end of the reign of the Yongzheng emperor, Castiglione painted *Spring's peaceful message* (no. 2), a portrait of the Yongzheng emperor and his fifth son Hongli, the future Qianlong emperor, standing by a clump of bamboo. The painting retains the Confucian notion of the ideal relationship between ruler and minister, father and son: Hongli, who was by then already

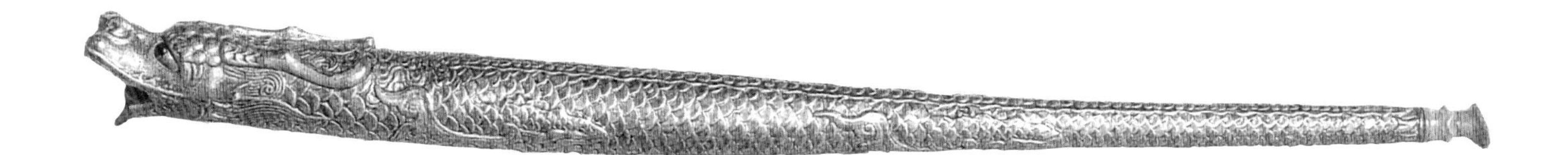

Horn for use in the deer-calling hunt, made of sandalwood, carved with dragons and gilded

a young adult, is shown shorter than his father, and in a position of respect, receiving from his father a sprig of plum blossom, symbol of luck and harbinger of the future. Yet, despite the obvious symbolism and adherence to Confucian moral principles, the painting displays a new hint of naturalism: the emperor's facial expression displays none of the solemnity and majesty found in other imperial portraits; rather, he is shown as a living individual. The painting *Hongli (the Qianlong emperor) and the royal children on New Year's eve* (no. 35), by Castiglione and the Chinese court artist Ding Guanpeng, shows even greater naturalism: the Qianlong emperor is in quite informal pose, playing with the children around him. Rather than falsely accentuating the height of the emperor to suggest his status, the artist plays on the natural differences in height between adult and children to highlight the emperor. The naturalistic pose of the emperor holding his youngest son in his arms and amusing him with a toy evokes a loving father devoted to his children. The work is imbued with the happy atmosphere of family life at the time of the Spring Festival, and the relationship between old and young appears so harmonious that the viewer might be forgiven for forgetting that this is in fact the portrait of a Chinese emperor. Castiglione and his Chinese collaborator have produced not only a true-to-life image of the emperor, but also a touching portrait of a loving father. Such a work was quite without precedence in the history of imperial portraiture in China.

The painting *Calling for deer* (no. 30) of 1741, by Castiglione and others, is another excellent example of the treatment of the relationship between ruler and subordinates. 'Calling' refers to the Manchu method of deer-hunting whereby the hunters went out at dawn wearing false deer heads and sounding a horn. The horn imitated the voice of a male deer in heat and would entice the female deer out of the woods, whereupon they could be easily captured. The Qianlong emperor advances towards the head of a large group of mounted figures, the last of whom holds the horn. From surviving examples of the emperor's clothing we know that he was of a similar stature to his ministers. In this painting Castiglione gives us a faithful representation of the mounted figures, who all appear in natural proportion to each other and to their surroundings. The emperor, third from the left, is no larger than his retainers; in fact, because of his position further into the picture, he appears slightly smaller than the two figures in front of him.

Artists had to be wary, however, of not making the emperor too small. When the emperor accompanied the tiger-hunting brigade on a hunt, he was with commanders who were sturdy and intrepid,

Detail of *Hongli stabbing the tiger*, anonymous and undated, hanging scroll, ink and colour on silk, H 258.3 cm, W 172 cm, Palace Museum, Beijing

and who tended to dwarf him. In the painting *Hongli stabbing the tiger* the artist does not hide the fact that the two commanders of the hunting brigade are taller than the emperor. However, so as not to demean the emperor in any way, the artist resorts to a compositional device: he places the emperor in a prominent position in the picture, thereby giving him the necessary stature and authority.

Paintings such as this one, and in particular those works that are collaborations between European missionary painters and Chinese artists, exemplify the new direction of court art in the eighteenth century during the reign of the Qianlong emperor. Prior to the arrival of missionary artists from Europe, Chinese court artists such as Jiao Bingzhen had relied on imported woodblock prints for any glimpse of European art. The advantage of the missionary artists was that they brought with them, in person, to the imperial court itself, scientific knowledge of anatomy, light and perspective, and more naturalistic means of representation. By tentatively introducing European painting techniques and theories to the Chinese court repertoire, the missionary painters were to bring about a transformation in court painting. For the first time European and Chinese painters were able to share their skills and collaborate on paintings, creating works that were a new fusion of western and eastern painting techniques.

Translation: Julian Ward

辛亥三月御筆
御筆

PAINTINGS AND CALLIGRAPHY BY THE QIANLONG EMPEROR

Yang Danxia

The reign of the Qianlong emperor was the final golden age of China's imperial period. Not only was this an age of great peace and prosperity that saw a vast increase in the population and astounding agricultural improvements, but it was also a time of enormous artistic creativity in many spheres. Han traditions and western ways were assimilated at the Manchu court, giving birth to a new type of court art. One important branch of this court art comprises the Qianlong emperor's own paintings and works of calligraphy which survive in prolific numbers, in exquisite mountings.

The relatively stable political and social climate allowed the Qianlong emperor time and energy to further his own artistic pursuits. The emperor had an extraordinary enthusiasm for literature and the fine arts, testified by the 40,000 poems and tens of thousands of paintings and works of calligraphy that he left behind. Despite his non-Han origins, he hoped to follow the role model of the Han Chinese emperor versed in Confucian doctrines as well as prove himself to be a more enlightened emperor than any of his forebears. Although he may have lacked the deep insight of a true artist, his commitment to literature and the arts was more comprehensive than that of many Han scholars. In addition, his imperial status gave to his paintings and calligraphy a significance which he alone could provide.

Qianlong was an extremely hardworking emperor who, from an early age, was exposed to Han culture. By the age of nine he was reading, by 14 he was writing compositions, and by 19 he was learning to paint, referring to himself throughout his life as a scholar. The depth of his scholarship gave weight to his own paintings and calligraphy. He lost no chance to show off his talents, even if he had to create such opportunities for himself, as for instance when he hosted banquets and literary gatherings for officials. Every winter, in the twelfth lunar month, the emperor would retire to the Hall for the Cultivation of the Mind and write the character *fu,* good fortune, one of the renditions of which was presented as a New Year gift to George III of Great Britain in 1793. On New Year's day he would paint a New Year picture, such as *Spring plants and fruit* (no. 69), with auspicious flowers, fruits and plants, and utensils from the palace; and as an obligatory annual task he would copy out the *Heart Sutra,* to which he would occasionally add a portrait of Guanyin, the bodhisattva Avalokitesvara, who is believed to have recited the sutra. In his old age, as a plea for longevity, the emperor would write out the *Heart Sutra* on the first and the fifteenth day of each month as well as on New Year's day. Some years he would paint something other than a New Year picture. In the thirteenth year of his reign (1748), the year of the death of his first wife, the Xiaoxian empress, and the time of the Jinchuan rebellion, the combination of deep personal sadness and the strain caused by political unrest made the emperor, not yet 40 years of age, particularly depressed and frustrated. On the first day of the following

Opposite:
Detail of *Mount Pan* (no. 50)

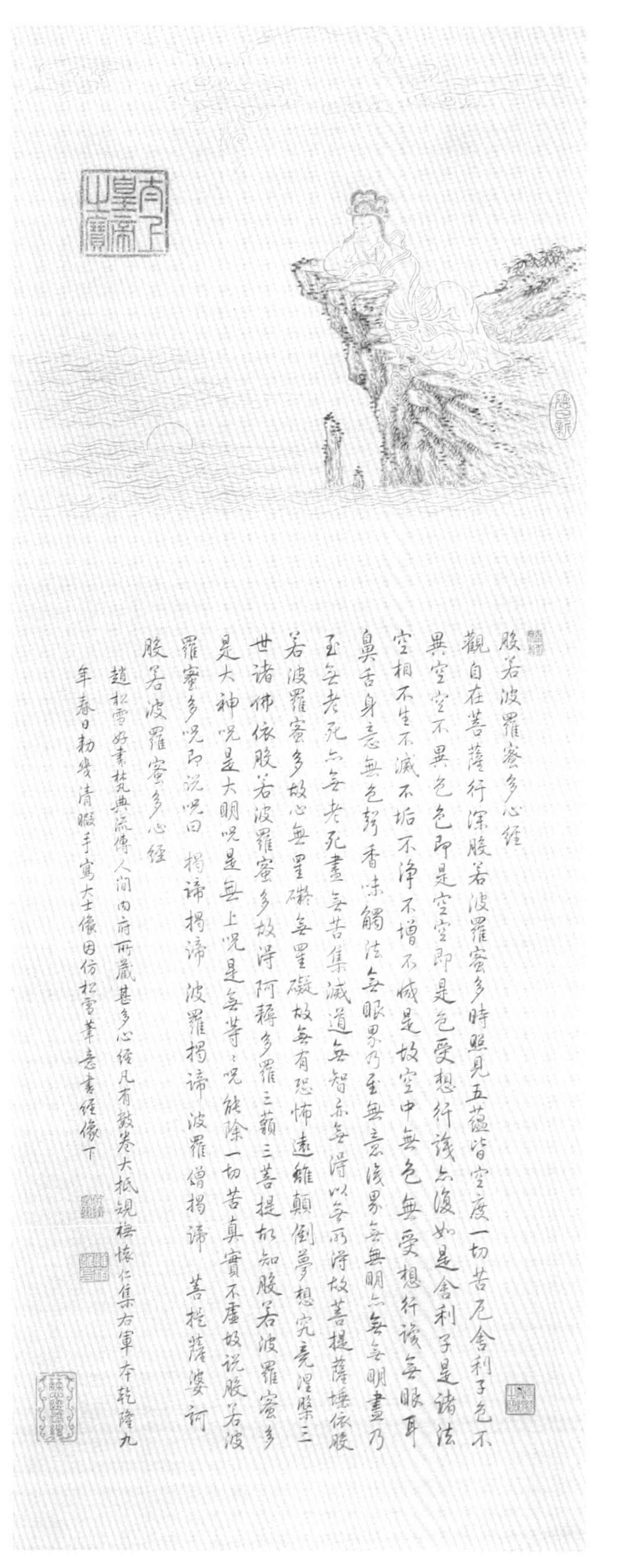

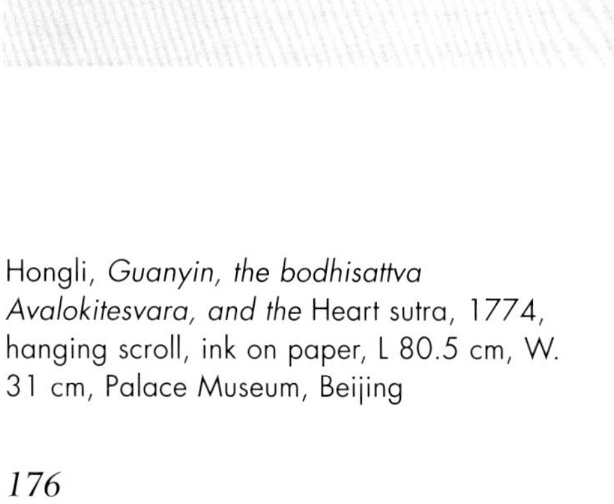

Hongli, *Guanyin, the bodhisattva Avalokitesvara, and the* Heart sutra, 1774, hanging scroll, ink on paper, L 80.5 cm, W. 31 cm, Palace Museum, Beijing

Hongli, *Rock, plum blossom and narcissi*, 1761, hanging scroll, ink on paper, L 56 cm, W 29.6 cm, Palace Museum, Beijing

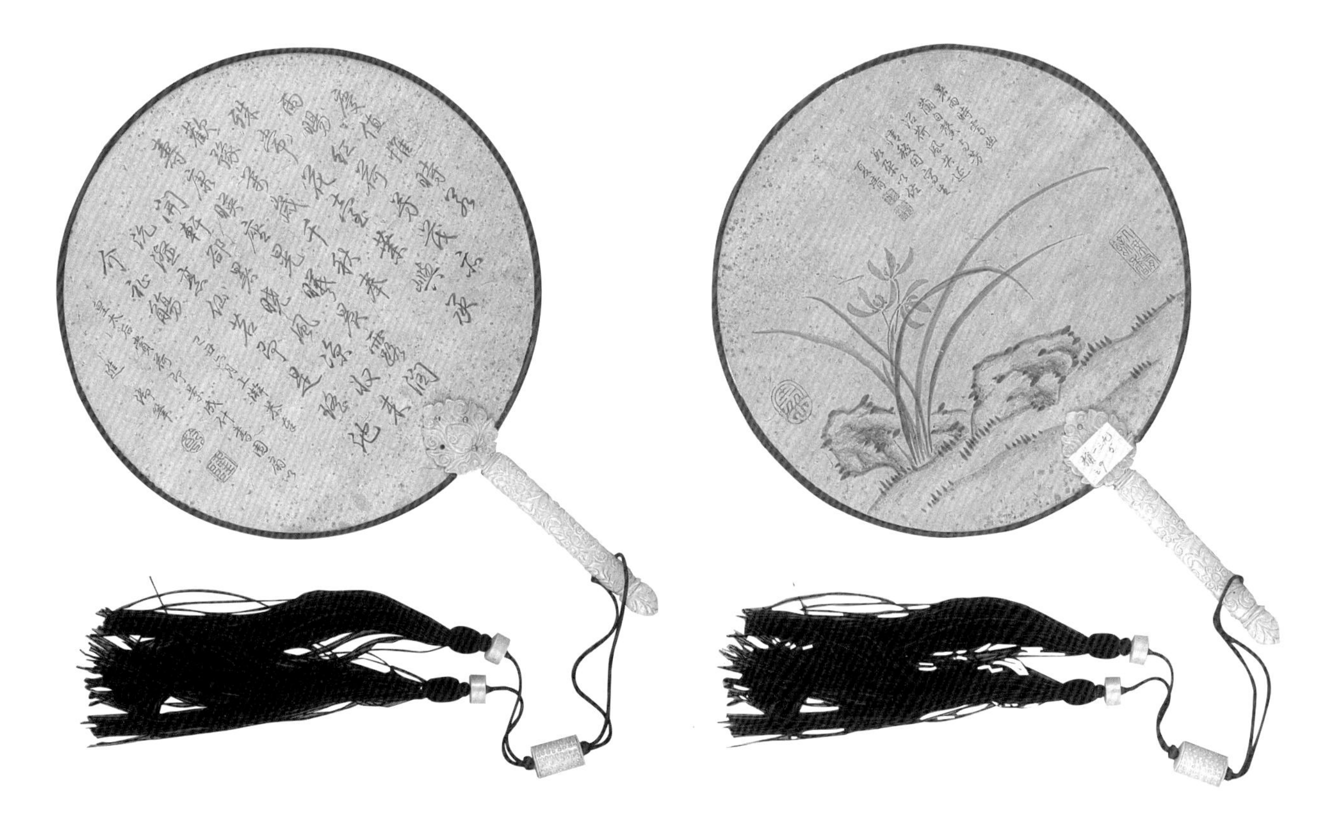

Hongli, *Orchid and rock*, 1769, fan, ink on paper, D 24.2 cm, Palace Museum, Beijing

year, news arrived from Jinchuan that Fuheng (?–1770) and Yue Zhongqi (1686–1754) had subdued the rebellion, at least temporarily. The depression that had engulfed the palace for so long was immediately lifted, and in a state of exhilaration the emperor created two versions of a painting entitled *Finding order amongst ten thousand threads* (no. 65). Although the paintings are simple ink sketches of bamboo, trees and a veranda by water, their very title and the inscription written by court officials express the emperor's relief that order might eventually have been created out of chaos, perhaps a metaphor for the victory in Jinchuan.

As well as the annual New Year picture, another mandatory annual activity was the creation of a small vignette by the emperor for his mother, the Xiaosheng empress (no. 7). The most exquisite of these are in the form of circular fans, such as *Orchid and rock* and *Three peaches* (no. 51), which were presented by the emperor to his mother on the occasion of a trip, a banquet or her birthday. The emperor also encouraged his son, Yongrong (1743–90) to amuse his grandmother. One New Year Yongrong gave the Xiaosheng empress one of his own paintings entitled *Ruyi and flowers* (no. 52), to which the emperor appended a poem in his own hand. The emperor's sense of filial piety towards his mother was particularly strong. He went to great lengths to make her happy, both at home in the palace and on the occasions when he invited her to accompany him on his grand tours. The majority of paintings created for her were finished personally by the emperor, with auspicious poems and greetings appended to the backs of all the fans, and no expense or effort was spared in the mounting, with the use of luxury materials such as red sandalwood, jade and precious stones. Not only are these fans fine examples of imperial craftsmanship but they also serve as records of the imperial family's intimacy.

Hongli, *Copy of 'Mountains enveloped by clouds' by Dong Qichang*, 1771, handscroll, ink on paper, L. 63.5 cm, H. 11.1 cm, Palace Museum, Beijing

So far no documentary evidence has been found to cast light on the Qianlong emperor's painting teachers. When Hongli, still a prince, was only twelve years old, his grandfather, the Kangxi emperor, insisted he be raised in the palace, and he instructed his own two sons Yinlu (1695–1767) and Yinxi (1711–43) to teach him, among other things, archery and shooting. These two uncles of Hongli were both highly skilled in the martial arts and well versed in poetry and painting. While both are considered competent painters, Yinxi in particular, a handsome man of many talents, was a versatile calligrapher and painter, creating landscapes in the style of the Yuan dynasty (1279–1368) masters. Many of his works are still extant. The young Hongli could not but have been influenced by his uncles in their daily encounters.

Of greatest inspiration to the young emperor must have been the huge collection of works of art amassed by his father and grandfather. The Qianlong emperor was to continue to build on this collection with an enthusiasm that far outstripped that of his forebears. Throughout his upbringing the Qianlong emperor was surrounded by scholars and painters who were highly educated in both the theoretical and practical aspects of painting and calligraphy. Men such as Liang Shizheng (1697–1763), Tangdai (1673–1752) and Zhang Zhao (1691–1745) each shared their skills with Hongli. With inspiration and guidance from such masters, Hongli was, by his teens, conscientiously studying the Confucian classics and developing his own poetic and artistic talents. His aim was to create the image of a multi-talented future ruler. Even his potential rival for the throne, his brother Hongzhou (1712–70), was convinced not only of Hongli's practical skills in statecraft, but also of his talents as a painter and poet.

According to the Qianlong emperor's own account, his study of painting began with the bird and flower paintings of professional artists at the Song dynasty court of the tenth to thirteenth century. But inadequate training in the basic skills of painting meant that a very small painting would often take him over a month to complete, and even then he could manage only a poor imitation of the original, and one that, in his opinion, lacked its vitality. He seemed to reach an awareness that his work was unlikely ever to be as good as that of the professionals, whose paintings combined both form and spirit. He therefore abandoned this aim, declaring that he would 'paint from the heart, let it take shape at will, and not be restricted by conventions'.

The emperor's painting was not about to undergo a transformation. Rather, his pronouncement can be seen as an admission of his shortcomings, and an attempt to justify mediocre techniques. Having abandoned the study of Song dynasty bird and flower paintings by skilled professional painters, the emperor became attracted to the more individual and scholarly approach of some of the Yuan dynasty painters, exemplified by Zhao Mengfu (1254–1322), who incidentally had had court connections. Zhao's influence is clearly obvious in the Qianlong emperor's calligraphy and painting, particularly in calligraphic works such as *Clearing after the night rain* (no. 44) and *Heaven's beneficence* (no. 77). The emperor's paintings on the other hand, in particular his copies of classical landscapes and of bird and flower paintings (no. 40), which make up over 80 per cent of his extant works, show the calligraphic style of Yuan dynasty ink painting, rather than the influence of any one particular artist. Typical of these paintings are his *Album in imitation of various painters of the Yuan dynasty*, *Copy of 'The study by old trees' by Wen Zhengming* (no. 48) and *Copy of 'Mountains enveloped by clouds' by Dong Qichang*. Although throughout his long reign the emperor never ceased to paint, his works never really rose above the level of 'ink play' by an amateur. His most outstanding paintings in terms of brushwork and design are *Copy of 'Studies of water' by Ma Yuan* (no. 72), *Copy of 'Arhat in red robe' by Zhao Mengfu* (no. 46), *Copy of 'Brewing tea' by Tang Yin* (no. 47) and *Copy of 'Chicks waiting to be fed' by Li Di* (no. 75), some of which may have been completed in conjunction with court artists. If we compare the copies made by the Qianlong emperor and his court artists with the original works, the faithfulness of the copies is surprising, not only in terms of the brushwork and ink washes, but also with regard to the dimensions of the pictures and the use of particular papers and paints. The explanation for this, of course, is not simply that the emperor was bored and wished to amuse himself by demanding exact technical imitations; rather, his aim was to impress upon his officials and descendants his own deep appreciation of ancient Han Chinese traditions. With each copy he wished to demonstrate a deepening of his understanding of religious issues, of people's daily lives and of the scholarly ideals of the recluse.

The Qianlong emperor, more than any other, was enormously fond of touring. Following in the footsteps of his grandfather the Kangxi emperor, and for purposes as varied as hunting, making sacrifices, inspecting sea and inland dams and nurturing relations with minority peoples, the Qianlong emperor travelled to every corner of his empire. There are numerous records and reflections in his poetry and paintings of these trips. Examples include the paintings entitled *View of the West Lake* (no. 49), *Copy of 'The Lion Grove Garden' by Ni Zan*, *The flowers at Dragon Well* and *Climbing up to the Jin Mountain temple*. On these trips the emperor made use of his free time to paint scenic spots and magnificent landscapes. The inscriptions on these paintings record the distances covered on the tours, the weather, his entourage, and information on the local people. The works are testimony to the emperor's deep love of his country and its natural landscapes, and to his yearning to emulate the life of a scholar in retreat in the countryside.

Naturally, an emperor was permitted to indulge his fantasies to the full: he made five trips to the Lion Grove Garden, his favourite miniature garden in Suzhou, executed four paintings of the garden in imitation of an original by Ni Zan (1301–74) (see no. 45) and composed over two hundred poems about it. He even spent over 200,000 taels of silver on two reconstructions of the Lion Grove Garden, one in Beijing and one in Rehe. The emperor also had gardens designed to replicate scenes from the West Lake in Hangzhou ('A stretch of cloud') and from Jiaxing ('The Tower of Mist and Rain', see no. 73). This tower appears in Dong Gao's painting *The Tower of Mist and Rain* (no. 73).

The topographic paintings made on his tours by both the emperor and his court painters expand the themes and subject matter of court painting, and reflect the fusion of northern and southern styles of garden design. They also provide an insight into the emperor's joys and sorrows on these trips. The sheer wealth of historical, political, economic and cultural detail they provide makes them an extremely valuable source of information on the life and times of the emperor and on the traditions of court art.

Translation: Frances Weightman

SUMMARY OF EVENTS 1711-99

1711

25 September: Birth of Hongli, future Qianlong emperor, in Residence of Prince Yong (Yinzhen, Hongli's father), Beijing.

1722

20 December: Death of Kangxi emperor.

1723

Yinzhen, Yongzheng emperor, succeeds throne. His princely residence renamed Palace of Complete Harmony.

16 September: Hongli secretly selected as heir apparent and begins formal education.

1727

Marriage of Hongli to Lady Fucha, future Xiaoxian empress. Move into living quarters in west of Forbidden City.

1730

Presentation by Hongli to court of *Anthology of studies from the Hall of Delight in Doing Good* (no. 4).

1735

8 October: Death of Yongzheng emperor.

18 October: Hongli succeeds throne as emperor (no. 11).

Beginning of military campaign against Miao people in southwest (completed 1736).

1736

First year of Qianlong reign. Emperor moves into Hall for the Cultivation of the Mind. His princely residence renovated and renamed Palace of Double Glory.

1739

First grand military review in South Park, Beijing (no. 34). Review takes place every three years thereafter.

1740

Completion of Palace for the Establishment of Happiness and its garden as Qianlong emperor's second residence in Forbidden City.

1741

First autumn hunting expedition in Rehe (Chengde) (no. 30). Thereafter becomes institutionalised annual event until 1775 with only six exceptions (1742, 1744, 1746, 1748, 1750, 1754).

1742

Han Chinese banner troops advised to leave army as precautionary measure to protect banner system.

1743

First pilgrimage by Qianlong emperor to Mukden (Shenyang), capital of Manchu heartland.

Qianlong emperor begins to learn Mongolian.

1744

Construction of mountain villa on Mount Pan (no. 50).

1745

Beginning of war in Jinchuan, Sichuan province (ends 1749).

Conversion of Palace of Complete Harmony, Qianlong emperor's birthplace, into lamaist temple, largest in Beijing.

Construction of mountain villa on Fragrant Hills near Beijing.

1746

Review of state seals. Revised number of seals set at 25 (no. 8).

1747

Completion of conservation of portraits of previous emperors and empresses; collection moved from Imperial Household Department to Nanxundian.

Completion of catalogues of imperial collection of paintings and works of calligraphy, *Shiqu baoji* and *Midian zhulin*.

Start of construction of European-style palaces in Summer Palace near Beijing (Yuanmingyuan) (main work completed 1759).

1748

8 April: Death of Xiaoxian empress in Dezhou on trip to Temple of Confucius, Qufu, Shandong province.

Creation of Manchu seal script for use on state seals.

First edition of Qianlong emperor's collected poems *Yuzhishi chuji*.

1749

Beginning of project to carve *Model works of calligraphy in the Hall of the Three Rarities* (no. 43) in stone (completed 1754).

Rebuilding of Shouhuangdian, imperial family ancestral hall in Sea Palaces, Beijing.

1750

Construction in Forbidden City of Palace of Compassion and Peace and its garden; also Pavilion of Rain Flowers, lamaist temple modelled on Tholing Monastery in Tibet.

Construction of Summer Palace near Beijing, Qingyiyuan (later Yiheyuan).

1751

8 February to 28 May: First southern tour of inspection.

Launch of painting project *Illustrated tributaries of the Qing empire* (no. 25) (completed 1775).

1755

February: Beginning of campaign against Western Mongols in Dzungaria (ends 1757).

Giuseppe Castiglione and other court artists commissioned to paint reception of Derbet tribe of Western Mongols in Garden of Ten Thousand Trees at Summer Palace in Rehe (no. 21).

Construction at Summer Palace in Rehe of Puning Monastery (modelled on Samye Monastery in Tibet) to commemorate victory in Dzungaria; also Yongyou Temple (modelled on Bao'en Temple in Nanjing and Liuhe Pagoda in Hangzhou).

Completion of catalogue of imperial collection of bronzes *Xiqing gujian.*

1757

28 February to 12 June: Second southern tour. First visit by Qianlong emperor to Lion Grove Garden in Suzhou (no. 45).

1758

February: Beginning of campaign against eastern Turkestan to suppress Muslim separatists (completed 1759).

Reception of Burut envoys from eastern Turkestan in Summer Palace in Rehe and in Beijing.

Giuseppe Castiglione commissioned to paint equestrian portrait of Qianlong emperor (no. 16).

1759

July: Completion of *Illustrated Regulations for Ceremonial Paraphernalia.*

1760

April: Uyghur girl from Kiramet family in eastern Turkestan becomes Qianlong emperor's concubine, given title Rongfei (no. 36).

Qianlong emperor learns Uyghur.

1761

6 February: Construction of Purple Light Pavilion in Sea Palaces, Beijing. Banquet held there to celebrate victory in Dzungaria and eastern Turkestan (no. 23).

Second edition of Qianlong emperor's collected poems *Yuzhishi erji.*

1762

5 February to 27 May: Third southern tour.

1763

Beijing lamas sent to Xinjiang province to assist in reconstruction of lamaist temples in Yili and elsewhere in Dzungaria.

1764

Construction at Summer Palace in Rehe of Anyuan Temple (modelled on Guerzha Temple in Yili).

Xu Yang commissioned to paint first southern tour (completed 1770).

1765

5 February to 9 June: Fourth southern tour on which emperor's second wife Ula Nara quarrels with him. As a result she shaves her hair and becomes a nun.

13 July: Dispatch of 16 drawings of *Conquest over Dzungaria and eastern Turkestan* through Guangzhou customs to court of Louis XV in France to make copper plates for 200 engravings.

1766

January: Break in war with Burma (armistice signed 1769).

16 July: Death of Giuseppe Castiglione.

Construction at Summer Palace in Rehe of Pule Temple (modelled on Hall of Prayers for Good Harvests in Beijing).

Compilation of dictionaries of languages of Eleuths, Uyghurs, Tibetans and Kokonors, *Xiyu tongwen zhi.*

1767

Beginning of construction at Summer Palace in Rehe of Putuozongcheng Temple, also known as Lesser Potala Palace (modelled on Potala Palace in Lhasa, completed 1771).

Death of Jin Tingbiao, painter (no. 63).

1768

Death of Jean-Denis Attiret, French missionary artist (no. 29).

1769

6 October: Death of Shen Deqian, poet and literary critic (no. 41).

Death of Dong Bangda, painter and scholar (no. 42).

1770

2 September: Death of Qianlong emperor's brother-in-law Fuheng.

1771

17 January: Migration of Turguts from Volga River region to Dzungaria.

August: Beginning of second military campaign in Jinchuan (completed 1776).

Start of construction in Forbidden City of Palace of Peaceful Longevity and its garden (completed 1776).

Replica made of Lion Grove Garden in Summer Palace near Beijing, Yuanmingyuan.

Third edition of Qianlong emperor's collected poems *Yuzhishi sanji.*

1772

7 February: Edict issued by Qianlong emperor to signal beginning of *The Four Treasuries* project.

1773

Beginning of translation of Buddhist sutras *Dazangjin* (*Great store of scriptures*) into Manchu language (completed 1790).

1774

January: Announcement by Qianlong emperor of intention to abdicate in 1795. Yongyan, future Jiaqing emperor, secretly selected as heir apparent.

17 February: Death of Qian Chenqun, poet (no. 71).

3 October to 2 November: Outbreak and suppression of Wang Lun uprising in Shandong province, first major peasant rebellion in Qing dynasty.

Construction at Summer Palace in Rehe of Hall of Arhats (modelled on Anguo Temple in Haining, Zhejiang province).

1775

Replica begun of Lion Grove Garden at Summer Palace in Rehe (completed 1778).

1776

26 December: Intensification of literary inquisition associated with *The Four Treasuries* project.

1778

Completion of catalogue of imperial collection of inkstones.

1780

16 February to 11 June: Fifth southern tour.

20 August: Reception of Panchen Lama at Summer Palace in Rehe. Panchen Lama stays in Xumifushouzhimiao (modelled on Zhaxilhunpo Monastery, his home in Tibet).

September: Carving of seal with inscription 'Treasure of the son of heaven, who is of an age seldom reached since antiquity' by Qianlong emperor to commemorate seventieth birthday (no. 74).

1781

October: Essay 'Knowing one's faults' by Qianlong emperor.

Replica built at Summer Palace in Rehe of Tower of Mist and Rain in Jiaxing, Zhejiang province.

1782

January: Completion of first copy of *The Four Treasuries*, for storage in Forbidden City.

August: Completion of seven more sets of *The Four Treasuries* for storage in Yuanmingyuan, Summer Palace in Rehe, imperial palace in Mukden (Shenyang), libraries in Yangzhou, Zhenjiang and Hangzhou.

1783

Fourth edition of Qianlong emperor's collected poems *Yuzhishi siji*.

1784

11 February to 10 June: Sixth southern tour.

1786

16 January: Outbreak of Lin Shuangwen uprising in Taiwan (suppressed 1788).

1788

10 October: Outbreak of war in Vietnam; Qing army intervenes (withdraws 1789).

1790

Carving of seal with inscription 'Treasure commemorating the advanced age of eighty' to celebrate Qianlong emperor's eightieth birthday (no. 74).

1791

13 November: Beginning of campaign against Gurkhas (ends 1792).

1792

26 September: George III's ambassador, Lord Macartney, leaves Britain for China.

1793

14 September: Reception of Lord Macartney at Garden of Ten Thousand Trees at Summer Palace in Rehe.

Completion of sequel to catalogues of imperial collection of paintings and works of calligraphy, *Shiqu baoji* and *Midian zhulin*.

Issue of Regulations for Tibetan Domestic Reconstruction.

1795

15 October: Announcement of succession of Yongyan, future Jiaqing emperor.

Fifth edition of Qianlong emperor's collected poems *Yuzhishi wuji*.

1796

9 February: Abdication ceremony of Qianlong emperor. Yongyan succeeds throne as Jiaqing emperor.

April: Outbreak of White Lotus rebellion (not suppressed until 1804).

1797

Destruction by fire of Palace of Heavenly Purity in Forbidden City (rebuilt 1798).

1799

7 February: Death of Qianlong emperor in Hall for the Cultivation of the Mind in Forbidden City. Buried in tomb named Yuling, situated at Eastern Tombs near Beijing.

BIBLIOGRAPHY

A CIDADE PROIBIDA 1992 *A Cidade Proibida (The Forbidden City)*, Fundacao Oriente 1992

AAS ABSTRACT 1995 *AAS Abstract* 1995, 'China session' 46, 65

BARTHOLOMEW 1997 Bartholomew, Terese Tse, 'Thangka of the Qianlong Period' in Jane Casey Singer and Philip Denwood, eds, *Tibetan Art: Towards a Definition of Style*, London: Laurence King 1997

BEURDELEY 1971 Beurdeley, Cécile and Michel, *Giuseppe Castiglione: A Jesuit Painter at the Court of the Chinese Emperors*, Rutland, Vermont: Tuttle 1971

BRUCKNER 2000 Bruckner, Christopher, ed., *Chinese Imperial Patronage: Treasures from Temples and Palaces*, London: Asian Art Gallery 2000

CHANG LIN-SHENG 1996 Chang Lin-Sheng, 'National Palace Museum: A History of the Collection' in Fong and Watt 1996, 3–26, 93–4

CHANG AND HSU 1999 Chang Hungshih and Jessica P P Hsu, *Tibetan Buddhist Images and Ritual Objects from the Qing Dynasty Summer Palace at Chengde*, Taibei 1999

CHEN JUANJUAN 1994 Chen Juanjuan, 'Qingdai fushi yishu', *Gugong bowuyuan yuankan* 1994.2: 81–97; 1994.3: 48–61

CHOU AND BROWN 1985 Chou, Ju-hsi and Claudia Brown, *The Elegant Brush: Chinese painting under the Qianlong emperor 1735–1795*, Phoenix Art Museum 1985

CHOU AND BROWN 1988 Chou, Ju-hsi and Claudia Brown, eds, *Chinese Painting under the Qianlong Emperor*, Phoebus 6, no. 1, Arizona State University 1988

COULING 1917 Couling, Samuel, *The Encyclopaedia Sinica*, Hong Kong: Oxford University Press 1917

CRANMER-BYNG 1962 Cranmer-Byng, J L, *An Embassy to China*, Hong Kong: Longmans 1962

CROSSLEY 1999 Crossley, Pamela Kyle, *A Translucent Mirror: History and Identity in Qing Imperial Ideology*, University of California Press 1999

CXSL 1980 *Chaoxian lichao (Yijo) shilu zhong zhongguo shiliao*, 12 vols, Beijing: Zhonghua shuju 1980

DAGYAB 1977 Dagyab, Loden Sherap, *Tibetan Religious Art*, part I: texts, Wiesbaden: Otto Harrassowitz 1977

DAI YI 1997 Dai Yi, *Qianlongdi jiqi shidai*, Beijing: Zhongguo renmin daxue chubanshe 1997

DANBY 1950 Danby, Hope, *The Garden of Perfect Brightness*, London 1950

DE VERBODEN STAD 1990 *De Verboden Stad (The Forbidden City: Court Culture of the Chinese Emperors 1644–1911)*, Rotterdam: Museum Boymans-van Beuningen 1990

DIE VERBOTENE STADT 1997 *Die Verbotene Stadt: Aus dem Leben der letzten Kaiser von China*, Reiss-Museum Mannheim 1997

DQHDT 1899 *Daqing huidian tu*, 270 *juan*, 1899

DU JIANG 1998 Du Jiang, *Qingdi chengde ligong*, Beijing: Zijincheng chubanshe 1998

EDWARDS 1976 Edwards, Richard, *The Art of Wen Cheng-ming (1470–1559)*, University of Michigan 1976

ELLIOT 2001 Elliot, Mark C, *The Manchu Way: Eight Banners and Ethnic Identity in Late Imperial China*, Stanford University Press 2001

FARQUHAR 1978 Farquhar, David, 'Emperor as Bodhisattva in the Governance of the Ch'ing Empire', *Harvard Journal of Asiatic Studies*, vol. 38, nos 1–2, 1978: 5–34

FONG AND WATT 1996 Fong, Wen C and James C Y Watt, *Possessing the Past: Treasures from the National Palace Museum, Taipei*, The Metropolitan Museum of Art 1996

FORÊT 2000 Forêt, Philippe, *Mapping Chengde: The Qing landscape enterprise*, University of Hawaii Press 2000

GCGS 1769 *Guochao gongshi*, 36 *juan*, reprinted Peiping: Palace Museum 1925

GCGSXB 1932 *Guochao gongshi xubian*, 100 *juan*, Peiping: Palace Museum 1932

GENG BAOCHANG 1983 Geng Baochang, 'Xuande qinghuaguan', *Zijincheng* 1983.5

GENG BAOCHANG 1993 Geng Baochang, *Mingqing ciqi jianding*, Beijing: Forbidden City Publishing House 1993

GUGONG 1988 Gugong bowuyuan, 'Qing gongting huajia Lang Shining nianpu', *Gugong bowuyuan yuankan* 1988.2: 29–71

GUGONG 1992 Gugong bowuyuan, *Life of the Emperors and Empresses in the Forbidden City 1644–1911*, Beijing: Zhongguo luyou chubanshe 1992: 14–15

GUO FUXIANG 1992 Guo Fuxiang, 'Qianlong yu Qingdai yin zhi', *Zijincheng* 1992.1

GUO FUXIANG 1993 Guo Fuxiang, 'Qianlong gongting yinzhang shujue', *Gugong bowuyuan yuankan* 1993.1: 36–43

HEARN 1988 Hearn, Maxwell, 'Document and Portrait: The Southern Tour Paintings of Kangxi and Qianlong' in Chou and Brown 1988: 91–131

HO 1992 Wai-kam Ho, *The Century of Tung Ch'i-Ch'ang 1555–1636*, vol. II, The Nelson-Atkins Museum of Art 1992

HU DESHENG 1986 Hu Desheng, 'Qianlong lujiaoqi', *Wenwu* 1986.7

HU JIANZHONG 1989 Hu Jianzhong, 'Qingdai wuchao huangdi de jiazhou', *Zijincheng* 1989.2: 36–41

HUMMEL 1949 Hummel, Arthur W, *Eminent Chinese of the Ch'ing Period (1644–1912)*, 2 vols, Washington: US Government Printing Office 1949

JU SHICHENG 1981 Ju Shicheng, 'Xunxiang he Gongting xiangyi', *Gugong bowuyuan yuankan* 1981.4: 56–61

KHAN 1971 Khan, Harold, *Monarchy in the Emperor's Eye*, Harvard University Press 1971

KHAN 1985 Khan, Harold, 'A Matter of Taste: The Monumental and Exotic in the Qianlong Riegn' in Chou and Brown 1985: 288–302

KUTCHER 1997 Kutcher, Norman, 'The Death of the Xiaoxian Empress: Bureaucratic Betrayals and the Crisis of Eighteenth Century Chinese Rule', *Journal of Asian Studies* 56 (3), August 1997, 708–25

LACHMAN 1996 Lachman, Charles, 'Blindness and Oversight: Some Comments on a Double Portrait of Qianlong and the New Sinology', *Journal of the American Oriental Society*, 1996 (116.4): 736–44

LANG XIUHUA 1989 Lang Xiuhua, 'Qingdai baqi jiazhou', *Zijincheng* 1989.2: 42

Ledderose and Butz 1985 Ledderose, Lothar and Herbert Butz, *Palastmuseum Peking: Schatze aus der Verbotenen Stadt*, Frankfurt am Main: Insel 1985

Legge 1882 Legge, James, *The Sacred Books of China: the texts of Confucianism, part II, The Yi King*, Oxford 1882

Li Xueqin 1989 Li Xueqin, 'Qianlongdi yu guyu', *Zijincheng* 1989.3: 3–4

Liu Lu 1996 Liu Lu, 'Kunninggong wei qingdi dahun dongfang lun', *Gugong bowuyuan yuankan* 1996.3

Liu Lu 2000.3 Liu Lu, 'Lun Qianlong huangdi shirenhua qingxiang', *Zhongguo wenhua yanjiu* 2000.3

Liu Lu 2000.4 Liu Lu, ' "Chong bo xin shiyi tu" yu "Qing Gaozong dayue tu"', *Gugong bowuyuan yuankan* 2000.4: 15–26

Liu Zhenwei 1995 Liu Zhenwei, *Zhongguo guditu jingxuan*, Zhongguo shijieyu chubanshe 1995

LSTQJ 1758 *Leshantang quanji* by Hongli, 30 *juan*, 1758

Medley 1982 Medley, Margaret, *The 'Illustrated Regulations for Ceremonial Paraphernalia of the Ch'ing Dynasty'*, London: Han-shan Tang 1982: 1–30

Millward 1994 Millward, James A, 'A Urghur Muslim in the Qianlong Court: the meanings of the Fragrant Concubine', *Journal of Asian Studies* 53, no. 2 (May 1994): 427–58

Museu de Arte de Macau 2000 Museu de Arte de Macau, *Splendors of a Flourishing Age*, 2000

Needham 1956 Needham, Joseph, *Science and Civilisation in China*, vol. 2, Cambridge: University Press 1956

Nie Chongzheng 1992 Nie Chongzheng, *Qingdai Gongting Huihua*, Beijing: Wenwu chubanshe 1992

Palace Museum 1991 Palace Museum, *Gugong bowuyuan lidai yishuguan chenleipin tumu*, Beijing: Wenwu chubanshe 1991

Palace Museum 1992 Palace Museum, *Life of the Emperors and Empresses in the Forbidden City 1644–1911*, Beijing: China Travel and Tourism Press 1992

Palace Museum 1994 Palace Museum, *Gugong wenwu dadian*, 4 vols, Fuzhou: Fujian renmin chubanshe 1994

Palace Museum 1995 Palace Museum, *Gugong bowuyuan cang wenwu zhenpin quanji*, 60 vols, Hong Kong: Commercial Press 1995–, vols 40, 42

Palace Museum 2000 Palace Museum, *The Imperial Packing Art of the Qing Dynasty*, Forbidden City Publishing House 2000

Pang 1989 Pang, Mae Anna, *Dragon Emperor: Treasures from the Forbidden City*, Melbourne: National Gallery of Victoria 1989

QSL-GZ *Qinggaozong chunhuangdi shilu*, 1500 *juan*

QSL-SZ *Qing shengzhu renhuangdi shilu*, 303 *juan*

Rawski 1998 Rawski, Evelyn S, *The Last Emperors: A Social History of Qing Imperial Institutions*, University of California Press 1998

RXJWK 1774 *Rixia jiuwen kao*, 160 *juan*, Beijing: Beijing guji chubanshe 1985

Spence 1974 Spence, Jonathan, *Emperor of China: self-portrait of K'ang-hsi*, New York and London: Knopf and Cape 1974

Stuart and Rawski 2001 Stuart, Jan and Evelyn S Rawski, *Worshiping the Ancestors: Chinese Commemorative Portraits*, The Freer Gallery and the Arthur M. Sackler Gallery 2001

Tang Bangzhi 1923 Tang Bangzhi, *Qing huangshi sipu*, 4 *juan*, Shanghai 1923

Tang and Luo 1994 Tang Wenji and Luo Qingsi, *Qianlong zhuan*, Beijing: Renmin chubanshe 1994

Tian Xiu 1992 Tian Xiu, 'Qianlong de tuzhang', *Zijincheng* 1992.5: 44–6

Trésors 1998 *Trésors du Musée National du Palais, Taipei : mémoire d'empire*, Paris: Galeries nationales du Grand Palais, 1998

Wan Yi 1980 Wan Yi, '"Sanxitang fatie" zha tan', *Gugong bowuyuan yuankan*, 1980.2: 72–8

Wan Yi 1988 Wan Yi *et al*, *Daily Life in the Forbidden City: The Qing Dynasty 1644–1912*, Viking 1988

Wan Yi 1996 Wan Yi, *Gugong cidian*, Beijing: Wenhui chubanshe 1996

Wang Baoguang 1983 Wang Baoguang, 'Shaolu yu "Shaolu tu"', *Zijincheng* 1983.2: 32

Wang Menggeng 1986 Wang Menggeng, 'Shenyang gugong cang Qing Gaozong Hongli shufa chutan', *Gugong bowuyuan yuankan* 1986.1: 42–8

Wang Yao-ting 1989 Wang Yao-ting, 'Paintings within Paintings' in *Pearls of the Middle Kingdom: A Selection of Articles from the National Palace Museum Monthly of Chinese Art* 1989: 80–7

Wang Zilin 1994 Wang Zilin, 'Qingdai gongshi', *Gugong bowuyuan yuankan* 1994.1: 86–97

Wei Dong 1992 Wei Dong, '"Huangqing zhigongtu" chuangzhi shimo', *Zijincheng* 1992.5: 8–12

Weidner 1994 Weidner, Marsha, *Latter Days of the Law: Images of Chinese Buddhism 850–1850*, Spencer Museum of Art, University of Kansas 1994

Wilheim 1965 Wilheim, Richard, *The I Ching, or Book of Changes*, London: Routledge and Kegan Paul 1965

Wu Boya 2000 Wu Boya, 'Qianlongdi he tade shichen Shen Deqian', *Zijincheng* 2000.2: 21–4

Wu Hung 1995 Wu Hung, 'Emperor's Masquerade: Costume Portraits of Yongzheng and Qianlong', *Orientations*, July–August 1995: 25–41

Wu Hung 1996 Wu Hung, *The Double Screen: Medium and Representation in Chinese Painting*, Reaktion Books 1996

Wu Hung 1997 Wu Hung, 'Beyond Stereotypes: The Twelve Beauties in Qing Court Art and the Dream of the Red Chamber' in Ellen Widmer and Kang-I Sun Chang, eds, *Writing Women in Late Imperial China*, Stanford University Press 1997: 306–65

Wu Kong 1994 Wu Kong, 'Ziguangge de yanyan', *Ziguangge* 1994.5: 47

Xihu jiuzong 1985 *Xihu jiuzong*, Zhejiang renmin meishu chubanshe 1985

Xu Bangda 1997 Xu Bangda, *Chongding qinggugong jiuchang shuhualu*, Renmin meishu chubanshe 1997

Xu Qixian 1995 Xu Qixian, 'Qing dai baoxi luetan', *Gugong bowuyuan yuankan* 1995.3: 62–6

Yang Boda 1982 Yang Boda, 'Qingdai gongting yuqi', *Gugong bowuyuan yuankan* 1982.1: 49–61

YANG BODA 1993 Yang Boda, *Qingdai Yuanhua,* Zijincheng chubanshe 1993

YANG BODA 1993.4 Yang Boda, 'Qing Qianlongdi yuqiguan chutan', *Gugong bowuyuan yuankan* 1993.4: 60–70

YANG DANXIA 2000 Yang Danxia, 'Qianlongdi huihua gaishu', unpublished manuscript 2000: 1–10

YANG RENKAI 1991 Yang Renkai, *Guobao chengfulu: Gugong sanyi shuhua jianwen kaolue,* Shanghai renmin meishu chubanshe 1991

YANG AND ZHU 2000 Yang Xin and Zhu Chengru, eds, *Secret World of the Forbidden City: Splendors from China's Imperial Palace,* Santa Ana: Bowers Museum of Cultural Art 2000

YIYUAN DUOYIN 1978 *Yiyuan duoyin,* no. 3, Shanghai renmin meishu chubanshe 1978

YU SHANPU 1980 Yu Shanpu, 'Guanyu Xiangfei chuanshuo de bianwei', *Gugong bowuyuan yuankan* 1980.2: 8–13

YU ZHUOYUN 1982 Yu Zhuoyun, *Zijincheng gongdian,* Hong Kong: Commercial Press 1982

YZSCJ 1748 *Yuzhishi chuji* by Hongli, 44 *juan,* 1748

YZSEJ 1761 *Yuzhishi erji* by Hongli, 90 *juan,* 1761

YZSSJ 1771 *Yuzhishi sanji* by Hongli, 100 *juan,* 1771

YZSSJ 1783 *Yuzhishi siji* by Hongli, 100 *juan,* 1783

YZSWJ 1795 *Yuzhishi wuji* by Hongli, 100 *juan,* 1795

YZSYJ 1800 *Yuzhishi yuji* by Hongli, 20 *juan,* 1800

ZHANG CHOU 1992 Zhang Chou, *Qinghe shuhuafang* (1616), in *Zhongguo shuhua quanshu,* vol. 4, Shanghai shuhua chubanshe 1992

ZHANG GUANGWEN 1990 Zhang Guangwen, 'Qingdai gongting fanggu yuqi', *Gugong bowuyuan yuankan* 1990.2: 39–51

ZHANG GUANGWEN 1991 Zhang Guangwen, 'Qianlongdi yu yugui', *Zijincheng* 1991.1: 30–1

ZHANG SHIYUN 1980 Zhang Shiyun, '"Jinouyonggu" bei', *Gugong bowuyuan yuankan* 1980.2: 80–1

ZHANG TANGRONG 1985 Zhang Tangrong, *Qinggong shuwen,* first edn 1937, reprinted Beijing: Beijing guji chubanshe 1985

ZHANG ZHANSHENG 1986 Zhang Zhansheng, 'Wanshuyuan da menggubao yan', *Zijincheng* 1986.1, 20–1

ZHAOLIAN 1980 Zhaolian, *Xiaoting zalu,* Beijing: Zhonghua shuju 1980

ZHOU NANQUAN 1991 Zhou Nanquan, 'Lun zhongguo gudai de yubi', *Gugong bowuyuan yuankan* 1991.1: 76–88

ZHU JIAJIN 1986 Zhu Jiajin, *Treasures of the Forbidden City,* Viking Penguin 1986

ZHU JIAJIN 1988 Zhu Jiajin, 'Castiglione's *tieluo* painting', *Orientations* 3, November 1988: 80–3

ZHU JIE 1999 Zhu Jie, 'Changchunyuan chunhuaxuan yu gugong leshoutang', *Gugong bowuyuan yuankan* 1999.3

ZITO 1997 Zito, Angela, *Of body and brush: Grand sacrifice as text/performance in eighteenth-century China,* University of Chicago Press 1997

GLOSSARY

Abode of the Hiding Dragon 潛龍邸
Aisin Gioro 愛新覺羅
Alantai 阿蘭泰
An Qi 安岐
Anguo Temple 安國寺
Anthology of studies from the Hall of Delight in Doing Good 樂善堂文鈔
Anyuan Temple 安遠廟
Attiret, Jean-Denis (Wang Zhicheng) 王致誠
Bai Shixiu 白世秀
bajixiang 八吉祥
Bao'en Temple 報恩寺
baoxianghua 寶相花
Bele 貝勒
Benoist, Father (Jiang Youren) 蔣友仁
bi 璧
Burhan-al-Din 波羅泥都
Buruts 布魯特
cakravartin 轉輪王
Cangca Khutuktu 章嘉呼圖克圖
Castiglione, Giuseppe (Lang Shining) 郎世寧
Changchun jushi 長春居士
Changchun shuwu 長春書屋
changle 長樂
Chen Mei 陳枚
Chen Min 陳敏
Chen Shijun 陳世俊
Chen Shu 陳書
Chen Zuzhang 陳祖章
Cheng Liang 程梁
Cheng Zhidao 程志道
Chengde 承德
Chongzhen 崇禎
chun 春
chuntiezi 春帖子
Chunyu 春雨
Commendation of Sakyamuni 文殊贊佛法身禮經
Dai Hong 戴洪
Dai Zheng 戴正
Dalai Lama 達賴喇嘛
Davatsi 達瓦齊
Dazangjin 大藏經
Derbets 杜爾伯特
dharani 陀羅尼(咒)
Dharmapala 護法神靈
Dharmaraja 法金剛
Dhritarashtra 多羅吒
Ding Guanpeng 丁觀鵬
Ding Yu 丁裕
Ding Yunpeng 丁雲鵬
Dong Bangda 董邦達
Dong Gao 董誥
Dong Qichang 董其昌
Dragon Boat Festival 端午節
Du Fu 杜甫
duoluorong 哆囉絨
Dzungars 准噶爾
Eidu 額亦都
Eleuths 厄魯特
fang 倣
feicui 翡翠
Feng, Lady 馮婕妤
Fengcheng 豐城
Four Treasuries 四庫全書
Fragrant Hills 香山
fu 黻
Fucha, Lady 富察氏
Fuheng 傅恒
Fupeng 福彭
Galdan 噶爾丹
Gansu 甘肅
ganzhi 干支
Gao Yu 高玉
Garden of Clear Waves 清漪園
Garden of Ten Thousand Trees 萬樹園
Gate of Dignity 端門
Gate of Supreme Harmony 太和門
Gu Fu 顧复
guan'geti 館閣體

Guangzhou	廣州
Guanyin (Avalokitesvara)	觀音
gui	圭
guiwei	癸未
guoyu qishe	國語騎射
Haining	海寧
Haiwang	海望
Hall for the Cultivation of the Mind	養心殿
Hall for Enjoying Longevity	樂壽堂
Hall for the Fulfilment of Promises	遂初堂
Hall for Serving Heaven	奉天殿
Hall of Abstinence	齋宮
Hall of Arhats	羅漢堂
Hall of Delight in Doing Good	樂善堂
Hall of Imperial Supremacy	皇極殿
Hall of Pleasant Breezes	卷阿勝境殿
Hall of Prayers for Good Harvests	祈年殿
Hall of Supreme Harmony	太和殿
Hall of the Three Rarities	三希堂
Hall of Union	交泰殿
Han Chinese	漢人
Han dynasty	漢(朝)
Hangzhou	杭州
Hanshan	寒山
He Yongqing	賀永清
Hepu	合浦
Heshen	和珅
Hill of Solitude	孤山
Hodja brothers	大小和卓
Hoja Erke Husein	額爾克和卓
Hongli	弘曆
Hongshi	弘時
Hongzhou	弘晝
Hu Shijie	胡世傑
Huai River	淮河
huang	璜
Huangtaiji	皇太極
Huashan	花善
hujun ying	護軍營
Illustrated regulations for ceremonial paraphernalia	皇朝禮器圖式
Imperial Household Department	內務府
Jade Spring Hill	玉泉山
Jialeba	嘉勒巴
Jiang Tingxi	蔣廷錫
Jiangnan	江南
Jiangsu	江蘇
Jiao Bingzhen	焦秉貞
Jiaqing	嘉慶
Jiaxing	嘉興
Jin Hong	金泓
Jin Kun	金昆
Jin Tingbiao	金廷標
Jinan	濟南
Jinchuan	金川
jinian	紀念
Jurmet Namjar	珠爾墨特那木扎勒
kang	炕
Kangxi	康熙
kapala	嘎巴拉碗
Kashgar	喀什噶爾
Khoits	輝特
Khoshotes	和碩
Khotan	和闐
Khozi Khan	霍集占
Kiramet	額喇瑪特
Kogler, Ignatius (Dai Jinxian)	戴進賢
Lake Dongting	洞庭湖
lanca	藍查(體)
Langka	郎卡(漢文音譯)
Leng Mei	冷枚
Lhasa	拉薩
Li Di	李迪
Liji	禮記
Li Song	李嵩
Li Yinpei	李因培
Li Zongwan	勵宗萬

Liang Shizheng	梁詩正
Liaoning	遼寧
lin	臨
Lin Bu	林逋
Lin Shuangwen	林爽文
lingzhi	靈芝
Lion Grove Garden	獅子林
Liuhe Pagoda	六和塔
Lodge for Retiring from Hard Work	倦勤齋
long (dragon)	龍
long (grandeur)	隆
Lu Hong	盧鴻
Lu Zhan	盧湛
Ma Yuan	馬遠
Magnolia Lodge	玉蘭館
Manchu	滿人，滿語
mandala	曼荼羅
Manjusri	文殊師利
mao	卯
meizhen	梅針
Meridian Gate	午門
Miao	苗
Mid-Autumn Festival	中秋節
Midian zhulin	秘殿珠林
Ming dynasty	明(朝)
mo	摹
Model works of calligraphy in the Hall of the Three Rarities	三希堂法帖
Mount Pan	盤山
Mount Tai	泰山
Mount Wutai	五台山
Mukden (Shenyang)	盛京
Mulan	木蘭
Naluoyanku (Narayana)	那羅延窟
nan wood	楠木
Nanjing	南京
Nanxundian	南薰殿
Ni Zan	倪瓚
Ningxia	寧夏
Niohuru	鈕祜祿
Nurhachi	努爾哈赤
Oertai	鄂爾泰
Orchid Pavilion	蘭亭
Palace for the Establishment of Happiness	建福宮
Palace of Blessing	毓慶宮
Palace of Compassion and Peace	慈寧宮
Palace of Complete Harmony	雍和宮
Palace of Complete Peace	咸安宮
Palace of Double Glory	重華宮
Palace of Earthly Peace	坤寧宮
Palace of Great Happiness	景福宮
Palace of Heavenly Purity	乾清宮
Palace of Peaceful Longevity	寧壽宮
Palace of Splendour	興慶宮
Panchen Lama	班禪喇嘛
Panzi, Joseph (Pan Tingzhang)	潘廷璋
Parsa	帕爾薩
Pavilion of Rain Flowers	雨花閣
Peng He	彭鶴
Potala Palace	布達拉宮
Pule Temple	普樂寺
Puning Monastery	普寧寺
Purple Light Pavilion	紫光閣
Putuozongcheng Temple	普陀宗乘之廟
qian	乾
Qian Chenqun	錢陳群
qianfeng ying	前鋒營
Qianlong	乾隆
qin (lute)	琴
qin (chime)	磬
Qing dynasty	清(朝)
Qingbi	清閟
Qu Yuan	屈原
Queen Mother of the West	西王母
Qufu	曲阜

Rehe (Chengde) 熱河
Rolpa'i Dorje 羅賴畢多爾吉
Rongfei 容妃
Room for the Pursuit of Leisure 得閑室
Room of Flowing Ink 墨雲室
Sakyamuni 釋迦牟尼
Samantabhadra 普賢
Sea Palaces 三海
Shaanxi 陝西
Shandong 山東
Shang dynasty 商(朝)
shen (deep) 深
Shen Deqian 沈德潛
Shen Yu 沈崳
Shen Yuan 沈源
Shen Zhou 沈周
Shijing 詩經
shinuhua 仕女畫
Shiqu baoji 石渠寶笈
Shiqu baoji xubian 石渠寶笈續編
Shouhuangdian 壽皇殿
Shuhe 舒和
Shuhede 舒赫德
Shujing 書經
Shun 舜
Shunzhi 順治
Sichuan 四川

Sickelbart, Ignatius (Ai Qiming) 艾啟蒙
Solobun 莎羅奔
Sonam Stobgyal 頗羅鼐
Song dynasty 宋(朝)
Songjiang 松江
South Park 南苑
Studio of Delicate Fragrance 漱芳齋
Studio of Restraint 抑齋
Study of Respect for Excellence 敬勝齋
Sui'an 隨安
suiyu eran 隨遇而安
Sumeru 須彌(座)
Sun Fu 孫阜
Sun Hu 孫祜
Sun Weifeng 孫威鳳
Suotong 索通
Suzhou 蘇州
Tang dynasty 唐(朝)
Tang Yin 唐寅
Tang Ying 唐英
Tangdai 唐岱
Tarbagatai 塔爾巴哈台
Tarim Basin 塔里木盆地
tatashi 他他士
Ten Thousand Feet of Snow 千尺雪
thangka 唐卡

tianqi 填漆
Tianru 天如
Tianshan 天山
tianxia 天下
Tower of Mist and Rain 煙雨樓
Treasure commemorating the advanced age of eighty 八徵耄念之寶
Treasure of the son of heaven 天子之寶 匱
Treasure of the son of heaven, who is of an age seldom reached since antiquity 古稀天子之寶
Tula 圖拉
Turdi 圖爾都
Turguts 土爾扈特
tusu 屠蘇
Ubasi 渥巴錫
Ula Nara 烏拉納喇
Uyghur 畏兀兒
Vaishravana 毘沙門
Veranda for Nourishing Harmony 頤和軒
Veranda for Three Friends 三友軒
Veranda of Serene Tranquillity 靜怡軒
Virudhaka 毘琉璃
Virupaksha 毗留博義
vitarka mudra 毘怛迦手印
Wang Bi 王弼

Wang Cen	王岑
Wang Jie	王玠
Wang Jun	王均
Wang Lun	王倫
Wang Mang	王莽
Wang Ruxue	王儒學
Wang Wei	王維
Wang Xianzhi	王獻之
Wang Xizhi	王羲之
Wang Xun	王珣
Wang Youdun	汪由敦
Wang Youxue	王幼學
Warring States period	戰國
wen	文
Wen Zhengming	文徵明
West Flowery Gate	西華門
West Lake	西湖
wu	武
Wu Gui	吳桂
Wu Yu	吳棫
Wucheng	烏程
wujuzu	五具足
Wumen	吳門
wutong	梧桐
Wuxi	無錫
Xia dynasty	夏(朝)
xiang (illusion)	相
xiang (image, elephant)	象
Xiang Shengmo	項聖謨
Xiang Yuanbian	項元汴
Xiangfei	香妃
xiangzun	象尊
xiaoqi ying	驍騎營
Xiaosheng	孝聖
Xiaoxian	孝賢
xin (heart, mind)	心
Xinjiang	新疆
xinletu	行樂圖
Xiqing gujian	西清古鑑
Xiyu tongwen zhi	西域同文志
Xu Tao	徐燾
Xu Yang	徐揚
Xu Zhang	徐璋
Xuande	宣德
Xun	恂
Yangzhou	揚州
Yao	堯
Yao Wenhan	姚文翰
Yarkand	葉爾羌
Ye Lüfeng	葉履豐
Yengi Hissar	英吉沙爾
Yijing	易經
Yichanga	伊昌阿
Yiheyuan	頤和園
Yili	伊犁
Yimianhuoluo	依綿豁羅(漢文音譯)
yin (term in *ganzhi* counting system)	寅
yin (sound)	音
yin-yang li	陰陽歷
ying (shadow)	影
Yin'e	胤䄉
Yinlu	胤祿
Yinreng	胤礽
Yinsi	胤禩
Yintang	胤禟
Yinti	胤禵
Yinxi	胤禧
Yinxiang	胤祥
Yinzhen	胤禛
yizisun	宜子孫
Yong, Prince	雍王
Yonghuang	永璜
Yongle	永樂
Yonglian	永璉
Yongrong	永瑢
Yongyan	永琰
Yongyou Temple	永佑寺
Yongzhang	永璋
Yongzheng	雍正
yu	玉
Yu Minzhong	于敏中
Yu Sheng	余省
Yu the Great	大禹

Yu Zhi	余穉
Yuan dynasty	元(朝)
Yuan emperor	元帝(漢)
Yuan Ying	袁瑛
Yuanmingyuan	圓明園
Yue Zhongqi	岳鍾琪
Yuling	裕陵
Yunlin	雲林
Yuzhishi chuji	御製詩初集
Yuzhishi erji	御製詩二集
Yuzhishi sanji	御製詩三集
Yuzhishi siji	御製詩四集
Yuzhishi wuji	御製詩五集
Zhan Xi	詹熹
Zhang Chou	張丑
Zhang Lin	張霖
Zhang Ruoai	張若靄
Zhang Tingyan	張廷彥
Zhang Tingyu	張廷玉
Zhang Weibang	張爲邦
Zhang Yusen	張雨森
Zhang Zeduan	張擇端
Zhang Zhao	張照
Zhang Zhen	張震
Zhang Zongcang	張宗蒼
Zhao Mengfu	趙孟頫
Zhao Yuan	趙原
Zhejiang	浙江
Zhenjiang	鎮江
Zhou dynasty	周(朝)
Zhou Dunyi	周敦頤
Zhou Kun	周鯤
zhuo	拙
Zou Yigui	鄒一桂
Zu Zijian	祖子兼